'C   le?

Writing Wales in English

Detail from 'Gwlad Canaan / The Land of Canaan' by Ap Dewi, 1900.
By permission of Llyfrgell Genedlaethol Cymru /
The National Library of Wales.

Whose People?

Wales, Israel, Palestine

Writing Wales in English

JASMINE DONAHAYE

UNIVERSITY OF WALES PRESS
CARDIFF
2012

British Library Cataloguing-in-Publication Data
A catalogue record for this book is available from the British Library.

ISBN   978-0-7083-2483-7
e-ISBN 978-0-7083-2484-4

AW

THE *A*SSOCIATION FOR
*W*ELSH *W*RITING IN *E*NGLISH
*C*YMDEITHAS *L*LÊN *S*AESNEG *C*YMRU

Typeset by Mark Heslington Ltd, Scarborough, North Yorkshire
Printed in Wales by Dinefwr Press, Llandybïe

CONTENTS

CREW

CREW series of Critical and Scholarly Studies
General Editor: Professor M. Wynn Thomas (CREW, Swansea University)

This *CREW* series is dedicated to Emyr Humphreys, a major figure in the literary culture of modern Wales, a founding patron of the *Centre for Research into the English Literature and Language of Wales*, and, along with Gillian Clarke and Seamus Heaney, one of *CREW*'s Honorary Associates. Grateful thanks are due to the late Richard Dynevor for making this series possible.

Other titles in the series

GENERAL EDITOR'S PREFACE

The aim of this series is to produce a body of scholarly and critical work that reflects the richness and variety of the English-language literature of modern Wales. Drawing upon the expertise both of established specialists and of younger scholars, it will seek to take advantage of the concepts, models and discourses current in the best contemporary studies to promote a better understanding of the literature's significance, viewed not only as an expression of Welsh culture but also as an instance of modern literatures in English worldwide. In addition, it will seek to make available the scholarly materials (such as bibliographies) necessary for this kind of advanced, informed study.

M. Wynn Thomas
*CREW (Centre for Research into the English
Literature and Language of Wales)*
Swansea University

Acknowledgements

Many people have helped and encouraged me in the research for this book. My thanks in particular to Professor M. Wynn Thomas for his interest and for his close, critical reading, to Dafydd Jones for his careful editing, and to the staff at the National Library for their help and patience. For interviews and correspondence I am grateful to the late Leo Abse, Lyn Ebenezer, the late Professor J. Gwyn Griffiths, Heini Gruffudd, Robat Gruffudd, Dorian Llywelyn and Judith Maro. My thanks also to John Harris for information on Caradoc Evans, to Peter Lord for originally bringing John Mills and a number of Jewish artists to my attention, to Anna Plodeck for generously sharing her research on Fred Uhlman, and to John Minkes for information on Lily Tobias. Finally, many people have passed on anecdotal and textual evidence to me, starting with Kathryn Klar of UC Berkeley in 1996 and ending with Matthew Jarvis who sent me a John Tripp Wales-Israel comparison just after this text was finalised. My thanks to them and to the very many others in between.

Introduction:
a beginning and an end

When I began to learn Welsh in the late 1990s at UC Berkeley, I harboured some hazy and romantic notions about Wales that included mist, sheep and political fervour: I knew little about the language or the place it came from, though I had visited Aberystwyth several times as a child, and as a teenager had been inspired by Port Talbot's satanic mills. It was a surprise, therefore, to find the Welsh language immediately familiar: its conjugated prepositions and initial consonantal mutations were instantly recognisable counterpoints to Hebrew prepositional forms and consonantal changes. Of course, I was not the first person to have noted these similarities. Linguistically speaking, the problem relationship between Celtic and Semitic language groups has been around in one form or other, and unresolved, for centuries, and papers on the so-called 'CHS problem' are regularly given at Linguistics and Celtic Studies conferences. I soon found, however, that the relationship was not only to do with language groups. I had learned Hebrew as a teenager on a kibbutz *ulpan* in Israel, a language intensive that had developed out of a need to enculturate new Jewish immigrants to the young state and its 'young-old' national language, and I was intrigued to discover that an intensive course of study in Welsh was also called an *ulpan* – spelled in Welsh as *wlpan*. Soon I found that many connections and comparisons had been made between Wales and Israel, between Welsh and Hebrew, and between Welsh political and cultural nationalism and Zionism, all of which were understood by commentators in the 1990s and early 2000s to constitute elements of a widespread, remarkable tradition of 'Welsh identification with the Jews', a tradition of identification that had its roots in the deep past.

Only, of course, it didn't – or not quite in the ways that were claimed. Ancient traditions, particularly traditions pertaining to national identity, may claim to have deep roots, but often don't have any such thing. On the contrary, as Benedict Anderson has argued, ideas of nation are constructed and imagined, and as Eric Hobsbawm and others have shown, ancient 'national' traditions are often of relatively recent invention. In *Invented Traditions*, the seminal publication edited by Hobsbawm and Terence Ranger, Prys Morgan traces just such traditions in Wales.[1]

Invented traditions and identities can be fluid and adaptable – 'Wales', as Gwyn A. Williams remarks so succinctly, 'is an artefact which the Welsh produce'.[2] But they can also become rigid and proscriptive, as is the case in Israel: according to Shlomo Sand, to choose not to use the rhetorically loaded terms that have shaped the 'traditional' Israeli national narrative is treated as 'heretical'.[3] If, over time, such invented traditions become the material of monolithic narratives of national history, they are nevertheless not always the clearly-delineated binary accounts that Sand describes as an '"Us" and "All the Others" division'.[4] Sometimes they are uncertain narratives of self in search of a model; sometimes, as is often the case in Wales, they are narratives of self in opposition to a specific rather than a universal 'other' – namely the English.

This study concerns such a narrative – a narrative of Welsh and Jewish culture and identity. It is not a literary or a historical study, but examines imaging and discussion of Jews in writing in both languages of Wales, across a very wide spectrum of publications.

To date there has been no monograph published on Welsh Jewish history or culture, or on Welsh Jewish relations. Nearly two decades have passed since the only scholarly book appeared on a Welsh Jewish subject, and that was a collection of essays covering the very limited terrain of south Wales Jewish history. This study does not fill that gap, but I hope it will point to the richness of the cultural material that invites further research.

When I began researching Welsh Jewish material years ago, time and again I was offered unsolicited anecdotal evidence of a 'tradition' of Welsh identification with Jews. Among older communicants the subject of my research needed no explanation: the idea of there having been some kind of Welsh identification with Jews was so widespread, especially among older Welsh speakers, that it was taken for granted. Clearly there was some such tradition in oral circulation. By odd chance, however, at the time when I began to follow up these intriguing indicators of some real or imagined relationship, this so-called 'tradition of Welsh identification with the Jews' was in the process of disappearing from national memory. Twelve years on, and a profound shift in political orientation later, it has been almost forgotten.

There are many reasons for that shift. One of these is the change in popular and political attitudes to Israel since the start of the second Palestinian intifada; another is the fading drama of modern Hebrew as a minority language 'reborn'. But there are also wider social and political factors in twentieth-century Wales that have contributed to this shift. These include the change from a country shaped by a nonconformist religious tradition into a country that is largely secular, and the development of a degree of self-government in the form of the National Assembly for Wales.

A younger generation registers no knowledge of such a 'tradition', and an older generation now qualifies, as a liability, the associations with Israel, which is seen by many as an aggressively militarist state. Although people still refer to the *wlpan*, after thirty-five years of its use the word may soon become something of an historical artefact: the names of Welsh-language courses run by county councils, universities or language centres include the term less and less.

Although evidence of a cultural tradition may be found in publications and other forms of cultural production, what that evidence derives from is nevertheless an organic process: a tradition lives in practices, in conscious-ness and, most importantly, in transmission. In rural Ceredigion, where I live, the New Year's Day folkloric tradition of collecting *calennig* is alive, even if its distribution has shrunk and its meaning and direction has changed, so that rather than walking from door to door in their community in a group, children are now driven by parents from selected house to selected house. By contrast, the Star of David emblem on the wall of a converted chapel or school (now a bird-hide) in Cwmrheidol is evidence of a tradition that is no longer transmitted. This was a tradition carried by a nonconformist chapel culture whose congregations visualised themselves as biblical inheritors in buildings and then in villages named, accordingly, Sion and Jerusalem – a tradition whose echoes resounded throughout the search for comparative and shaping national models long into the second half of the twentieth century.[5] Those older people for whom the subject of my research was so instantly familiar had been exposed to that religious culture as children, but this particular religious tradition and community is now largely gone.

A closer examination of this so-called tradition reveals that it is of much more recent vintage than is usually supposed. In various forms – ethnic and linguistic, spiritual and moral, national and international, historical and biblical – Wales has indeed imagined 'Israel' as place and a people for several centuries. But the notion that there is a long-standing, warm and positive tradition of Welsh identification with Jews is an early twentieth-century invention: as far as I have been able to discover, the compilation of its disparate elements, including the affixing of origins in the sixth or seventeenth centuries, began in 1901.

An examination of that compilation, the purposes it served, and the ways in which it was reinvented through the twentieth century constitutes the subject of the first chapter in this study. What emerge are several discrete areas of discussion. On the one hand, there exists a centuries-old tradition in which the Welsh have prominently identified themselves as the biblical Jews, and have compared Welsh with ancient Hebrew. This tradition has roots in mythical narratives of the deep national past – those narratives that constitute what historians have called 'traditional Welsh historiography'. On the other hand, a political discussion emerges primarily in the twentieth century that concerns itself with Jewish national aspirations, with Zionist efforts, and with the Hebrew language revival as a comparative model for Wales and the Welsh language. In addition – both separate from these, but also overlapping in some cases – there is abundant evidence of a persistent interest in and discourse on post-biblical Jews. This interest is usually overtly or covertly conversionist, or informed by conversionist understandings of 'the Jew' as a pitiable (because not Christian) subject. But there is also a recurring pattern of familiar stereotyped imaging of Jews in more incidental ways, particularly in fiction and poetry. Finally, in the twentieth century, some of the evidence from all three of these areas of discussion has-been conflated in accounts of a long-standing 'tradition of identification with the Jews', beginning with a Reverend D. Wynne Evans in the early 1900s.

The invention and reinvention of this so-called 'tradition' has entailed omissions and elisions, which are helpfully facilitated by an approach that assesses attitudes to Jews in simple binary terms of hostility (antisemitism) or warmth, love and support (philosemitism). Some of these omissions and elisions are the subjects of the subsequent chapters.

One of these omissions is a consideration of Welsh conversionism. Neither Welsh support for conversionist activity nor Welsh conversionist imaging of Jews has been analysed: although on occasion it has been acknowledged in passing by historians, it is usually glossed over or downplayed. In chapter 2, therefore, I examine the work of writers who were interested either hypothetically or practically in the conversion of the Jews. This includes the series of influential essays by D. Wynne Evans which posit, for the first time, a tradition of affiliation or identification between the Welsh and the Jews. I also look at the work of Margaret Jones, 'y Gymraes o Ganaan' (the Welshwoman from Canaan), who wrote home from Palestine and Morocco where she worked for Christian missionaries in the later nineteenth century. Most importantly, I look at accounts by the Reverend John Mills of his twelve-year mission to convert the Jews of London in the mid-nineteenth century, and of his travels in Ottoman Palestine, which, he proposed, would be an ideal location for a Welsh colony.

Conversionism doesn't fit tidily within the confines of positive or negative attitudes to Jews, but this is how Welsh imaging of Jews has until now been categorised. In chapter 3, therefore, I explore the way in which a mutually exclusive 'philosemitic' or 'antisemitic' interpretation of Jewish imaging restricts the understanding of its meaning and deployment, and, more importantly, permits the isolation of unwelcome expressions of hostility from the mainstream. In its place, I propose that it is more productive to examine in a wider context the use to which writers put Jewish stereotype, whether negative or positive. When examined as 'semitic discourse' – what David Cesarani, for example, defines as 'a discourse about the Jews which operates through stereotypes that can be either positive or negative depending upon the intention of the agent employing them' – the stereotyped imaging of Jews in twentieth-century Welsh literature in both languages begins to look very mainstream indeed, but with characteristics and purposes that are particular to the Welsh situation.[6] Sometimes those purposes are surprising, however, as a forgotten novel by Caradoc Evans indicates.

In many cases, evidence of hostile imaging of Jews, particularly by Saunders Lewis, one of the founders of Plaid Cymru, has been used by some to make anti-nationalist arguments. Such arguments are premised on the claim that the 'philosemitic' Labour tradition (of south Wales in particular) is the sole legitimate political expression of Wales, and that the nationalists are covert or overt fascists. At the same time, the Zionist movement and the revival of Hebrew were strong points of comparison for the national movement in Wales. So, in chapter 4, I look at the changing imaging of Jews in the nationalist narrative of the twentieth century, including a survey of Plaid Cymru's official publications from 1926. The use of Hebrew as a model for the revival of Welsh emerges in the 1940s, and it takes on new life in the 1960s and 1970s in the context of the rise of Cymdeithas yr Iaith Gymraeg (The Welsh Language Society) and the introduction in Wales of the word *wlpan*. Here, as with John Mills's proposals for a Welsh colonial project in Palestine, there is a quite serious sleight of hand: in the use of Israel and Hebrew as models, the Jewish claim on Palestine is reinforced, and the non-Jewish population is either marginalised or not acknowledged. Wales is thus implicated in the tangled complexity of the Israel-Palestine situation in the present by the promotion of this colonial fantasy, by the promotion of the Hebrew revival without acknowledgement of its costs, and also by Wales's contribution to British imperial control of Palestine during the Mandate. All of this lends itself to what one might term a post-Zionist analysis, which I attempt at the conclusion to this chapter. While those who have been termed 'post-Zionist' historians analyse the costs, to others and to Jews, of the establishment of a Jewish state in Palestine, and reassess the validity of the Zionist narrative and its claims, my intention here is to ask in what ways Welsh writers collude in the validation of that narrative and the marginalisation of those costs.

This engagement with Hebrew and with Israel did not occur in isolation, however, and nor does Welsh imaging of Jews more generally. Instead, it is part of a dialogue with its subject. In chapter 5, therefore, I examine Jewish responses to Welsh culture, whether in the early twentieth-century example of the *South Wales Jewish Review*, in writing by Jewish visitors and immigrants, or in writing by Jewish authors born or raised in Wales. Some, particularly those with strong socialist or Marxist views, reveal in their work a deep suspicion of national and nationalist sentiment, and a hostility to the Welsh-speaking community more generally.

But the evidence suggests that others, for a range of reasons, have been active agents in the promotion of notions of Welsh identification with and 'love' of Jews. In some cases, on the back of legitimising a Zionist narrative in a Welsh context, Jewish writers have been the chief means by which such a 'tradition' has been transmitted. Their work also lends itself to a post-Zionist analysis, as does the mutual reinforcement that emerges between Jewish and non-Jewish Welsh writers in the 1970s in particular.

This study attempts to bring back into dialogue the material of two cultural commentaries that was in fact the product of such a dialogue. It does not set out to be either comprehensive or representative. On the contrary, it constitutes preliminary studies of particular areas of Welsh imaging of Jews and uses of Jewish models that suggest themselves as being the most urgent, or most overlooked, or that in one way or another have been misrepresented. However, I have left out the most misrepresented subject, which is also the most often cited – that of the Tredegar riot of 1911. As I have argued elsewhere, in most British-Jewish studies Wales is mentioned almost exclusively in relation to the riot, which is presented as its sole distinguishing feature.[7] In Jewish scholarship there is often an overly comfortable slippage between the terms 'Anglo' or 'English', and 'British', which permits Wales to be seen and sometimes named as a typical province of England. By presenting the particularity of the Welsh cultural context, I aim to demonstrate that it is not possible to characterise it as 'typical' in the context of so-called British-Jewish experience, notwithstanding the fact that both Jewish experience and the imaging of Jews in Wales may nevertheless share many features with such experience and imaging throughout the UK. I hope that this study will make it difficult, for example, to repeat Michael Woolf's suggestion in a review of Bernice Rubens's novel *Set on Edge* that 'the location could be Rubens' native Wales *or any other small town*' (the added emphasis is mine).[8] However, I hope that it will also, in part, contribute to a broader survey that is needed, which takes into account and considers the particularity of the constituent nations of the UK in relation to one another.

By examining some of the typicality of Welsh imaging of Jews, I also seek to challenge the notion of Wales as unusually tolerant and liberal.[9] Welsh writing in both languages shares the full range of what can be seen as stereotypical Jewish motifs, and Welsh missionaries have been as enthusiastic participants as English missionaries in the project of converting Jews. They have also been as enthusiastic as English missionaries in the role of colonial agent and imperial forerunner. In addition, claims of unusual Welsh tolerance and 'love' of Jews must be as tenuous and perhaps spurious as a claim of fundamental English 'philosemitism' would be. While some historians of British Jews have marginalised or subsumed Wales, equally problematically some studies in Wales have made overstated claims about the uniqueness of Welsh 'love' of Jews. Consequently, while I hope that, as an outcome of this study, it will be difficult to equate Wales with 'any other small town', I hope it will also be difficult to repeat the claim made by W. D. Rubinstein when he proposes that 'it is no exaggeration to say that [philosemitism] permeated every aspect of Welsh culture until very recent times'.[10]

I should emphasise, however, that by challenging received notions of Welsh attitudes to Jews, I have no intention of making an argument about some marked cultural *intolerance*. Instead I wish to shift the argument away from competing claims of 'hostility' or 'welcome', and focus instead on the conflicting and nuanced imaging of Jews by Welsh writers and commentators (and, where relevant, on the support of this by publishers). This focus reveals how such imaging serves a purpose that often has very little to do with Jews at all, and everything to do with Welshness and Wales.

When it comes to recognising the particular cultural context of Wales, Eitan Bar-Yosef's *The Holy Land in English Culture 1799–1917* is, I believe, the exception in Jewish studies. In his introduction he defines carefully how he uses the terms 'English' and 'British', explaining that his study sets out 'to reveal the various cross-exchanges between the imperial project of exploring, representing, and eventually conquering Palestine and between the long tradition of internalizing those central biblical images – "Promised Land", "Chosen People", "Zion" – and applying them to England and the English'.[11] He adds in a footnote:

> Many of these observations hold true for the British isle (if not isles) as a whole. My study excludes other parts of Britain, not simply because Jerusalem is to be built in *England*'s green and pleasant land, but because Scotland, Wales, and Ireland raise questions which simply cannot be explored here.[12]

This study does not seek to be an answer to Eitan Bar-Yosef's observations or exclusions, nor is it an attempt to fill lacunae in the two books dealing with Wales-Israel matters that Bar-Yosef cites, namely Dorian Llywelyn's *Sacred Place, Chosen People: Land and National Identity in Welsh Spirituality*, and John Harvey's *Image of the Invisible: the Visualization of Religion in Welsh Nonconformist Tradition*, both of which I consider in chapter 1.[13] Unlike Bar-Yosef, whose book explores Palestine as an object of English colonial desire, Llywelyn and Harvey both restrict themselves to an examination of biblical religious traditions and their influence in the wider culture of Wales. Nevertheless, though I cannot aspire to filling the gaps left by these complementary texts, I do hope that this study might constitute something of a bridge between them, and that it may also serve as a bridge to other recent foundational texts of British Jewish studies by scholars such as Bryan Cheyette, Nadia Valman and David Cesarani.

There are rich literary-critical pickings in research on Wales, and in Jewish studies, and several theoretical approaches to understanding the texts under consideration here jostle for position. Kirsti Bohata's *Postcolonialism Revisited* and Stephen Knight's *A Hundred Years of Fiction*, as well as Bryan Cheyette's *Constructions of 'the Jew' in English Literature and Society: Racial Representations 1875–1945* and 'Neither Black Nor White: the Figure of "the Jew" in Imperial British Literature', suggest some possible ways forward.[14] Similarly, Benedict Anderson's *Imagined Communities*, Shlomo Sand's *The Invention of the Jewish People*, and Gwyn A. Williams's *When Was Wales?* all suggest further comparative investigation.[15] In addition, Nadia Valman's extensive work on Jewish women writers offers a way of looking in more comparative detail at conversionist discourse and the construction of the literary image of 'the Jewess' in English literature and in Welsh culture.[16]

Nadia Valman, Bryan Cheyette and others consider how 'the Jew' as ambivalent image is woven into the fabric of canonical English literature, and how such imaging challenges what Cheyette calls 'the humanizing pretensions of the Anglo-American literary canon and liberal culture in general'.[17] It is certainly the case that this kind of imaging of Jews in Welsh canonical literature in both languages troubles equivalent (but by no means identical) humanising pretensions, and a comprehensive examination of the Welsh literary canon in this light would be invaluable, particularly one that takes a more theoretically-driven approach like that of Cheyette's. Although this study does take in some canonical literary texts along the way, it also ranges very far from the canon. Nevertheless, I hope that the approach I take helps to accommodate the complex imaging of Jews in Welsh writing, and can facilitate an analysis of why such imaging is used.

Given that Wales barely figures in Anglo-Jewish studies, no matter if these are sometimes termed 'British-Jewish' studies, there is a considerable amount of groundwork to be done, and a process of uncovering and rehabilitation to be undertaken, much as has been the case with women's writing (and, indeed, with Welsh women's writing). Although this study is shaped by forms of enquiry undertaken by researchers in related fields, in large part it constitutes a project of recovering overlooked texts, and it is therefore necessarily descriptive and historical. While the imaging of Jews in Wales needs to be considered simultaneously in Welsh terms and in broader Jewish literary and cultural terms, the Jewish considerations can occlude some of the specificities of the Welsh cultural context. Like any theoretical approach, it can sometimes prove overbearing to the material itself. Consequently, I use the term 'semitic discourse' with some diffidence. 'Semitic' to denote 'Jewish' is in itself problematic, given the shift from its original philological meaning in which it included the peoples and cultures of the Semitic language group; it is more problematic yet in the context of Israel and Palestine, around which a great deal of the Welsh discussion revolves.

David Cesarani's definition of semitic *discourse* might suggest a theoretically 'innocent' or neutral use of the latter term to describe, simply, a specific rhetorical framework that is used in different ways according to context. Nevertheless, the power of that rhetorical framework to determine attitudes and social relations is evident, and whether or not it affects how people behave towards Jews, it certainly informs how Jews see their social position. So the term indicates both discourse in a neutral descriptive sense, and Discourse in the sense in which the interpreters of Michel Foucault have often deployed it to denote the use of language as an instrument of social power and control.[18] There is inevitably a slippage between the two in this study, though I endeavour to use it for the most part in a theoretically neutral way.

However much I might hope for an Eden of theoretical innocence, this is not entirely possible where postcolonial approaches to Welsh literature are concerned – not least because of the argument over whether Wales was a colony, internal or otherwise, and whether it is now post-colonial, and because of Wales's contribution to imperialist endeavours elsewhere, particularly in Ottoman and British Mandate Palestine. Questions of colonialism and postcolonialism, particularly with respect to Palestine and in the context of Zionism, are persistent subtexts of this study and are sometimes its subject – though the approach might be better characterised as post-Zionist than postcolonial. Relatively little postcolonial analysis has been carried out on British imperial literary texts that deal with Palestine, either before, during or after its colonial presence there, and Eitan Bar-Yosef's *The Holy Land in English Culture* is a major intervention in the field. Perhaps the question of British colonialism in Palestine has been displaced (or replaced) by the more immediately gripping evidence of what many see as Jewish colonialism, and the Palestinian post-colonial experience. Similarly, although a considerable amount of attention has been paid to postcolonial theory and its applicability to Wales, there has been relatively little analysis of Wales's own colonial enterprises and aspirations (in Palestine, India and Argentina, for example), and its willing participation in British imperial endeavour.[19] Nevertheless, as I hope this study shows in small part, Wales is as implicated as any of the constituent nations of the UK in the postcolonial legacy of the British Mandate in Palestine, and 'Palestine' as a geographical, historical and metaphorical figure has left a deep and perhaps ineradicable print on Wales.

1

Tracing the Wales-Israel tradition

'The Welsh-Israelite tradition is, I believe, the most resonant bourdon in
Welsh history, both spiritual and political.'
— Dorian Llywelyn, *Sacred Place, Chosen People*

A CENTURIES-LONG TRADITION?

At the close of the twentieth century, and into the early years of the
twenty-first, several publications appeared that laid claim to a continuing,
pervasive and ancient tradition of Welsh identification with the Jews. The
proliferation of publications between 1999 and 2002 dealing with Welsh
attitudes to Jews was not entirely coincidental: in 1997, residents of Wales
voted in a second national referendum on a devolved assembly, and in
1999 the first National Assembly for Wales was elected. Although the
research for Dorian Llywelyn's book *Sacred Place, Chosen People*
preceded these events, it was a time when publisher support for a
re-imagining of Wales was widespread and varied: in the same year the
University of Wales Press also published John Harvey's *Image of the
Invisible: the Visualization of Religion in Welsh Nonconformist Tradition*,
which, like Llywelyn's book, as discussed below, explored a tradition of
Wales-Israel connections and Welsh-Jewish relationships.

The late 1990s was a time of national narrative reinvented on a grand
scale for a new national status and identity, including comprehensive
surveys of the literature in both languages (such as *The New Companion to
the Literature of Wales* published in 1998), and of visual art (such as Peter
Lord's three-volume Visual Culture of Wales series, published between

1998 and 2003).[1] But while that new narrative re-imagined the past, including past religious traditions put to new purpose, it also engaged with a multicultural civic present and future: 1999 saw the publication of titles such as *Nation, Identity and Social Theory: Perspectives from Wales*, followed not long after by *A Tolerant Nation?: Exploring Ethnic Diversity in Wales*.[2] Smaller presses also engaged in the newly self-conscious project of imagining an inclusive civic Wales, with Planet publishing *Sugar and Slate* by Charlotte Williams and Seren producing an anthology of Welsh writings on Jews, *Chosen People: Wales and the Jews*, edited by poet Grahame Davies.[3] Some of these developments had their earlier partial research expression in magazines and journals – indeed, W. D. Rubinstein's 're-examination' of the Tredegar riots of 1911 had appeared in *Welsh History Review* in 1997.[4]

The appearance at the close of the twentieth century of accounts dealing with Jews – those by Llewelyn, Harvey, Davies and Rubinstein – had its forerunner a hundred years earlier: at the beginning of the century and in different circumstances, but under the pressure of a parallel need for a reinvented national tradition following the disappointing demise of the Cymru Fydd movement, D. Wynne Evans published a series of essays dealing in direct and indirect ways with Jews in the prominent cultural journal *Young Wales*.

Produced at the beginning of the century between 1901 and 1905, and at the end between 1997 and 2002, these accounts took a variety of forms, and served apparently widely divergent purposes, but they have in common a strongly politically-motivated argument about Welsh particularity, and about a notional 'true' Welshness.[5] They also have in common a claim that the Welsh are particularly well-disposed towards the Jews, that Jews have experienced a welcome in Wales distinct from their reception elsewhere, and that the Welsh have taken a unique and disproportionate interest in their social welfare and their political status. The evidence used to support these claims ranges from historical material relating to Welsh support for Jewish causes; visual imaging that compares biblical Palestine with Wales; the adaptation of the Hebrew *ulpan* system to the Welsh *wlpan*; comparisons made by Welsh writers from the seventeenth century to the present; statements and actions of prominent Welsh individuals, and positive 'philosemitic' or 'loving' and 'admiring' treatment of 'the Jew' in Welsh literature in both languages.[6] All of this constitutes a tradition, which, it is argued, derives from the strongly Old Testament biblical orientation of Welsh nonconformity, in which the Welsh identified themselves closely with biblical Jews. Such an identification purportedly predisposed the Welsh also to identify closely with post-biblical, historical Jews. This preponderance of interest in and 'supportive' attitude towards Jews also derives, it is argued, from earlier 'traditional Welsh historiography', a body of pre-twentieth century writing that posits ancient foundations for the Welsh nation, including biblical ethnic and linguistic descent. This latter tradition is traced back in various forms to the seventeenth century (and, by Dorian Llywelyn, to the sixth).

At the beginning of the twentieth century, the source for this account of a Jewish narrative thread in Welsh cultural life was a nonconformist minister. At the end of the twentieth century the sources were a historian, a poet, an art historian and an academic Catholic priest, all writing in English. The form the more recent accounts take – three substantial books published by Welsh presses, and articles in a literary journal and a history quarterly – is indicative of the significant change that took place in Welsh literary and cultural life in the twentieth century: the emergence of a substantial, Wales-based, English-language book-publishing infrastructure. At the beginning of the century there was nothing like this. Instead, a diversity of small, high-quality and voraciously-read cultural journals came and went at considerable speed.[7] The absence of institutional book publishers meant that any attempt at an overarching narrative was necessarily fragmented and occasional, and relied also on oral transmission – indeed oral tradition heavily coloured popular historiography and other forms of publishing in both languages in Wales in the early years of the twentieth century. In contrast, the development of stable and substantial structures by the end of the century helped to support the emergence and then reinforcement of the kind of grand nation-building narrative to which these more recent books contribute. However, the institutional *gravitas* provided by substantial publishing structures does not make these accounts any less subject to critical scrutiny as imagined national narrative than their more fragmented predecessors.

There is indeed a considerable body of work, consisting of both poetry and non-fiction prose produced over several centuries, in which 'the Jew' or 'the Jews' are the subject of apparently positive investigation or comment, and Welsh and Jewish cultural and national aspirations are compared. However, the nature of that interest in Jews is considerably more ambiguous and complex than its commentators have so far acknowledged. For example, there appears to be a significant degree of confusion between, on the one hand, *notional* Jews and, on the other, *historical* Jews. My distinction here might at first seem itself to be notional. By 'notional Jews' I mean those representative or metaphorical Jews – often referred to collectively as 'the Jews' – who include and derive from biblical textual Jews (one might say 'imagined' Jews in Benedict Anderson's terms, though this is an imagined 'other' rather than the imagined self).[8] By 'historical Jews' I mean post-biblical contemporary Jews of a particular present moment, whether directly encountered or not. I should emphasise, however, that by distinguishing between historical and notional Jews in this way I am not commenting on the historical reality of the deep Jewish past, nor on continuities or discontinuities between biblical and contemporary Jewish identity.

I diverge from Bryan Cheyette here in his distinction between 'the Jew' as signifier, and Jews as living reality, and I do so because of peculiarities of the Welsh context that will, I hope, become apparent.[9] In accounts of Welsh interest in Jews, evidence of interest in notional Jews is frequently and seemingly unconsciously conflated with evidence of interest in historical Jews, and this has led to a quite skewed impression of the imprint that these various forms of interest (and putative support) have left on the culture.

The disparity between claims made about this tradition of Welsh identification and the evidence to support such claims derives not only from the conflation of notional and historical Jews, but also from the sometimes deliberate entanglement of distinct areas of discourse from the preceding several hundred years. Although it is not possible to categorise this discourse tidily, and although the simplification in such categorisation is ultimately somewhat misleading, it is useful to identify several interrelated but distinct narrative threads that will be explored in more detail later.

The first to emerge, chronologically speaking, is the kind of commentary generally identified by historians of religion as 'traditional Welsh historiography', which posits mythical biblical and Brythonic (ancient Celtic) ethnic origins for the Welsh people, and Hebrew roots for the Welsh language. As discussed below, Dorian Llywelyn argues that elements of this commentary may be traced in its earliest form to the sixth-century monk Gildas, author of *De Excidio Britanniae* (The Ruin of Britain), but it was popularised in the eighteenth century by Theophilus Evans, author of the work *Drych y Prif Oesoedd* (The Mirror of the First Ages).[10]

A second category concerns the Welsh self-identification *as* biblical Jews or Israelites, in which notional and historical Jews bear little if any relation to one another (that is, Jews are considered as almost a legendary image rather than as a continued historical reality). This commentary intertwines with 'traditional historiography', but in its most overt form emerges as a product of the late nineteenth-century height of Welsh nonconformity, particularly with the growth of the Sunday School movement. This might be termed the 'Welsh-Israelite' tradition, along the lines of Llywelyn's arguments about a religious or spiritual tradition (although, as I shall indicate in my discussion of Caradoc Evans, the legacy of this 'spiritual tradition' is perhaps more ambiguous than the one Llywelyn describes).

A later development, emerging in the very early twentieth century, constitutes more overt political discourse and consists of commentary that compares the historical experience and social and political status of historical Jews and the Welsh, including the status of the Hebrew and Welsh languages. Although aspects of it appear earlier (and for some, such as Gwynfor Evans, this remained a religiously-informed comparison), this is for the most part a twentieth-century concern of a largely secular, post-nonconformist Welsh-language culture. For the sake of convenience, this might be termed a 'Wales-Israel' tradition, as it deals primarily with questions of national self-determination and national language revival.

Finally there is a very long history of commentary on the abject status of post-biblical Jews, which includes expressions of sympathy for their condition and support for their emancipation. This commentary in the very great majority of cases constitutes conversionist discourse, which is perhaps the least acknowledged or analysed of all commentary about Jews in the Welsh context.[11]

The conflation of putative Welsh attitudes to notional and historical Jews can be traced to the beginning of the twentieth century when, in the context of the Celtic Revival, the growth of cultural nationalism, and of Welsh patriotism within a British Empire framework, D. Wynne Evans twined together motifs of 'traditional historiography', Welsh self-identification as biblical Jews, Hebrew and Welsh language relationships, political comparisons, and millenarian 'admiration' and 'support' for Jews. If Evans was a selective and deliberate compiler, he was nevertheless redacting for his new purposes a widespread cultural tradition drawn from a multiplicity of sources, including traditional historiography. Importantly, this bringing together of notional and historical Jews by Evans, and his accompanying claim of peculiar Welsh tolerance, may be seen as the root source of some late twentieth-century writers' conclusions about a long-lived 'tradition of identification'.

However, even within those areas of discussion relating only to *notional* Jews, the evidence of continuity and influence over a long period is questionable. It is, for example, debatable whether or to what degree 'traditional historiography', which incorporates foundation myths such as descent from the biblical figure of Gomer, exerted an influence on Welsh nonconformity and particularly on Calvinistic Methodism, a powerful Welsh denomination in the nineteenth century. Consequently, if there was little continuity, the argument that this traditional historiography predisposed the Welsh to any particular attitude towards Jews becomes, effectively, spurious. In addition, while it seems clear that the nineteenth-century chapel tradition of identification *as* biblical Jews (whatever its sources), itself predisposed Welsh people to take a certain interest in historical Jews, it is not clear that this interest was either positive or even necessarily benign. Nevertheless, in late twentieth-century retellings of the 'tradition' that D. Wynne Evans had articulated in 1901 and 1902, it is widely assumed (but not demonstrated) that these culturally prominent attitudes to notional (biblical) Jews had an influence on the development of decidedly positive attitudes to historical Jews. The evidence, however, seems to point to a different conclusion and suggests that the complex of Welsh attitudes to historical Jews derives as much from a tradition of conversionism (including a relatively recent tradition of applied conversionism) as from any long-standing tradition of 'identification'.

THE LATE TWENTIETH-CENTURY PROMULGATORS

Who, then, are these writers who cite a tradition of identification, and what exactly do they claim about such a tradition? Between 1997 and 2002, such a tradition is articulated (although not critically analysed) by, among others, historian W. D. Rubinstein and poet Grahame Davies. John Harvey's survey, *Image of the Invisible* (to which Eitan Bar-Yosef refers in his seminal volume *The Holy Land in English Culture*), explores biblical influences in Welsh visual culture.[12] Quite distinct from these, and considered separately, is Dorian Llywelyn's work, which is also cited by Bar-Yosef. This book, *Sacred Place, Chosen People*, constitutes a rigorous analysis, in a specifically religious and spiritual framework, of what Llywelyn calls the 'Welsh-Israelite tradition', though it omits consideration of the Jewish element in the Welsh-Israelite equation.

The increase, at the end of the twentieth century, in references to the 'tradition of Welsh identification with the Jews', and the emergence of several publications dealing with it either centrally or in passing, is suggestive. It is perhaps the demise of the prominent religious and political movements that were informed by the belief in such a tradition that makes it ripe for reinvention – and makes the national narrative ripe for reinvention, too.

W. D. Rubinstein, however, does not appear to be concerned with a reinvention of Welshness; on the contrary, he states that the larger purpose of his intervention is to argue that philosemitism rather than antisemitism predominated in Britain generally, a subject on which he has published several times.[13] In his article on the Tredegar riots, published in 1997 in *Welsh History Review*, in which he reassesses and then dismisses earlier 'antisemitic' interpretations of the 1911 riots, he provides a formulation of Welsh 'philosemitism' that usefully illustrates the way in which an idea of Welsh identification *with* Jews has developed:

> Philosemitism – support and admiration for Jews, *both* ancient and modern – became a recognizable and distinctive part of Welsh culture and national identity with the rise of nonconformity and the fundamental importance of the Bible and of the saga of the ancient Hebrews. It is no exaggeration to say that it permeated every aspect of Welsh culture until very recent times . . . Identification with, and knowledge of, the Old Testament Hebrews was pervasive in nineteenth-century Welsh culture.[14]

The considerable problems of Rubinstein's definition of 'philosemitism', and his division of attitudes towards Jews into a binary opposition between 'philosemitism' and 'antisemitism', are discussed in chapter 3, but it is his argument that '*philo*-semitism . . . was virtually ubiquitous in Edwardian Wales and, indeed, an important component of Welsh national identity as it emerged during the nineteenth century', that is useful here.[15]

Rubinstein's conflation of philosemitism and identification with biblical Jews recurs throughout the article. Indeed, he makes explicit a direct causal link between this religious identification and expressions of sympathy to Jews, though this is not supported by his evidence:

> The reaffirmation of Welsh national identity in the nineteenth century, so heavily religious and bound up with nonconformity, emphasized even more strongly than previously the association between the Old Testament Hebrews and the Welsh people.
>
> This continuing linkage resulted in an extraordinary outpouring of sympathy and support for persecuted Jews throughout the world during each instance in the late Victorian and Edwardian periods when the oppression of Jews became international incidents.[16]

As Rubinstein details such an outpouring of sympathy in Britain more widely, this does not seem to support the 'extraordinary' case of Wales. His promotion of David Lloyd George and the Reverend John Mills as examples of 'philosemites' is also deeply problematic: as will be shown, their attitudes are very much more complex and multiform than this simple binary designation of philosemitism or antisemitism permits. Nevertheless, he concludes:

> It seems abundantly clear from these examples – which are only the tip of an enormous iceberg – that philo-semitism and the specific identification of the Welsh people with the Jews have been a real and important component of modern Welsh national identity . . . It probably remained a factor in the late 1990s. Furthermore, it is extremely difficult to identify any element among Wales's opinion leaders and notables in modern times that dissented from this pattern or for which anti-semitism comprised a perceptible strand in its world view.[17]

These statements are somewhat amplified a few years later in Rubinstein's review of *The Chosen People: Wales and the Jews*, an anthology of writing on Jews edited by poet Grahame Davies. Here he argues that

> the Jews have had an impact upon the cultural and religious evolution of modern Wales unequivocally out of all proportion to their numbers; in some respects Old Testament and Hebrew images, terminology, and morality have been virtually coterminous with Welsh national identity as it developed from the mid-eighteenth to the mid-twentieth century. For generation after generation until living memory, the Old Testament account of the history of the ancient Jewish people was voluntarily grafted upon Wales, such that Non-conformist Wales almost became surrogate Jews of a kind [*sic*].[18]

This characterisation of Welsh nonconformity is somewhat monolithic, but perhaps more telling here is Rubinstein's compression of 'Non-conformist Wales' into that strange 'surrogate Jews of a kind'. This apparently unnoticed slippage is significant and, as it happens, accurate: as discussed below, identification *as* Jews is a wholly different matter from identification *with* Jews.

Grahame Davies, the editor of the anthology that Rubinstein reviews, is considerably more attentive to the range of attitudes that have been expressed by Welsh writers towards Jews. Such attentiveness is apparent in his choice of material for the anthology, and in his introductory notes to each entry. Nevertheless, he too is limited by this binary opposition of antisemitism and philosemitism, which demonstrably precludes understanding a good deal of nuance and complexity. For his purpose, however, this either/or understanding serves not as a constraint but as a blessing: it allows him, like Rubinstein, to isolate expressions of hostility from normative discourse and label them as an exception, rather than consider them in the context of a spectrum of complex and contradictory attitudes.

Usefully, Davies attempts to distinguish Welsh responses to historical Jews from references to biblical Jews, but explains the difficulty in making such a separation:

> There is inevitable overlap between the two categories, of course: for the majority of their history, most Welsh people's attitudes to the real Jews of their own day were profoundly influenced by the Bible. However, I have tried to confine myself to the material . . . which truly reflects an encounter – however conceptual – between two contemporary peoples, an encounter that is therefore the real material of a study in ethnic relations.[19]

Davies suggests that if 'imitation is the sincerest form of flattery, then the Welsh have certainly flattered the Jews' (p. 19), and the material collected in his anthology lends considerable weight to an argument about a sustained interest in Jews on the part of Welsh writers. However, the selections often constitute discourse on 'the Jew' and, indeed in more complex ways, on 'the Jewess', which complicates the argument of identification implicit in that 'flattery', and implicit, as he suggests, throughout the anthology. Overtly conversionist poems such as 'The Virgin of Israel' by David Owen, 'The Jews' by Henry Vaughan and 'The Jews' by George Herbert, are presented as examples of Welsh 'identification' and 'engagement', but although Davies acknowledges their conversionism, he does not comment upon its implications. For example, according to Davies, 'The Jews' by George Herbert shows the poet 'recognising the Christian debt to the Jews, and, while desiring their conversion, nonetheless regarding their state with compassion rather than condemnation' (p. 48).

However, in acknowledging the millenarianism and conversionism of Morgan Llwyd, Henry Vaughan, George Herbert and others in his introduction, Davies does recognise that conversionism is 'an attitude which usually combines varying degrees of admiration and sensitivity towards the Jewish people with a desire – wholly offensive to a Jewish sensibility – to change them into something different' (p. 13). Davies struggles with this contradiction, arguing, for example, that the poem 'Wal yr Wylofain' (The Wailing Wall) by Gwenallt 'depicts both an instinctive human and communal sympathy tempered by a reservation based on an ideological Christian position. As such, it is a late illustration of how Welsh Christians encountering the Jews have held in tension the two responses of affinity and apprehension' (p. 74). Similarly, he proposes that Gwenallt's work, despite being 'consistent with the traditional Christian position that the Jews need to recognise Christ as their Saviour . . . does not indicate any prejudice' (p. 184). Another poem by Gwenallt 'deplores the persecution of the Jews' (ibid.). However, this is to overlook the equivocations in that poem, 'Y Coed' (The Trees), which ameliorate or qualify such condemnation of Jewish persecution.[20]

Davies chooses not to quote the early nineteenth-century book-length poem *Golwg ar gyflwr yr Iuddewon* (A look at the state of the Jews) by Daniel Evans, though he does refer to it as another example of 'this widespread Welsh response to Jewish history' (p. 47). The poem provides even stronger conversionist material than is found in David Owen's poem 'The Virgin of Israel', and would perhaps make Davies's own equivocations more difficult to sustain. *Golwg ar gyflwr yr Iuddewon*, published in Aberystwyth in 1826, includes stanzas that begin: 'Gwargaled, O Israel, gwargaled yn wir' (Obstinate, Oh Israel, truly obstinate), and 'O Israel, gan addef addefwch eich bai' (Oh Israel, in confessing, admit your fault).[21] Unfortunately, Davies explains that 'this interest and identification, although motivated largely by a conversionist motive [*sic*], nonetheless prepared the ground for Christian sympathy with 19th [*sic*] and early twentieth century Zionist aspirations . . . a project in which the Welsh played an important part' (p. 47).

In his notes on the award-winning early twentieth-century poet Crwys, Davies finds 'a more magnanimous attitude again, more concerned with understanding and explaining, and less with bending the Jewish people to fit a Christian scheme' (p. 65). According to Davies, the poet displays

> a response which largely repudiates earlier prejudices about the Jews (although it does still endorse some lingering suspicious [*sic*] relating to Jewish religious intransigence and supposed Jewish financial greed) . . . Written in January 1918, only a month after the conquest of Jerusalem . . . it shows a predominantly admiring picture of the Jewish people. (p. 65)

Despite these claims, the translated extract from Crwys that follows shows a highly racialised and Orientalist essentialism in a discourse on 'the Jew' as unchangeably other, complete with reference to Shylock, jealous protection of Jewish communal membership, and simultaneously depraved and cunning financial characteristics. It is not clear how a text that reads, 'Yes, such a person as the Jew exists, and there is no device that can either estrange his hand and skin nor that can exile Galilee from his speech' can be understood as 'magnanimous' or 'admiring'.[22]

These apologetics by Davies for the material he introduces, his equivocation about conversionism and its implications, and his oversight of some common stereotyped imaging of Jews, all make his shock at discovering instances of less ambiguous hostile stereotypes more comprehensible. In describing that discovery, Davies also reveals where his particular intervention in promoting this 'tradition of identification' fits. With the exception of 'the single and often-quoted example of Saunders Lewis', he explains, he had expected to find that his research would reveal work 'animated by the values on which the Welsh pride themselves: respect for cultural diversity; compassion towards suffering; solidarity with the oppressed, and an instinctive feeling for the spiritual' (p. 9). Instead, he goes on, although 'the broad mass of material is characterised by those qualities of empathy . . . there is also material ranging from the well-meaning but patronising, through the insensitive to the prejudiced and downright offensive' (p. 10). Of his discovery of antisemitic stereotype in O. M. Edwards he confesses:

> I found the actual passage almost unbelievable. However . . . it is all too real, and it must be recorded that such a great servant of Welsh culture as O. M. Edwards produced this shameful, credulous, extended endorsement of the age-old conspiracy theory about Jewish greed. (p. 157)

Because this is an isolated example by the author, Davies concludes that the passage shows 'how even an otherwise generous nature like O. M. Edwards's can prove vulnerable to the irrational virus of anti-semitism' (p. 158).

The overt hostile stereotyping by Edwards is, in its period, common enough – and, as Hazel Walford Davies observes, this particular example of it was probably 'met with silent acquiescence by the majority of Edwards's readers in 1889'.[23] What is surprising here, therefore, is not Edwards's aside on the Jews but Davies's shock at discovering it. But belief in the now rather battered myth of pure, liberal Wales has been widespread and resilient – a myth in which people saw themselves as 'the most upright, God-fearing, radical, moral, philosophical, cultured and tolerant in the world', in the words of Neil Evans.[24] It was in order to help preserve that myth, perhaps, that an editor of O. M. Edwards, sensitive to changed attitudes, chose not to reproduce the passage in a later edition of the book in which it had originally appeared.[25]

Though he acknowledges that the results of his research challenged his notions of marked Welsh tolerance, Davies still isolates such material from normative discourse of 'empathy' and 'identification' with Jews, taking pains, for example, to dismiss some truly offensive statements (given the timing) made by W. J. Gruffydd in 1941 in *Y Llenor* as being 'entirely out of touch with the Welsh Nonconformity and liberalism for which Gruffydd was otherwise such an eloquent spokesman'.[26] As W. J. Gruffydd was author of a biography of O. M. Edwards, this is evidently not the case: he was very much in touch with that tradition – and expressed contradictory positions in ways that are quite typical of a broad general discourse on Jews in the 1930s and 1940s, as is discussed in chapter 3.

In a somewhat intemperate aside to his discussion of O. M. Edwards, Davies goes further yet with Caradoc Evans, the extraordinary modernist fiction writer of the early twentieth century, whose depiction of Wales for an English readership was so widely condemned. Davies accuses Caradoc Evans of both antisemitism and a treachery comparable to that of a nineteenth-century Jewish convert to Christianity, Jacob Brafman (given in the text as Joseph Brafman). 'For its part', he observes, 'Wales too has produced its share of anti-Welsh Welshmen . . . Caradoc Evans made a career out of calumniating his own people for the delectation of English prejudice in a way very similar to that in which Brafman exposed his fellow-Jews to Gentile hatred'.[27] In fact, as discussed later in chapter 3, Caradoc Evans's writing provides one of the more important examples of the other tradition from which Davies seeks, effectively, to isolate the work in his anthology: that of Welsh identification *as* Jews. Indeed Evans proves to be a kind of literary primate 'missing link' between a tradition of Welsh identification *as* biblical Jews and identification or 'friendliness' (in his spiky deployment of the word) *with* historical Jews.

By isolating instances of overt hostility as exceptional, and by overlooking the often ambivalent nuance of purported Welsh 'admiration', both Rubinstein and Davies reinforce the image of Wales as being peculiarly well-disposed towards Jews and, by extension, peculiarly tolerant in a wider sense, when work by Charlotte Williams, Neil Evans, Paul O'Leary and, subsequently, Glenn Jordan, among others, undermines the foundations of that comfortable notion.[28] Rubinstein and Davies have also both inherited and repeated a merging of disparate areas of discourse that, under examination, reveal a somewhat different story. Consequently, the way in which they invoke an older 'tradition' is perhaps as interesting for what it says about their social and political agendas in the present as it is interesting for the material evidence they use to argue their case.

In contrast, John Harvey's argument in *Image of the Invisible* about a tradition of Welsh identification with Jews in *visual* culture rather struggles for lack of material. Unlike Welsh literature, Welsh art does not show a significant imaging of Jews, and Harvey's survey is primarily interesting in this context for the source material upon which he relies. He locates this 'tradition of identification' in the turn-of-the century Celtic Revival, and reproduces as evidence the first page of O. M. Edwards's *Hanes Cymru*, in which an image of Snowdon is juxtaposed with a text of Moses blessing the twelve tribes of Israel. Here Harvey combines biblical and historical Jews in a now-familiar way:

> For Edwards, Wales, tokenly represented by the painting, evoked Israel and was thus heir to its spiritual prosperity. This coupling was one expression of a more general identification established between the two peoples which assumed a particular intensity and pervasive influence around the turn of the twentieth century. This was at the height of the so-called Celtic Renaissance and a period of burgeoning national prestige.[29]

One striking image that Harvey does find is a map from 1900, which shows the names of the tribes and areas of biblical Israel superimposed upon the Welsh counties.[30] A publication of the Sunday School Union of Great Britain, it is an unusually strong visual representation of the identification of Wales as a new Israel, and suggests one of the means by which children were educated in the topography of Palestine (a biblical topography) through the Sunday schools.[31] But with the exception of this image, and geographic comparisons made by Welsh travellers to Palestine, Harvey provides little evidence to support this tradition as being widespread in the visual culture.[32] Much of his evidence for this turn-of-the-century claim is the work of D. Wynne Evans, a writer whom Rubinstein also cites, and whose essays are discussed in detail in the next chapter.[33] In this way late twentieth-century promulgators of the 'tradition' rely on the early twentieth-century compiler. However, unlike Rubinstein, Harvey recognises those origins in the twentieth century, and does not take as evidence the claims D. Wynne Evans himself makes for the existence of an ancient tradition.

DORIAN LLYWELYN'S WELSH-ISRAELITE TRADITION

In contrast to these other authors, Dorian Llywelyn does not make claims about Welsh attitudes to either historical or notional Jews in his *Sacred*

Place, Chosen People. Instead he focuses on a spiritual tradition in which the collective, 'Israel' (that is, the collective of biblical Jews), is always a representation, a religious or spiritual metaphor of origin and example. His text is remarkable for the near-total absence of historical Jews, and in this regard he repeats and reinforces a separation long established in the texts that he discusses. Indeed, in the 'tradition of identification' that he investigates, historical Jews are effectively removed from the picture, and replaced by the Welsh.

Although Llywelyn is by no means the first to discuss the influence of the Bible on Welsh literature (he is preceded, for example, by Glanmor Williams and Derec Llwyd Morgan), his survey provides a new analytical approach of sacred space, notions of 'election', and a consideration of the risk of idolatry of the land in a Catholic theological framework.[34] Llywelyn identifies a 'substratum' to a religiously-inflected formulation of nation and nationalism that has roots as far back as the sixth century, makes appearances through the seventeenth and eighteenth centuries, and emerges most powerfully in the nineteenth. He locates the beginnings of this 'Welsh-Israelite tradition', as he calls it (sometimes referred to, confusingly, as a 'Wales-Israel' tradition), in Gildas's *De Excidio Britanniae*.[35] Gildas exhorts the new Chosen of the Christian church, his Christianised Romano-British countrymen – the proto-Welsh-as-Jews – to strive for moral rectitude, and he castigates the decadence and depravity of religious leaders, warning that the disasters of pagan proto-English Saxon invasions are (in Llywelyn's words), 'a punishment from God'.[36] By implication Gildas assigns a biblical lineage to the British (which is to say the Welsh), giving his readers, according to Llywelyn, 'the image of Britain as a holy land, a new land of Israel for a new people of God'.[37] Importantly for subsequent developments, Llywelyn explains:

> Gildas's theologically based scheme of things . . . leads him famously to identify the people of Britain as *praesens Israel*. We should note that this is not just a simile, in which x is said to be *like* y. The metaphor, where x *is* y, identifies or joins the two realities . . . Gildas's description is more than a literary device: in a typological sense the Christian Britons *are* the inheritors of the Old Testament promise.[38]

Llywelyn's equation unequivocally identifies this discourse as one of identification *as* Jews, rather than *with* Jews (which is to say as biblical Jews), and it is an equation maintained throughout his discussion of writers subsequent to Gildas.

Llywelyn traces the course of this self-depiction as the biblical chosen after it first appears in Gildas, and locates its re-emergence in the

seventeenth century with *Y Ffydd Ddi-ffuant* (The Unfeigned Faith) by
Charles Edwards, which was published in Oxford in 1667. The first edition
of this work was 'no more than an uninspired abridgement of John Foxe's
Acts and Monuments', according to one account, but the third and much
enlarged edition, published in 1677, became 'one of the classics of the
Welsh language'.[39] According to Llywelyn, 'it is difficult to overstate the
influence of *Y Ffydd Ddi-ffuant*'.[40]

In this text, Edwards builds on the Welsh-biblical associations made by
Gildas, but adds both biblical linguistic and genealogical roots – if indeed
not genetic ones. Although this was not original to Edwards, it was
Edwards who 'gave full expression to an instinct which had been suggested
in muffled tones over the previous century or so'.[41] Edwards devotes an
entire chapter to the purported linguistic connections between Hebrew and
Welsh, a connection explored later by Theophilus Evans in *Drych y Prif
Oesoedd* in 1716, and also explored by Henry Rowlands in *Mona Antiqua
Restaurata* in 1723.[42]

The extensive comparison of Welsh and Hebrew vocabulary and
linguistic structures by Edwards is dismissed by Llywelyn as 'logically
and philologically . . . deliciously eccentric nonsense', which, according
to Orin Gensler and other contemporary linguists, is not at all the case.[43]
On the contrary, the so-called Celtic/Hamo-Semitic 'problem' continues to
dog the discipline of linguistics.[44] Nevertheless, Llywelyn concedes,
'theologically and politically, it is highly significant nonsense', for, as he
argues, 'Edwards's linguistic fantasy is part of his attempt to strengthen
the grafting of Welsh national identity on to the trunk of Israel'.[45] Edwards
suggests that the Welsh came originally 'from the countries of the east, for
there is so much agreement between our tongue and the tongues of these
parts'; consequently, according to Llywelyn, in Edwards's formulation
'not only are the Welsh *praesens* Israel. They carry in their veins as well as
on their lips something of ancient Israel.'[46] However, what Llywelyn
quotes from Edwards suggests something else: 'Some suppose that we are
the offspring of Cam, and some of the remnant of the Gentiles who escaped
from the land of Canaan towards the West'. This attribution of descent
from *Gentiles* rather than Jews is curiously indicative: even when identifying the Jewish origins of the Welsh, Edwards stops short of an ethnic
attribution, though it is not a reluctance that Llywelyn appears to notice.[47]

Election and denominational differences

While Llywelyn may be sceptical about the linguistic connections made
by Edwards, it is the matter that this linguistic correlation *supports* which

is perhaps most important – namely the insertion by Edwards of the question of 'election', of 'chosenness', in this story of Welsh origin.[48]

The importance of belief in the Christian inheritance of election is a common attribute of Protestant tradition and, across a range of Protestant denominations, has given rise to similar formulations of particular nations as 'elect' and identified as biblical Jews in this way – among them, for example, the Dutch and the English (indeed the Anglo-Israel or British-Israel theory, discussed in the next chapter, elaborates on this identification in disturbing ways). If the association or identification is by no means unique to Welsh religious tradition (and the cultural and political nationalism arising out of it), nevertheless it takes a unique Welsh expression. Perhaps the near-total absence of Jews in Britain in the period to trouble such an association, as well as the apparently close similarities between Welsh and Hebrew, helped to facilitate the co-option of the biblical covenant between the Jews and God, so that a belief in a new covenant between the Welsh and God became integral to the sense of Welsh identity.[49]

The theme of the Welsh as the new Chosen articulated by Charles Edwards reappears in altered form in the Welsh or Calvinistic Methodism of the eighteenth and nineteenth centuries.[50] E. Wyn James suggests that while Welsh Methodists would have inherited traditional Welsh historiography in part through Charles Edwards, Morgan Llwyd, the popular verse of Rhys Prichard ('Vicar Prichard'), and through oral tradition, the main source was probably Theophilus Evans's *Drych y Prif Oesoedd*, which, according to Prys Morgan, was 'the most widely read history book in Welsh in the eighteenth and nineteenth centuries' and, according to Glanmor Williams, was 'the most influential book on the subject of the history of religion in Wales'.[51] It was this book, published in 1716, that popularised ideas of election, of the relationship between Welsh and Hebrew, and of the relationship between the Welsh and the biblical Jews. It was Theophilus Evans who articulated a national genealogy and a mythological origin in the biblical Gomer (a name which, through a contorted linguistic derivation, becomes cognate with 'Cymru' – Wales), and in so doing gave to the Welsh, according to Glanmor Williams, 'an impeccable Old Testament origin'.[52] Theophilus Evans believed Welsh to be the language closest in form to Hebrew, 'which conferred upon it unrivalled linguistic purity and distinction'.[53] Less than a century later, in 1802, the Methodist leader Thomas Charles of Bala, for example, cites the connection between Welsh and Hebrew in his *Geiriadur Ysgrythurol* (Scriptural Dictionary). In the entry on language, he posits that, in James's words,

'Welsh is closely related to Hebrew, that it is the oldest and purest language in the West, and only one step removed from the original language of the world'.[54]

This claim was used in arguments for the preservation and teaching of the language, and through the Sunday School movement the association of Welsh and Hebrew became part of generations of Welsh enculturation. Glanmor Williams observes:

> Sixteenth-century authors . . . or again John Lewis and Charles Edwards in the seventeenth century, had pressed the theme that in preserving the Welsh and their language God had some historic mission in store for them. Such earlier motifs were powerfully reinforced in Theophilus Evans's mind by the close affinities which he saw between the old Celts and the chosen people of the Old Testament. It led him to give a renewed and more graphic emphasis to the parallel between the Welsh and the Hebrews as an elect people, who had flourished as long as they remained faithful to divine commands but who had been subjected to condign punishment when they followed their own sinful and wayward paths.[55]

This latter consequence is of particular relevance to the marked nonconformist interest in historical Jews, which is discussed in the next chapter: the Jews' abject state, seen as a consequence of the 'sin' of rejecting Jesus as the Messiah (rather than a consequence of prejudice arising out of viewing this as a sin), could be redeemed and transformed through conversion (and, indeed, must be redeemed as a fulfilment of conditions for messianic 'return').

Glanmor Williams and others might ascribe to this work by Theophilus Evans a lasting influence, but the degree of his influence and that of Charles Edwards on Welsh Methodism in particular is contested. On the one hand, making the case for it, E. Wyn James objects to a tendency among historians of Methodism in Wales 'to emphasise a break with the past', and instead emphasises himself 'that the eighteenth-century Welsh Methodist leaders were *the heirs of traditional Welsh historiography*'.[56] In a footnote, James identifies earlier origins than Theophilus Evans for Gomeric descent, but adds that, nevertheless, 'it seems not to have gained widespread popularity in Welsh-speaking circles until the eighteenth century'.[57]

In contrast, Eryn White claims that, unlike writers such as Theophilus Evans and others, 'Methodists did not appeal to the past or refer to the traditional links between the Christian faith and the Welsh language. They preferred to celebrate their connections with other evangelical movements across the world.'[58] Dorian Llywelyn appears to agree with the latter view put forward by White, for he observes that 'as neither the material *place* of Wales nor the spiritual meaning of nationality . . . were among the concerns of early Welsh Methodism', the themes of election and of 'Wales as Israel' would not be found in prominent early Methodist writers such as William Williams, Pantycelyn or Ann Griffiths.[59] This is not to say that these writers did not use imagery from the Hebrew scriptures, for they did, but Llywelyn separates the use of such imagery from the formulation of Welsh election and the place of Wales as akin to that of biblical Israel. Nevertheless, the silence of early Welsh Methodism on traditional Welsh historiography, its associated 'Welsh-Israelite' strains, and the absence of concerns with nationality and election were only temporary. By the mid-nineteenth century, Llywelyn explains, 'the current of religious nationalism had begun to rise to the surface again, with the beginnings of a secular national consciousness', informed by continental Romanticism and Romantic Nationalism.[60]

These are perhaps fine distinctions of denominational historiography, but this disagreement over the influence of 'traditional Welsh historiography' has implications for claims that have been made about the orientation of a general 'Welsh nonconformity' and how this might or might not have predisposed the Welsh to have positive attitudes to Jews.[61]

Other denominational differences also have implications for such putative attitudes towards Jews. In a history of religion in Wales that challenges popular perceptions about the dominance of the Calvinistic Methodist movement in the nineteenth century and the actual degree of religious observance in the period, E. T. Davies distinguishes Calvinistic Methodism from other forms of nonconformity (such as the Baptists, the Independents and the Presbyterians, all of which had Puritan roots), and attributes to it a strong continued connection with the established Church from which it only separated in 1811. Consequently, Davies suggests, the Calvinistic Methodists did not play such a prominent part as the Baptists or Independents in the political campaign that led to disestablishment.[62] Nor, it appears, did the Calvinistic Methodists share the commitment to Catholic and Jewish emancipation held by the Dissenting denominations, such as the Baptists and Independents. In the 1838 Independent Assembly, for example, Hugh Pugh, a prominent Independent minister, 'maintained that it was the glory of nonconformity' (from which he excluded the Calvinistic Methodists), 'that it could not deprive others of this liberty without denying their own faith'.[63]

Nevertheless, nonconformists in general – and none more so, from the second half of the nineteenth century onwards, than the Calvinistic

Methodists – were also Christian evangelists (in the American sense of the word), and were therefore interested in the conversion of the Jews. The tension between the kind of liberal humanism expressed by Pugh on the one hand and conversionism on the other is one of the many complexities in nonconformist attitudes that have been glossed over by late twentieth-century claims about a tradition of Welsh identification with Jews. This tension is exemplified in the poetry of Gwenallt, but it is also evident in the applied missionary work of John Mills, a Welsh Calvinistic Methodist, and Margaret Jones, an Independent, both of whom sought Jewish proselytes, as discussed in the next chapter.

According to E. T. Davies, Calvinistic Methodists came into line with other nonconformist groups, at least on social issues such as emancipation from the Church of England, subsequent to the national crisis of the Blue Books of 1847, in which the Welsh were accused of moral depravity and educational poverty. The rapid expansion of the Sunday School movement that resulted as a reaction to such condemnation gave rise to a widespread childhood familiarity with the topography and history of Palestine (though this was probably a specifically biblical topography and history).[64] This 'imagined' geographical Palestine, arising from the Sunday School movement, joins apparently seamlessly with those elements of 'traditional Welsh historiography' that deal with linguistic and ethnic biblical descent, and these create the kind of coherent whole expressed in the 1900 map published in this volume as a frontispiece, where the tribes and regions of biblical Palestine are mapped onto the counties of Wales.[65]

In another such compression, E. T. Davies asserts that in the nineteenth-century Sunday schools, 'the words and phrases of the Bible were so well known as to pass into current speech, and the history and literature of the Jewish people became far more familiar to the regular attenders than that of their own people'.[66] Again, this 'Jewish people' is almost entirely a notional one, a biblical one: that history and literature ceases, suspended in time some two thousand years in the past. In this way Jews stand outside history, so that an encounter with a Jewish individual is effectively an encounter with a living anachronism. Such a response is evident, in fact, in initial reports by John Mills in London in the mid-nineteenth century, and is also described by Welsh-Jewish writers.[67] Nevertheless, this slippage between biblical Jewish history and modern Jewish history by a religious historian suggests the continued strength of that cultural compression achieved in the Welsh religious tradition.

The widespread Sunday school familiarity with this largely notional Palestine and this notional Jewish people (as against a historical, geographical Palestine and historical Jews) has been repeated frequently enough to become received wisdom. The most well-known and often-cited example is, of course, that of David Lloyd George – an example discussed by Eitan Bar-Yosef, though he removes it from its very particular Welsh context.[68] But Lloyd George's own writings about Jews, which are explored in chapter 3, further complicate simple claims of familiarity and sympathy.

The work of Charles Edwards, Theophilus Evans and other formulators of 'traditional historiography' may or may not have continued to inform the various denominations of Welsh nonconformity directly in the nineteenth century, but in less specific ways the spiritual 'Welsh-Israelite' tradition continued to flow – sometimes openly, sometimes underground, according to Llywelyn's metaphor of the tradition as a river. With its theme of the Welsh inheritance of 'election', this 'Wales-Israel spiritual tradition' is for him

> the most resonant bourdon in Welsh history, both spiritual and political. Certainly it is heard time and again – in hymnology, in poetry, in political writings, in sermons and in place-names – and its semi-conscious, instinctive echoes are to be heard in many places even today.[69]

The Welsh as biblical Jews

As I have suggested, what is made clear from Llywelyn's theological analysis is that this 'tradition' is one of Welsh identification *as* the chosen people, rather than identification *with* the chosen people. While there are innumerable instances in the late nineteenth and twentieth centuries of an invocation of Jewish biblical suffering as a metaphor for Welsh suffering, this is informed by a spiritual and theological tradition in which the Welsh *become* the children of Israel, notwithstanding the fact that Charles Edwards himself refers to ideas of descent from the 'gentile' remnant, rather than from Jews.

Derec Llwyd Morgan tackles this equation from another angle in his discussion of the influence on Welsh-language literature of a Welsh identification *as* Jews. Here the boundaries between notional and historical Jews are more fluid and confusing than ever: the 'chosen people' in his published lecture, *'Canys Bechan Yw': y Genedl Etholedig yn Ein Llenyddiaeth* ('For she is small': the chosen people in our literature), are metaphorical Jews.[70] Llwyd Morgan claims that followers of the Reformation developed a national spirit in opposition to Catholic internationalism, but he also begins to distinguish between a small elect nation whose elect status is deferred, and 'successful' nations whose dominance is seen as evidence of divine favour. Perhaps one might understand this as a theological description of the psychology of colonised nationhood as against the psychology of the coloniser:

> Beth sy'n dod yn amlwg i'r neb a astudia phenomen y genedl etholedig Brotestannaidd o'r cyfnod modern cynnar hyd y dydd heddiw yw hyn – sef bod dau ddosbarth o genhedloedd etholedig, dau deip, dau fath. Y rhai llwyddiannus, a dybiant mai llwyddiant yw eu rhan yn wastadol; a'r rhai methiannus y mae eu llwyddiant eto i ddod.[71]

> (What becomes obvious to anyone who studies the phenomenon of the elect Protestant nation from the early modern period to the present day is this – that there are two classes of elect nations, two types, two kinds. The successful ones, who imagine that success is their perpetual fate, and the failed ones, whose success is yet to come.)

The English are one of those 'successful' elect nations, who believe that God is on their side: their success as an imperial power is a signal of divine favour. 'Nid bechan yw', Llwyd Morgan concludes – 'she is *not* small'.[72] In contrast, of course, the Welsh are the latter kind, a chosen people whose success is yet to come, and he finds the evidence of this self-image and the 'hope-against-hope' myth of the small and powerless nation and its deferred glory throughout Welsh writing from the sixteenth century to the present. Theology gives an odd explanation of history, he remarks, but this is what it provides:

> darlun o Israel lân y gorffennol yn syrthio i alaeth yn y presennol, ac yn aml yn ysglyfaeth i'r cenhedloedd o amgylch (ys gelwir hwy), fel nad oes ganddi ddim i'w chalonogi ond rhyw obaith am a ddaw. A'r bobl a gyflawna'r gobaith hwnnw yn Llyfr Eseia yw'r gweddill, y 'gweddill cyfiawn'. 'Y gweddill a ddychwel'.[73]

> (a picture of a pure Israel of the past, reduced to lamentation in the present, and often a prey to the surrounding nations (as they say), for there is nothing to hearten her but some hope of what is to come. And the people who will fulfil that hope, in the Book of Isaiah, are the remnant, 'the righteous remnant'. 'The remnant who will return'.)

An odd explanation, perhaps, because it is theological typology that he is describing: in the comparison that Charles Edwards makes between English treatment of the Welsh and Assyrian treatment of 'Israel', for example, he equates Wales and Israel; the equation is also implicit in the assertion by Edwards that 'one must accept on faith that the Lord God will have mercy on "Pure Wales" exactly as, time after time, he had mercy on Israel'.[74]

Given the strength of the tradition of biblical identification, Llwyd Morgan finds it natural that what most appeals to Welsh writers is 'the myth of our Israeliteness'.[75] However, and importantly, in discussing the influence of this tradition in Gwenallt's poem 'Cymru' (Wales), he observes:

> cerdd Gristnogol nid Israelaidd yw hon mewn gwirionedd, er bod ynddi elfennau Hen Destamentyddol . . . Ynddi gwelir Cymru fel Israel arall, ond Israel anhanesyddol a dderbyniodd y Meseia yw'r Israel arall honno, Israel na fu eriod mewn gwirionedd.[76]

> (this is really not an 'Israelite' poem but a Christian one, despite the Old Testament elements that it contains . . . In it Wales is seen as another Israel, but that other Israel is an ahistorical Israel which accepted the Messiah – an Israel that never was, really.)

This is a religious identification of the Welsh *as* biblical Jews – Israelites – as distinct from any engagement with historical Jews, though perhaps, given the conversionist tendencies elsewhere in Gwenallt's poetry, one might see this as a retroactive conversion of the Jews by the poet, if only as a metaphor.

Dorian Llywelyn places Gwenallt centrally in the spiritual tradition he describes: like Gildas, Gwenallt rails against his countrymen for their degeneracy and depravity, and invokes a high moral past to which to aspire. Similarly, as with Charles Edwards's English Assyrians, English imperialism is depicted by Gwenallt as Jezebel, and, in the poem 'Cwm Tryweryn' (the Tryweryn Valley), as Goliath – 'Y dienwaededig gawr' (the uncircumcised giant). In this latter poem the Welsh *are* the biblical Jews.[77] In similar vein, Moses and the Maccabees are equated with the heroic Welsh figures Glyndŵr and Emrys ap Iwan, but in the poem 'Sir Forgannwg a Sir Gaerfyrddin' (Glamorganshire and Carmarthenshire) there is a hierarchy: 'Canaan a Chymru, daear a nef', he writes – 'Canaan and Wales, earth and heaven'.[78]

In these discussions by Derec Llwyd Morgan and Dorian Llywelyn, and in the treatment of 'traditional Welsh historiography' and Welsh religious history by Glanmor Williams, Eryn White, E. Wyn James and others, the absence of reference to historical Jews complicates the claim that the Welsh identified themselves *with* the 'chosen people'. In this Welsh-Israelite tradition, the Jews themselves have effectively been replaced by the Welsh. Where the (biblical) Jews do appear as a distinct group, it is in terms of the model offered by the consequences of their sinfulness. The attitudes towards Jews expressed in the texts by Gildas, Charles Edwards, Theophilus Evans and others, and the discussions about these texts by subsequent commentators, suggest neither like nor dislike of Jews, neither hostility nor support, nor identification or sympathy – because the Jews themselves are simply absented from the discourse. One might therefore usefully see this 'Welsh-Israelite tradition' as effectively 'dejudaised' semitic discourse.

AN IMAGINED COMMUNITY, AN INVENTED TRADITION

This Welsh-Israelite tradition, and the traditional Welsh historiography on which it sometimes draws, constitutes a kind of Welsh meta-narrative of identity, and has been used to help characterise Welshness as unique, legitimate and ancient. It supports a claim of mythical and *aboriginal* belonging, an image of the Welsh nation as a repository of moral purity, and the Welsh as inheritors of biblical 'election': in this tradition, the Welsh are the new 'cenedl etholedig' – the chosen people. In its later more secular re-imaginings as a broader 'tradition of Welsh identification with Jews', religious moral purity and election cede to the social moral purity of unusual tolerance and liberality, as in W. D. Rubinstein's and Grahame Davies's formulations.

The Jews as rendered here constitute a rather interesting variation on Benedict Anderson's 'imagined communities'. If, as Anderson proposes, 'all communities larger than primordial villages of face-to-face contact . . . are imagined', so too, surely, must other communities be imagined in order to distinguish what constitutes the self from what constitutes the other.[79] Indeed, the ways in which Welsh writers have imagined unique Welsh characteristics, have attempted to legitimise and normalise Welsh nationhood (whether in cultural or political terms), and have deployed – or excluded – particular 'national' others (in this case Jews, whether notional or historical) in order to define the self, provides an appropriate context to consider some of Anderson's claims.

In the preceding overview of late twentieth-century promulgators of this tradition, I have sought to identify the ways in which an apparently monolithic and ancient tradition is, in fact, the result of a perhaps entirely ingenuous conflation of quite distinct areas of discussion; it is a conjoining of diverse histories much like the grafting, in traditional Welsh historiography, of a recent history onto a deep past, and one that relies on a slippage between notional and historical Jews.

Anderson's promotion of an anthropological approach, in which he suggests that communities 'are to be distinguished, not by their falsity/

genuineness, but by the style in which they are imagined', is certainly pertinent to these twentieth-century interpretations, as well as to the reading of texts in the following chapters, because the tradition under consideration concerns 'qualities' and imagined or actual relationships rather than political history.[80] The paradoxes of nationalism that he identifies ('the objective modernity of nations to the historian's eye vs. their subjective antiquity in the eyes of nationalists'; the 'universality of nationality as a socio-cultural concept' as against its particular expressions, and the effective 'power of nationalisms vs. their philosophical poverty and even incoherence') all map rather tidily onto the Welsh example (though perhaps less tidily onto the political nationalism of the later twentieth century).[81] However, his picture of the relationship between 'imagined communities of nations' and the decline of religious communities and dynastic systems does not at first glance reflect so clearly the Welsh context.[82] The nonconformist imagined Welsh 'community of nation' was formulated specifically as a religious one – indeed as one of unifying distinction: distinction from the English, and from Anglicanism. However, that very formulation may hint at the insecurity of the increasing independence of Welsh religious thought and practice from the dominant Anglican church from the eighteenth century, and on into the early twentieth. A fusion of national and religious identity perhaps provides a structure with which to replace the centralised and dominant Anglican – and English-language – church. In the early Edwardian period, the manifestation of the Welsh religious revival, informed by an idea of inherited national 'moral purity', might again be seen as constituting a structural buffer against what was being lost, or against external threats. Perhaps, therefore, this Welsh-Israelite tradition, with the attached ancient provenance provided by traditional Welsh historiography, as much as the development of political Wales-Israel comparisons, can be seen to express this pattern of emergence identified by Anderson, though not in the most direct or obvious terms.

Anderson's rebuke of Ernest Gellner for associating 'invention' with falsity rather than with imagination is a useful warning not to be overly concerned with 'fabrication', but it is nevertheless still valuable to consider in this particular context what such 'fabrication' permits and what it proscribes. A less-than-salutary formulation of the Welsh-as-biblical-Jews as an imagined community in Anderson's terms is expressed concretely and disturbingly in Caradoc Evans's stories, for example.[83] In 1915, Evans turned on its head a religiously-infused and idealised image of nationhood bound together by an imagined past, an imagined future, and a moral inheritance and imperative. Evans's inversion of that high moral tradition suggests how proscriptive and constraining such a national narrative can be. Indeed, where Anderson perhaps over-optimistically stresses the creative and organic potential of 'imagined communities', Eric Hobsbawm suggests something of this potential constraint when he describes a tradition as a 'set of practices . . . which seek to inculcate certain values and norms of behaviour by repetition, which automatically implies continuity with the past. In fact, where possible, they normally attempt to establish continuity with a suitable historic past.'[84] This closely describes a process in play, particularly where ancient provenance and a 'suitable history' are concerned, in the Welsh-Israelite tradition and in the traditional Welsh historiography from which it in part developed. It also describes the late twentieth-century 'retellings' by Grahame Davies and W. D. Rubinstein, whose claims about a tradition of Welsh identification with Jews Hobsbawm might be describing when he observes that traditions 'which appear or claim to be old are often quite recent in origin and sometimes invented'.[85]

Of course neither the Welsh-Israelite tradition nor the twentieth-century tradition of Welsh identification with Jews consists of a 'set of practices' along the lines of Hobsbawm's definition; instead they might be said to constitute a recurrent set of motifs. These motifs can be grouped roughly in the following ways: linguistic origin or relationship; geographical and ethnic origin or relationship; spiritual inheritance and election; political-historical parallels; and sympathy, 'tolerance', philosemitism or conversionism. Dorian Llywelyn sees in these repeating motifs a form of theological 'type', in which one occurrence prefigures a future fulfilment, so that Gildas functions as a foreshadowing of, if not necessarily influence on, Charles Edwards in the 1660s and Gwenallt in the 1960s. Llywelyn's work itself can therefore be seen as a continuation of this 'typological' relationship: in *De Excidio Britanniae* as in *Sacred Place, Chosen People*, there is an invocation of a high moral past, and a warning against present or future moral degeneration, an approach that draws on the prophetic model in the Hebrew Bible.[86]

Perhaps the theological worldview that shapes Llywelyn's work (and, in different form, the work of Glanmor Williams and Derec Llwyd Morgan), is precisely what has permitted the omission from their work of a consideration of the Jews themselves. J. R. Jones, whose exploration of the 'interpenetration' of people and place informs Llywelyn's analysis, does acknowledge in the conclusion to his essay 'Troedle' (A Foothold), the case of 'modern Israel' as still being 'the best example' of the relationship between geographical place and nation.[87] However, even here the frame-work is a biblical one: 'Modern Israel' for Jones is the almost notional or symbolic collective of the people 'Israel' that returns to 'Canaan'.[88]

It is easy to see how, given the absence of historical Jews from this Welsh-Israelite identification, and from discussion of such identification, slippages can conveniently occur. This absence allows W. D. Rubinstein to conflate notional and historical Jews, for example, in his description of Welsh 'support and admiration for Jews, *both* ancient and modern'.[89] A similar slippage occurs when he claims that 'the Jews have had an impact upon the cultural and religious evolution of modern Wales unequivocally out of all proportion to their numbers', and continues seamlessly from this reference to the limited number of 'historical' (post-biblical) Jews in Wales, to how 'Old Testament and Hebrew images, terminology, and morality have been virtually coterminous with Welsh national identity' from the eighteenth to twentieth centuries.[90]

Historical Jews are removed from traditional Welsh historiography and from the Welsh-Israelite tradition that grew out of it, and Jews are replaced in that tradition by the Welsh. But in the tradition of 'Welsh identification with the Jews' that Davies and Rubinstein present, a set of attitudes to historical Jews is grafted onto this 'dejudaised' Welsh-Israelite tradition, creating a continuity in attitudes to Jews (and a conflation of notional and historical Jews) that is, at least in Anderson's 'creative' sense of the word, imagined.

The notion of continuity in identity between biblical and modern Jews has itself been challenged – by Arthur Koestler in *The Thirteenth Tribe: the Khazar Empire and its Heritage* (1976), and most recently by Shlomo Sand. In *The Invention of the Jewish People*, Sand examines critically one of the purposes to which the idea of such continuity has been put, and its cost: namely, the historical outcome of a Zionist meta-narrative of aborig-inal belonging, diaspora, exile and return. It is these 'creative' imaginings – or in Gellner's terms, perhaps, 'fabrications' – that J. R. Jones reinforces when he describes a return of modern 'Israel' to 'Canaan'. To examine and challenge the one invention leads inevitably and perhaps painfully to a challenging examination of the other to which it is related; to take a so-called post-Zionist view such as Sand's of the Jewish nationalist narra-tive in the context of Wales requires taking a post-Zionist view of the Welsh national narrative, too. This leads inevitably to the question of how this narrative and its inventors collude with and reinforce Zionist aspira-tions, elisions and omissions – and their costs.

SOME NEW MAPPING

What, then, is the outcome of examining the claims made by the late twentieth-century promulgators of a tradition of Welsh identification with Jews? One outcome is, surely, that a separation needs to be made between Welsh attitudes to historical Jews on the one hand, and 'the Welsh-Israelite tradition', an effectively dejudaised tradition in which the Welsh identify *as* biblical Jews, on the other. If such a distinction highlights a kind of slippage, it does so to useful effect: that slippage marks the precise location of an elision or an omission, or, perhaps, a rhetorical sleight of hand – as, for example, the case of J. R. Jones's 'modern Israel' suggests. The ambiguities of Welsh engagement with Zionism are discussed in more detail in chapters 4 and 5, but two equally important sleights of hand have occurred in this conjoining of two traditions by writers at the end of the twentieth century. One is the isolation of hostile stereotyped imaging of Jews from the mainstream, and the presentation of this hostile imaging as untypical and marginal. As is explored in chapter 3, this is not at all the case. The other is the downplaying of ambiguities in conversionism. By conflating responses to historical Jews with the imaging of notional or biblical Jews, the difficult evidence of a sustained conversionist and millenarian discourse remains safely concealed or subtextual. When these are separated, however, attitudes towards Jews qua Jews stand more clearly exposed, as is explored in the next chapter.

Overall, Welsh imaging of Jews, whether modern and historical, or biblical and notional, can now perhaps be usefully separated into three discrete threads, as follows: a religious or spiritual tradition of identification *as* biblical Jews arising from, or at least informed by, so-called traditional Welsh historiography; a *twentieth-century* tradition of Welsh identification with and sympathy for Jews; and a nineteenth- and twentieth-century applied interest in historical Jews.

Dorian Llywelyn is responsible for the most thorough 'reinvention' of this first strand, while, as an articulated tradition, the second – the twentieth-century 'Welsh identification with Jews' – has its roots in 1901–2, in the redaction by D. Wynne Evans in the journal *Young Wales*. Evans, compiling, at the beginning of the twentieth century, the motif references that later commentators cite as evidence of a long-standing identification, plays a role equivalent in many ways to the seventeenth-century 'traditional' historiographer, Theophilus Evans, who compiled and popularised Welsh foundation myths. Like Theophilus

Evans, D. Wynne Evans himself had earlier sources, among whom the most important was probably John Mills.

The late twentieth-century promulgators have dispensed with some elements that no longer serve a purpose but which, for Evans in 1901 and 1902, were highly resonant and deployable – such as the motifs of linguistic comparison and ethnic descent. In his series of articles in *Young Wales*, an influential cultural-nationalist journal, Evans formulated a kind of structural taxonomy of 'Wales-Israel' or Welsh/Jewish motifs – linguistic, ethnic, spiritual and political – in an argument about the nature of Welsh nationality and the part the Welsh nation had to play in the British Empire. Successive twentieth-century expressions of or references to a 'tradition of Welsh identification with Jews' cite and echo his work. However, using his writings as evidence of a tradition of philosemitism, as W. D. Rubinstein does, for example, is deeply problematic for, as discussed in the next chapter, Evans was influenced by the millenarian British-Israel or Anglo-Israel movement (though he offered a Welsh version of it), and he was an overt conversionist.

2

The mission to convert the Jews

'Gwargaled, O Israel, gwargaled yn wir'
(Obstinate, Oh Israel, truly obstinate)
– Daniel Evans, *Golwg ar gyflwr yr Iuddewon*

DEALING WITH CONVERSIONISM

During the late Victorian period, the growing Jewish community of Britain
was subjected to increasing pressure from conversionist activity, activity
that was enthusiastically endorsed and supported by English and Welsh
congregations. Michael Ragussis observes that such conversionist efforts
were viewed on the continent as 'the English madness', while Eitan
Bar-Yosef picks up on this motif of madness and eccentricity among
colonisation and conversionist societies to explore how their attitudes
existed at the margins rather than within 'the cultural consensus' in
England.[1] As his analysis indicates, nineteenth-century English support for
Jewish settlement in Palestine, and anticipation of Jewish conversion to
Christianity, were bound up with millenarian and pre-millenarian thought,
which saw the 'restoration' of the Jews as fulfilment of prophecy about the
End of Days.[2] There were therefore fluid boundaries between missionary
efforts and early proto-Zionist support, both of which fit loosely under the
rubric of 'Christian Zionism' in the period (as indeed they do now under
modern Christian Zionism).

In Wales, the boundary between 'restoration' and 'conversion' did not
exist in the language: 'dychweliad' could mean both 'return' and 'conversion'. Nor, in practical terms, were these conversionist efforts of the early

to mid-nineteenth century only an 'English' madness. A major mid-nineteenth century conversionist effort in London was sponsored by the Calvinistic Methodists in Wales and, unlike its English counterpart, this was for a period towards the centre of the 'cultural consensus' (though, as discussed below, its tenor was later challenged). Indeed the later 1904–5 religious revival, which retains a kind of iconic status in Welsh historiography, and which was a defining social and political movement with effects that were felt long into the twentieth century, developed out of the religious/political nonconformist movement, which, in the nineteenth century, had been deeply engaged in conversionist activity.

It was in the mid-nineteenth century that the status of contemporary rather than biblical Jews entered public discussion on a large scale in Wales. The fate of Jews in Britain had been historically closely caught up with the fate of the Welsh, though this seems to have passed largely unnoticed in Wales: in the thirteenth century, Edward I had borrowed heavily to fund his Welsh wars. Shortly after his defeat of Llywelyn ap Gruffudd, the last Welsh prince, in 1282, Edward expelled all the Jews from Britain, thereby inheriting monies owed to them and alleviating his own debt. In the early 1700s, subsequent to the formal readmission of the Jews by Oliver Cromwell in the seventeenth century, Jewish individuals began to arrive in Wales, and the first non-metropolitan Jewish community in Britain appears to have been established in Swansea in the mid-eighteenth century. However, the expansion of the Jewish population outside the south and north coast clusters did not really take place until the late nineteenth century, following the pattern set by the arrival of those fleeing hardship or persecution in Russia and eastern Europe.[3]

An encounter with living rather than imagined Jews therefore became possible in many parts of Wales by the end of the nineteenth century, and the 'Jewish community' as a whole became an object of direct rather than merely theoretical interest. Even if it did not often take the form of applied conversionist activity, a great deal of Welsh writing indicates that such interest was, nevertheless, often influenced by conversionist sentiment and orientation. However, the purportedly forcible conversion case of Esther Lyons in 1868 has received, like the Tredegar riots, a disproportionate amount of attention in the limited survey of Jewish experience in south Wales.[4] This apparent attempt by two Baptists to effect the religious conversion of a young Jewish woman in Cardiff (which attracted dramatic speculations about kidnapping and forcible conversion), has been used on the one hand to prop up arguments about widespread religious hostility and intolerance (by Geoffrey Alderman, for example), and on the other has

been isolated as an exceptional incident by W. D. Rubinstein.[5] This occurrence and the Tredegar riots have become two spikes on which to impale
attitudes to, and the experience of, Jews in Wales, but they lend themselves
to this endeavour only insofar as such attitudes and experiences are considered in terms of the binary opposites of so-called antisemitism and
philosemitism, a frame of reference used, without exception as far as I
have been able to discover, by all commentators on Jews in Wales.

While it is difficult to see enthusiastic conversionism as anything
approaching benign interest in Jews, neither can it be read as simple
hostility (even as hostility to Judaism if not to Jews). Inconveniently,
neither conversionist sentiment nor conversionist activity, and least of all
conversionist discourse, fits tidily within this binary antisemitism-
philosemitism opposition. Consequently, less overt conversionism than
the Esther Lyons case has been either overlooked, downplayed, isolated or
marginalised.[6] While the lingering Welsh interest in Jews expressed in
twentieth-century literature, including interest in Zionism, clearly does not
derive solely from conversionist sentiment, it is nevertheless evidently
informed by it. Millenarianism, and the conversionism that accompanied
it, if not always dominant themes across Welsh Christian denominations,
certainly were (and continue in some cases to be) a substratum.

The neglect of this substratum of conversionism – overt, covert or
residual, neither categorically hostile nor innocently benign – may in part
result from the available critical framework, which cannot adequately
account for its contradictory attitudes. Self-styled Protestant 'philosemites'
prided themselves on desiring to convert Jews out of love – the mystic
Morgan Llwyd being an early, Puritan example.[7] This claim of 'loving'
conversionism may be seen as a Protestant self-positioning in contradis-
tinction to the continental Catholic one, with its history of forcible
conversionist tactics. However, the ambiguity of this purportedly loving
Protestant intolerance of cultural and religious difference highlights one of
the problems inherent in an analysis of attitudes to Jews, from banal to
malign, 'along a continuum where the measured quality is "virulence"', to
use Matthew Biberman's description.[8]

D. WYNNE EVANS: COMPILER AND CONVERSIONIST

One such 'loving' conversionist was the Reverend D. Wynne Evans, who
relied heavily on Morgan Llwyd in his writing. As touched on in the
previous chapter, the promotion of Evans's work by W. D. Rubinstein and

John Harvey as evidence of a tradition of identification with Jews illustrates how conversionist discourse might be elided by an approach that
measures 'virulence': there is nothing in Evans's writing that is virulent,
and a great deal that is, on the surface of it, 'positive' – but this is often not
as simple as it at first appears.

In a series of essays published in 1901 and 1902 in *Young Wales*, the
prominent journal of the Cymru Fydd movement, Evans presents a complicated muddle of eschatology, Romantic nationalism, and British Empire
patriotism, arguing for the crucial contribution of Wales and Welsh culture
to British – and more broadly Christian – endeavours.[9] Along the way, in
his attempt to make a case for the religious purity of Wales, he repeatedly
draws parallels between the Welsh and the Jews, whether through invoking
Charles Edwards's seventeenth-century work, *Y Ffydd Ddi-ffuant*, or
Theophilus Evans's eighteenth-century *Drych y Prif Oesoedd*, through
citing linguistic relationships between Hebrew and Welsh, or presenting
the example of the Reverend John Mills and his reception by Jews in
Palestine.[10] Primarily, however, he is concerned with Puritan eschatology,
and each of the five articles uses an epigraph from the seventeenth-century
Puritan writer, Morgan Llwyd. Evans was one of three who initiated the
Llandrindod Wells Convention, a foundation stone of the religious revival
of 1904–5, and these essays may be seen as a slightly earlier articulation of
the millenarian hope that suffused that movement. At the same time he
attempts to reconcile a Welsh 'national' spirituality within a British
imperial framework.[11]

If Evans's arguments are often condensed and muddled, his millenarianism is always clear. The epigraph to his first article, 'Studies in Welsh
Chiliastic History', is Morgan Llwyd's 'watchword', 'Our Lord is coming
once againe [*sic*]'. The article proceeds to several columns on millenarian
and pre-millenarian thought, in which the only reference to Jews is conversionist: 'Popery and Mohamedanism still remain to be destroyed – the
Jews, as a people, are not converted to Christ'.[12] The epigraph to the second
article, 'Studies in Iberic=Hebraic Eschatology' (the equation rather than
hyphen seems to operate as a deliberate conceit in the original title), is four
lines of conversionist poetry, again by Morgan Llwyd:

> Make way, Remoove the blocks, stand by
> O wellcome Jewes by mee
> A Shulamite in Jesus coach
> I long thy face to see.[13]

Evans follows this with an exploration, characterised by a kind of ethnic essentialism, of the wild poetic Celt, who is 'needed to give fire and speed to an English stock', in which the Celtic 'strain' is itself composed of the 'Iberian' and the Celt. It is in this context that Evans introduces 'Hebrews' as possible 'brothers from the wilderness'. However, in its first appearance, this 'brothers' is qualified. The text may or may not be a direct quotation from a 'Prof. Lloyd' (either Evans or the editor is unreliable with quotation marks):

> The historian himself would not be surprised if it were proved that it was from the boundless wilderness of the east the Cymro came . . . The theory of phrenological students is to say that it was from the east and from the wilderness the Iberian came; but when it is remembered how adapted to the Cymro's mind is the Old Testament, it is not difficult to believe that the Welshman and the Hebrew are brothers from the wilderness. (p. 121)

On the next page Evans repeats this as a quotation from 'Prof. Lloyd' (but doesn't provide a closing quote mark), and elaborates:

> When it is remembered how adapted to the Cymro's mind is the Old Testament, it is not difficult to believe that the Welshman and the Hebrew are brothers from the wilderness. These two things stand out in bold relief in the history of Cromwell and the Commonwealth. The absorbing interest in the Old Testament, in particular, exhibited by the Puritans, is a fact which historians never fail to direct attention to. And the other, related to it, is the unprecedented sympathy with, and interest in, the Jews manifested at that time – sympathy and interest that demanded, through Cromwell, the return to Britain after a banishment of well nigh four centuries, of this Hebrew wilderness brother, for whom the Cymro-Celt in particular has always had an affectionate regard.[14]

This sympathy and interest in the Jews is conversionist, both on the part of Cromwell as Evans imagines him, and on the part of Evans himself, as his millenarian analysis suggests.[15] It is in this context that he ruminates on Welsh attitudes to Jews more widely, citing, for example, the editor of 'Everyman', Ernest Rhys, who is reported by Evans as having 'touched on this Hebrew-Celtic chord, which must have vibrated sympathetically in many hearts belonging to the two nations'.[16] He quotes from a review of the *Jewish Encyclopaedia*, in which Rhys states:

> It is not a mere ingenious idea that the Welsh people have felt at times in their history that it had a very strange parallel in the history of the Jews. There is even a spiritual affinity between the two races that lies deeper than we know; and when a Welshman thinks of the Holy Land he is very apt to think of it as another Wales in the East. So today there is no section of readers more eager

than ours for anything that helps to lighten and explain the inner and outer world of Jewish life and all that belongs to it.[17]

For Evans this is an example of how 'the checkered [*sic*] career of Israel finds a sympathetic echo in the warm Cymric heart'.[18] In addition he details the claims made in a lecture by Anglican Dean David Howell (also known by his Bardic name 'Llawdden'), who commented on 'points of resemblance', citing 'a striking similarity in the geographical features of Wales and of Palestine'; parallel sentiments of 'intense and undying patriotism, which is characteristic of the two nationalities'; commonalities between Welsh and Hebrew, and the claim – 'on good authority' – that 'the Welsh translation of the Old Testament Scriptures comes nearer to the Hebrew original than almost any other'.[19] Howell slips, however, into reference to biblical Jews, for he goes on to compare open-air Welsh revival meetings with 'the large concourse of people at the Jewish festivals', and the volume of Welsh praise to that of 'King David's choir'.

Given the detail in this lecture by Howell, as reported by Evans, one might expect to find some such comparisons in Howell's pamphlet on 'Welsh nationality', which was published in 1892. However, although, like Evans's essays, it articulates a familiar Welsh cultural nationalism within a patriotic British imperial framework, it does not touch in any part on these matters.[20]

Defending his country's 'philosemitic' tradition, Evans recounts how he sent a report of Howell's lecture to Chief Rabbi Adler, who wrote back agreeing that the Welsh and the Irish were the only nationalities not to have persecuted the Jews. This shows, Evans explains, 'that the Celtic race, in its Welsh and Irish branches, is the one solitary exception among the nations of the earth that has never suffered from that periodical epidemic of suicidal madness, called anti-Semitism'.[21] This claim is an important element in the case he builds, across his five articles, of Welsh moral superiority to England – indeed to any nation.

In the third article, Evans's Iberic-Hebraic explorations begin to meander off into popular nineteenth-century philological notions of Iberians as original Druids, and Druidism as a kind of 'heathenized Israelism', in which he suggests that 'the peculiarity of the Iberian is in keeping with the peculiarity of the Hebrew. The splendid isolation of British Druidism is, in many respects, like that of Judaism.'[22] However with the fourth essay, once more sporting a conversionist epigraph from Morgan Llwyd ('Harke what a sound the dead bones make / The Jews with Jesus rise' – but juxtaposed with a verse beginning 'Oh Wales, poore Rachel'), he opens again with this Hebrew 'brothers from the wilderness'.[23] It is this essay

that W. D. Rubinstein quotes, and from which he deduces that 'the intimate knowledge of the ancient Hebrews, and the identification of
nonconformist Welshmen with the ancient Hebrews, was extraordinarily
widespread'.[24] However, in this essay, Evans stumbles into Anglo-Israel or
British-Israel territory, and his millenarian beliefs and the argument for
the essential Welsh contribution to the British Empire need to be considered in that context: something less than a straightforward 'sympathy' is
suggested in Evans's careful distinctions in the 'brothers from the wilderness' phrase.

The Anglo-Israel or British-Israel theory, which, through complex
eschatological arguments, posits that the English are descended from the
lost tribes of Israel and that the English language is descended from
Hebrew, enjoyed wide debate in England both within and outside the
Church of England in the late nineteenth and early twentieth centuries. The
theory has roots in Puritan eschatology, the Fifth Monarchy Men movement and Cromwellian millenarianism; it has influenced white suprematist
groups in the USA and it still enjoys support in the form of the Anglo-Israel
Federation.[25] Anglo-Israel theorists point to England's international prominence as being an indication of divine favour and fulfilment of biblical
prophecy – the 'successful' form of election identified by Derec Llwyd
Morgan in his lecture *Canys Bechan Yw* discussed in the previous chapter.[26]

The two interpretations of election mark strong divergence between the
Anglo-Israel theory and the Welsh-Israelite tradition, but perhaps more
important is the careful clarification made by Anglo-Israel theory expo-
nents that the English are descended from 'Israel' and not from 'Judah'
– they argue that it is from the latter tribe that both Judas and the Jews are
descended, and these distinctions often rely on overtly hostile and stereotyped characterisation of Jews. In the Welsh context, Theophilus Evans
and others since him posit Welsh descent neither from Judah nor Israel, but
from Gomer. Indeed, as indicated in the previous chapter, Charles Edwards
suggests in *Y Ffydd Ddi-ffuant* that the Welsh are perhaps the descendants
of the 'remnant of the Gentiles who escaped from the land of Canaan
towards the West'.[27] However, in his fifth essay, D. Wynne Evans makes
this division clear, and he brings 'Judah' and 'Israel' back together in a
conversionist vision that follows Morgan Llwyd. Quoting again the quat-
rain that begins 'Harke what a sound the dead bones make', Evans claims
that Morgan Llwyd

> evidently thought that the Commonwealth period was a great crisis in the
> history of Israel – both the house of Judah and the house of Israel. The
> prophecy of Ezekiel, concerning the vision of the dry bones, embracing both

houses which are to be joined and restored together, is referred to as beginning to be fulfilled.[28]

In 1879, Philo-Israel, editor of the Anglo-Israel journal, had commented on the relation of Welsh to Hebrew, citing, among others, Henry Rowlands, author of the eighteenth-century *Mona Antiqua Restaurata*, which compares Hebrew and Welsh linguistic structures.[29] But a year later Philo-Israel produced publications specifically geared towards the Welsh, including *Proofs for the Welsh that the British are the lost tribes of Israel. The Abrahamic Covenant*, and *Y Genedl Gymreig yn deillio oddiwrth ddeg llwyth colledig Tŷ Israel: sef, epistol at y Cymry*.[30] It would be difficult to reconstruct the way in which publications such as these might have come to combine with the influence of Theophilus Evans, and with the topological evidence of place-names and personal names in Wales which express the Welsh-Israelite tradition in the landscape and in human relationships; nevertheless, the motif of the Welsh as 'the lost ten tribes of Israel' recurs again and again in literature and is still current in oral tradition.[31]

Beyond the sources D. Wynne Evans specifically identifies, including Morgan Llwyd, it would appear that in these essays he draws as much on publications by the British-Israel group, as well as on Theophilus Evans. Whether it lies in one of these publications, or whether he is picking up on something that had, for decades, been discussed quite widely, his reference to the Welsh having a relationship with the 'boundless wilderness of the east' has its source somewhere here.

British-Israelism is perhaps more worthy of the term 'deliciously eccentric nonsense' that, in *Sacred Place, Chosen People*, Dorian Llywelyn attributed to the linguistic comparisons made by Charles Edwards, but I would argue, like Llywelyn, that 'politically, it is highly significant nonsense', for it provides eschatological justifications for British imperialism, it influenced white supremacist groups that still operate today, and it undoubtedly shaped some forms of Christian Zionism, as Eitan Bar-Yosef has indicated.[32]

Eric Michael Reisenauer promotes British-Israelism as an important late expression of a long tradition of English-Hebraic associations – a tradition that is comparable to (and which Reisenauer sometimes conflates with) traditional Welsh historiography.[33] Unfortunately, he relies on a somewhat hegemonic notion of 'the British nation' and 'Britons', and does not appear to recognise differences between British imperial and constituent national traditions. On the other hand, Eitan Bar-Yosef questions the degree of influence not only of British-Israelism but also of most such nineteenth-century 'eccentricities' in the context of Christian Zionism.

If D. Wynne Evans shows the clear influence of British-Israelism, it is a British-Israelism redeployed for peculiarly Welsh purposes. Although he is an admirer of empire, he does not quite as overtly provide a Welsh biblical exegesis that invokes divine justification for national expansion and imperialism, as the British-Israel theory does. Instead he argues that in addition to the physical resources of coal and water, Wales offers a necessary contribution to the British imperial project: a pure form of nationalism. Indeed, because of the moral purity of Wales, even the coal it offers to the work of empire has 'moral significance'.[34] Describing the worldwide travels of the English royal family and of the steamship the *Ophir*, which was fuelled by Welsh coal, he sums up: 'This was a parable of the powers of the principles of the Principality in the progress of the Empire.'[35]

But it is Wales as inheritor of election that underpins its moral superiority in Evans's formulation. Quoting heavily from J. H. Edwards, the editor of *Young Wales* from 1895 to 1904, Evans reports how Edwards proposed that every country had 'some special purpose to accomplish – some special destiny to fulfil in the Divine economy of the world', and the one allotted to Wales was that 'the Celt was destined to carry on the work of the Hebrew as bearers of a message to the hearts of the people'.[36] Edwards, Evans continues,

> looked to the Celts to rescue England from the danger of becoming grossly materialistic, and to the conquered, in this case, establishing a moral and beneficent superiority over their conquerors, so that all-powerful England might turn to Wales, not only for its coal and water supply, but also for purer national aspirations and nobler national ideals.[37]

Importantly, these 'purer national aspirations and nobler national ideals' are premised in part on the assertion that Wales is not contaminated by the 'suicidal madness called anti-Semitism' and, in this regard, Wales provides a model for England to follow. One might see again in this characterisation in relation to England the 'small nation' nationalism of Derec Llwyd Morgan's analysis. Nevertheless, if the claim of this more morally pure Welshness becomes in effect a discourse of racism, Evans is saved from the accusation by his slippage, in the final essay, between Wales, Britain and England, a confusing slippage that appears to arise from his need simultaneously to argue Welsh distinctiveness from England, and Welsh centrality to the glory of the British Empire.[38]

In the period that D. Wynne Evans is writing, traditional Welsh historiography was challenged by the Welsh cultural renaissance, which had begun to discover a more useable indigenous Welsh past – expressed, for example, by the publication in 1911 of J. E. Lloyd's Welsh history, which dispensed with 'traditional historiography'.[39] Evans's work is remarkably representative of this transition, straddling, as it does, the older, essentially religious interest in notional or biblical Jews, an encounter with historical Jews, and a combination of Romantic Home Rule nationalism and British Empire patriotism.

Some of his observations, when lifted out of context – particularly his claims of a 'traditional sympathy and good feeling existing between the two peoples' – do appear to provide strong evidence of a long-standing set of decidedly positive attitude to Jews.[40] But when seen in the whole, Evans's essays prove an odd source to cite in support of philosemitism or a tradition of identification with Jews. Instead they reveal themselves to be strongly millenarian and, at the very least, covertly conversionist, which the words 'eschatology' and 'chiliastic' in the essay titles alone indicate, reinforced by quotation from Morgan Llwyd.

Evans's millenarianism and conversionism, intertwined with a 'brothers from the wilderness' sympathy, effectively illustrates the kind of contra-dictory position that an analysis based on an antisemitic-philosemitic opposition cannot very easily accommodate or elucidate. Evans argues with pride for the 'affectionate' attitude of the Welsh to the Jews, but to place such conversionist 'affection' on the supportive and loving side of this opposition is to conceal the ways in which it is internally contradictory and far from benign. Nor does Eric Michael Reisenauer's notion of 'the bifurcation of the Jew into the Hebraic and the Judaic' (and his related distinction between philo-Semitism, or philo-Hebraism, and anti-Judaism) prove very much more useful in understanding the ambivalence of a great deal of conversionist writing, or of writing on Jews more widely (particu-larly in the twentieth century), as it still limits the view to one of binary opposition.[41] Indeed much if not most discussion and imaging of Jews does not easily fit into this kind of dualism: to consider it in dualistic terms, therefore, is to overlook a great deal of nuance and complexity.

Welsh conversionist texts are problematically – if typically – contradic-tory. The Jews, depicted as stubborn and blind and responsible for their abject state (a consequence of their refusal to recognise Jesus as the Messiah), are treated with the same mixture of voyeuristic interest, pity and contempt in Morgan Llwyd in the seventeenth century as in Daniel Evans's *Golwg ar gyflwr yr Iuddewon* in the early nineteenth, or, again, a hundred years later, by the poet Elfed (Howell Elvet Lewis).[42]

If Morgan Llwyd's 'Make way, Remoove the blocks, stand by / O well-come Jewes by mee / A Shulamite in Jesus coach / I long thy face to see' is characterised by a paternalistic pity, Daniel Evans is less sympathetic: 'Gwargaled, O Israel, gwargaled yn wir' (Obstinate, Oh Israel, truly obstinate), he declares in his book-length 1826 poem *Golwg ar gyflwr yr Iuddewon* (A look at the state of the Jews). 'O Israel, gan addef addefwch eich bai' (Oh Israel, in confessing, admit your fault), he implores, and his long lament is reprised by the poet Elfed in an English-language collection entitled *Israel and Other Poems*, published by Foyles in 1930.[43] Typical of Welsh conversionist rhetoric in both languages, these two works trace biblical Jewish history, Jewish deicide, the Jewish fall from grace, and Jewish diaspora and homelessness, with asides on character flaws and essentialist racial traits.

Elfed was, to say the least, a prominent poet: he won the Crown at the National Eisteddfod in 1888 and 1891, and the Chair in 1894, and was Archdruid between 1924 and 1928. He was instrumental in setting up the organisation 'Wales International' in 1948, which continues today to create links between Welsh diasporic communities and Wales.[44] On Jewish deicide he writes in 1930:

> His God he served with a Cross,
> He creeps in its shadow still!
> He crushèd the Heavenly Rose,
> In his rage, on a little Hill.[45]

This species of conversionist doggerel includes lines such as 'Unwelcomed, unbrothered, unhomed, — / Hating, and hated of all', and 'Soiled with the userer's filth'.[46] But all will be well, the poem suggests, once the Jews, now addressed directly, embrace truth:

> And, at last, with the Gentle and Meek,
> Who wrought into Love thy Law,
> Wilt thou not, in charity, speak,
> And unto Him sweetly draw?[47]

Despite its prominence, conversionist discourse in Welsh literature has not been addressed as a problem, but instead its ambivalence has been either ignored, minimised, or glossed over. Perhaps this is in part because, within a religious worldview, the ambivalence it expresses does not appear to constitute a contradictory attitude. It is difficult to understand on its own terms, without appearing to apologise for it, an historical attitude that in the present day we might see at its best as being ethnocentric and intolerant of religious and cultural difference. But in the present as in the past, no matter how liberal, a religious worldview (like any worldview) can still operate as a constraint. It might be such a constraint that accounts in part for this oversight of conversionism – suggested, for example, in the case of Derec Llwyd Morgan, when, under the heading 'Morgan Llwyd a'r Iddewon' (Morgan Llwyd and the Jews), he examines the author's End of Days vision and the necessary conversion of the Jews, without considering the impact on or meaning for Jews of that vision.[48]

APPLIED CONVERSIONISM: JOHN MILLS, CALVINISTIC METHODIST MISSIONARY TO THE JEWS

Welsh writers may have taken a particularly keen interest bordering on voyeurism in the abject 'state of the Jews', but some also took practical action to relieve such abjection.[49] The most important figure in this context, one whose practical example and literary influence in both languages was considerable, was the missionary, the Reverend John Mills. Mills is better remembered as a hymnologist, but his writing on Jews and on Ottoman Palestine was extensive, and provides something of a case study for the problem of how one might consider conversionism in the context of Wales.

In 1859 Mills was castigated for that very consideration that I suggest is lacking in the critics cited previously: his opponents, and erstwhile supporters, asserted that his failure to convert the Jews of London had resulted from an overly sympathetic attitude to and respect for the Jewish culture he encountered. For that sensitivity and interest, he was accused of courting conversion to Judaism himself.

The influence of John Mills on some Welsh attitudes to Jews would have been considerable. He was a prolific writer, and for the twelve years he spent in London in the 1840s and 1850s he wrote a monthly column in *Y Drysorfa* which would have been read by many if not most Calvinistic Methodists in Wales, and in the substantial Welsh communities in Liverpool, London and elsewhere. According to D. Wynne Evans, Mills, 'whose book on the "British Jews" is still regarded as an authority, did more than any man in Britain to remove the prejudices of Christians against Jews and *vice versa*'.[50] Reception of that book, *The British Jews: their religious ceremonies, social condition, domestic habits, literature, political statistics etc.*, published in 1853, was enthusiastic in England, particularly in the church papers, whose reviews appear on the covers of a later book by Mills. The *Jewish Herald*, organ of the London Society for Promoting Christianity among the Jews, commented: 'while we trust his volume will be read with interest by thousands, we are certain that it cannot fail to quicken the feelings of those who are concerned to promote the spiritual welfare of this remarkable people'.[51]

Mission to the Jews of London

Mills, whose Bardic name was Ieuan Glan Alarch, was born in 1812, and served in Ruthin as a minister from 1841, before moving to London in December 1846.[52] In the early nineteenth century, several denominations sponsored joint missionary activity among the Jews, but after inter-denominational disagreement over missionary activity in the UK and abroad, the Welsh Calvinistic Methodists supported their own missionary labourers from 1840 onwards. Despite internal arguments over whether a mission to the Jews of London would more appropriately fall under the category of 'Foreign' or 'Home' mission (which in itself indicates the ambiguous position of British Jews with respect to Empire), the Calvinistic Methodists sent John Mills to London in 1847 to bring the People of the Book to knowledge and truth.

In his work *Gwalia in Khasia*, which explores the better-known Welsh mission in India, Nigel Jenkins expresses some surprise that so little has been written on the subject, but the mission to the Jews has been similarly overlooked. Jenkins himself only states in passing that missionaries were sent 'to do battle in Brittany' with Catholicism, and that 'they also sent a missionary to the Jews in London, but neither venture resulted in many converts'.[53] Yet for twelve years Mills published in *Y Drysorfa*, the journal of the Calvinistic Methodists, a monthly piece under the heading 'The Jewish Mission', a column that for some years enjoyed a status equal to if not greater than the column on 'The Overseas Mission', which included the mission in Khasia. Articles on all things Jewish that appear in most issues of *Y Drysorfa* in the years leading up to Mills's mission are almost always millenarian in tone, and Mills's own early articles prove no exception: in his first report he presents his work among the Jews as 'one of the chief signs of the times: a sign that the great event is approaching' – namely the return of the Messiah and the End of Days.[54]

His encounter with the Jews of London challenged the theoretical knowledge he had no doubt gleaned earlier from the pages of *Y Drysorfa* and, at an even further remove, from the Bible. He was distressed to discover that the People of the Book were *not*, in fact, in his opinion, people of the book: they were Talmudists, under the thumb of the rabbis and, like Catholics, ignorant about the scriptures. In education, he asserts, the Jews everywhere else were better off than the Jews of Britain; few of the Jews he met understood the grammar of their own language (he means

Hebrew here, not Yiddish), and their knowledge of the practices and laws of their religion were poorer still. 'They are as much a stranger to the Old Testament as are the Papists to the New', he remarks, and 'the names of Isaiah, Jeremiah, Daniel &c. are as strange to most of Jewry of these parts as are the names of Taliesin, Tydain or Dafydd ap Gwilym'.[55]

The chief explanation he advances for this ignorance is the Jews' 'commercial spirit'.[56] The interest in wealth marks the Jew wherever he is, he reports, and he elaborates on this at some length, in a piece that includes familiar negative stereotyped motifs that are common in a great deal of nineteenth-century and early twentieth-century English literature.[57] In the next monthly article, Mills writes in a tone of paternalistic affection rather than contempt: he compares the mind of the Jew to that of a fifteen-year-old boy. The Jews are beginning to wake up, he believes: 'they are beginning to see the word of the Rabbi as the word of a failing man . . . the spirit of the nation is as if waking from a long sleep. The boy is freeing himself from the law of his father, and is starting to walk of his own will.'[58]

The rhetoric of the childlike native, and the shaking off of superstition, of blindness and ignorance, are of course familiar colonial as well as conversionist motifs. What is of interest here, however, is not so much the typicality of this rhetoric, as the change it undergoes. By the time Mills comes to publish *Iddewon Prydain* (The Jews of Britain) in 1852 for a Welsh-speaking readership, and a year later the English-language *The British Jews: their religious ceremonies, social condition, domestic habits, literature, political statistics etc.*, his attitude has shifted to one of respect. In the latter work he challenges stereotypes, admires Jewish learning and ethics, and details closely and objectively the domestic and religious customs and traditions that he observes. Although his studies are not without shortcomings, after several years of a kind of proto-anthropological participant observation he is no longer paternalistic, and no longer presents the Jew as blind to the truth and stubborn in his ways.

In comparison, his contemporary, the infamous Robert Knox, finds everywhere reinforcement of his prejudices, which he published in 1850 in his notorious racist work *The Races of Men*. In an aside to his ruminations on the unchangeable nature of Jewish racial traits, Knox remarks: 'Societies are got up for their conversion! Be it so. Nothing can be said against them; but in one hundred years they will not convert one hundred Jews – not even one real Jew. This is my opinion and solemn conviction. Nature alters not.'[59] Knox was correct in his prediction that missionaries would achieve little, though the reason for Mills's failure in particular probably did not lie in the biologically unchanging nature of the Jew. In 1851, support for the mission was nearly withdrawn because, according to one commentator, 'great divergence of opinion existed as to the methods employed by the missionary', and whether to continue the mission 'was warmly discussed'.[60] The controversy – over 'philosemitic' versus 'coercive' conversionist methods – was lampooned a few years later in two cartoons in the satirical paper, *Y Punch Cymraeg*, after Mills's work was once again criticised in the annual meeting of the Methodist Missionary Society in 1858. One cartoon, entitled 'Y Ddau Allu' (The Two Powers), depicts the argument between methods: a figure on the left shows the way to a cross, and a central figure, pitchfork in hand, pulls a Jew along by his beard. With an informed pun on the Yiddish word for synagogue ('shul'), the text makes fun of the 'two shools of thought', and describes how criticism of Mills prevailed: 'The Chairman arose, his eyes flashing with anger, and having given the boot to the Missionary, grabbed the Jew's beard and commenced to drag him unceremoniously to the Cross.'[61]

Mills lost support for the mission in 1859 in part for his failure to achieve conversions, but also for allegedly courting conversion to Judaism himself.[62] His troubling sympathy and respect had emerged in *Iddewon Prydain* in 1852, and *The British Jews* in 1853.

The British Jews
The British Jews opens with a dedication to Lord John Russell who, in 1844, had sponsored the parliamentary bill removing some Jewish civil disabilities. In addressing Russell, Mills emphasises this issue, commenting on 'the conditions of the Jews of this country', commending the part Russell played in 'recent efforts to remove the last remnants of Jewish disabilities', and asserting that his name is associated with 'all other enlightened measures to improve the condition of the nation, and to place all sections of Her Majesty's subjects on equal civil ground'.[63] Here Mills is linking interest in 'the condition of the Jews' to the removal of civil constraints on Welsh nonconformists as well. However, in the earlier Welsh-language book, Mills's purpose is different, for he writes that 'the chief aim . . . in preparing [the volume] was to win over the Christian feelings of [the author's] compatriots to pray for the Jewish nation, and to endeavour to win them to the truth that is in Jesus'.[64] There continues to be a slippage between his Welsh and his English texts: those in Welsh are overtly millenarian, and stress the need for Jews to embrace truth; those in English are more anthropological and objective in tone and only covertly conversionist.

The British Jews is perhaps intended in part as a rebuttal to Robert Knox, for Mills remarks in the book's rather fussy style: 'we must confess that we have no sympathy with those authors, who, reckless of facts and history both sacred and profane, would lead us, for the sake of building up a theory, to believe that the difference of character among the nations is founded upon constitutional and unchangeable principles'.[65] He goes further, however, and expresses his belief that 'the British Jews are not guilty of any habitual vice peculiar to themselves; but on the other hand ... are less addicted to the immoralities that so frequently disgrace their Gentile neighbours' (p. 348).

Nevertheless, for Mills, the Jews constitute a fascinating eastern other, and it is in this framework that he understands those traits he finds distasteful – namely what he calls 'a love of finery', which, he observes, 'may be, in part at least, a relic of their oriental taste' (p. 352). Another unfortunate trait is their passionate and intolerant nature: 'The Jew', he remarks, 'seems to retain much of his oriental warmth – not having had the advantages of a training calculated to smoothe [*sic*] down the passions, we meet with but little of that sedateness so valuable in general society' (p. 353). Fortunately these less appealing eastern traits are soon to be eradi- cated, for 'as education, founded upon the true knowledge of God, progresses, all vices that now deface human society will be removed from both Jew and Gentile' (p. 355).

Mills touches on another intent, common both to his mission and to his book, which opens with a summary history of Jews in Britain, but with an anti-Catholic rhetoric that makes the nonconformist agenda explicit:

> From an early period, they found a quiet home in this island, until Popery was matured, and began to exert its influence in this country. The first decree on record, of a menacing character to the Jews, is that of Egbert, Archbishop of York, in the year 740, prohibiting the Popish population to appear at Jewish feasts. From that period their interest became very insecure. At times they found peace ... but anon a storm of persecution would arise ... In these barbarities, the priests generally took the lead. (p. 1)

Mills links the expulsion of the Jews in 1290 to this Popish fiendishness, whereas, in contrast, the Protestant attitude was, according to him, one of love and welcome, for in 1655 Menasseh Ben Israel, a Dutch Jew, was able to appeal to the millenarian Cromwell for the readmission of the Jews to Britain (we may see here a source for D. Wynne Evans some fifty years later). According to Mills, Menasseh Ben Israel was

> by nature a noble-minded man; and deep learning, with a knowledge of the world, made him exceedingly kind and urbane. He had raised himself above

the prejudices of his nation, and courted the friendship of enlightened Christians . . . The liberty and kindness which Protestantism was extending to the Jews on all hands, had attracted the attention and aroused the fondest expectations of Menasseh for years. He looked with anxiety to Britain – that his persecuted race might find in it an asylum. (pp. 2–3)

In 1860, when Mills visits the Middle East, the role of Papist fiends is replaced by what he invariably calls 'bigoted Mohammedans', which, as D. Wynne Evans's work indicates, was entirely consistent with Puritan eschatological thought that looked for signs of the approaching millennium not only in the conversion of the Jews, but also in the destruction of Catholicism and Islam.

The conversion of the Jews, for Mills, is a religious obligation and of millenarian inspiration, but as some of the foregoing and the address to Lord John Russell indicates, it is also an anglicising and assimilationist task. I use the term *anglicising* in this context to mean quite specifically assimilation to English ways and the English language as much as conversion to Christianity. The uncertainty about classifying the mission to the Jews within a 'Home' or 'Foreign' framework suggests that the position of this mission with respect to Empire is an odd one for the Calvinistic Methodists, particularly as their missionary efforts elsewhere, conducted through the medium of Welsh, were certainly *not* anglicising ones, though they operated within the framework of clear British imperial interests.[66]

This is one of the curious tensions in John Mills's work among the Jews of London: he was not only a Welsh speaker, reporting to his sponsors in Welsh, but was the missionary of a uniquely Welsh denomination, for whose members Christian belief was bound up with the Welsh language, with Welsh traditions, and with Welsh nationhood.

A Welsh colony in Palestine

That tension emerges in Mills's response to Palestine, which he visited in 1855 as part of a missionary effort to relieve (and convert) the destitute Jews of Jerusalem with money collected from Welsh congregations. While in the Middle East, he wrote his monthly article for *Y Drysorfa* from Alexandria and Jerusalem, and he published a book-length account of that visit in 1858 as *Palestina: sef Hanes Taith Ymweld ag Iuddewon Gwlad Canaan* (Palestine: namely the history of a journey to visit the Jews of the Land of Canaan).[67] Near the end, he slips in a piece of Welsh imperialism coloured by colonialist rhetoric and assumptions that might prove somewhat challenging to those who subscribe on the one hand to the tidy equation of Wales as colonised and therefore anti-imperialist, and, on the other (and related to it), to the myth that the Welsh have always and quite naturally had a sympathy for the situation of the Palestinian people.

Mills was profoundly nationalist in the context of Wales, and simultaneously patriotically imperial and evangelist, and he saw in Palestine an intoxicating possibility. At the end of *Palestina* he sets out his arguments for why Palestine was 'the best place in the world' for a 'gwladychfa', a Welsh colony or settlement.[68] At the outset, he dispenses with what he expects will be 'the inevitable objection' from those who believe that Palestine belongs to 'Israel' and that 'it is they who will possess her again', by suggesting, in somewhat familiar terms, that the territory is sufficiently large to accommodate the Welsh settlers.[69] He advances a four-part argument about the suitability of Palestine for a Welsh colony: the quality of the land; its economic situation; the opportunity it offers for Welsh settler independence, and its religious advantages.

Palestine is a country rich in natural assets, he claims; it is sleeping through a long Sabbath and is only waiting to be awoken – by honourable Welsh labour. He objects to the idea of both Patagonia and America as appropriate places of settlement, as was being proposed at the time by Michael D. Jones. Mills's objection is one based on the need for Welsh independence, which he emphasises repeatedly. Although he gives no detail about the practical organisation of the proposed settlement, he argues that the widespread shared interest in the Holy Land among the major powers of Europe would ensure its autonomy. There would be a kind of spiritual Cold War of mutual interest in keeping the status quo: 'The Welsh colony in Palestine would be under the continual gaze of the various European powers and this would ensure no one could interfere with its independence', he suggests.[70] It is not, therefore, a Welsh colony within a British imperial structure that he proposes, but a politically independent Welsh national home in Palestine – a place which, as he observes, would be extremely valuable in the near future and one where such a settlement would facilitate European and particularly British imperial interests in India.

Mills describes the incomparable untapped natural resources of the country (untapped, as he explains, because of eastern sloth), whose exploitation would not require the kind of hard labour that Wales itself exacts. On the contrary, unlike in Wales and America, he suggests, in Palestine 'nature does more than half the work'.[71] Not only the necessities but also luxuries would be easily obtained, which would in turn leave time and energy for the cultivation of the mind and for the service 'of virtue and belief'.[72] Where better to do this than in the Holy Land, he asks – and, one might infer, who better to develop the land than the Welsh?

Mills stresses the need for Welsh emigrants to be able to 'live as a community of Welshmen – live on their own land; earn their own bread; speak their own language; formulate their own laws – in a word, carry on their whole being as a community independent from any other government'.[73] As a consequence of Wales losing her independence, the Welsh have also lost their place on the world map, and Palestine, he suggests, offers the chance for Wales to reassert herself. Unlike the colony in Patagonia, which, even if it were to prove successful, 'is so remote, and so out of sight of the civilised world, that there is no hope that it would ever be noticed', where Palestine is concerned, 'every country feels so much of an interest in it' that the Welsh settlement would carry the weight that would enable it – and, implicitly also Wales – to gain a place on the map of the world.[74]

With quite extraordinary casualness, Mills disposes of the problem of an existing population in Palestine: Jew, Muslim and Christian, he remarks in passing, will quickly be won around to the idea when they see what wonderful benefits the Welsh will bring. As the state of religious belief in Palestine is so dire, he claims, there is very little difference between the three main religions, and there is no place more desperately in need of missionary activity. He feels sure, he concludes blithely, that Muslims, Christians 'and especially the Jews, would very quickly be full of kind feelings for the settlement, and eager to serve it'.[75] The settlers would lead by example, and would quickly win their neighbours round to virtue and truth.

This proposal by Mills was not so absurd that it was merely made and dropped, and not so idiosyncratic that it could be dismissed as one man's fantasy. It is probably the case that in the missionary circles in which he had been moving in London, he would have been exposed to many of the proposals, practical and otherwise, of both Jewish and English colonial settlement in Palestine that were current in the mid-nineteenth century.[76] Mills discussed his ideas with the British representative in Jerusalem, who reputedly responded favourably, and he lectured on the subject on his return to Wales.[77] More than forty years later, and long after the establishment of the Welsh colony in Patagonia, the Reverend D. Wynne Evans picked up on the proposal in one of his articles in *Young Wales*, and elaborated on its fantasy:

Mr Mills was so struck with the fertility of the Jordan valley that he suggested the establishing of a Welsh Colony there. His fellow countrymen, however,

chose the West rather than the East – Patagonia rather than Palestine. It is
curious to note that a colony of Jews followed the example of the Welsh and
settled near the same regions . . . Who knows but that the Welsh will, again,
act upon John Mills' suggestion, join their 'Hebrew brothers from the wilderness,' and leave Patagonia for Palestine, and the Chubat Valley for the Jordan
Valley, saying 'We will go with you; for we have heard that God is with you.'[78]

Mills may have been touching on a widespread religious tendency to see
Palestine as a Wales in the east, but he conceives of his imagined *gwladfa*
in terms of a quite concrete *political* proposal for Welsh independence,
rather than in a kind of millenarian Welsh-Israelite version of the
British-Israel framework pertaining in England. This emphasis on cultural
and political independence may well have contributed to the later political
comparisons made between the two countries in the twentieth century.

Mills and the Samaritans

Two years after the publication of *Palestina*, and after the abrupt conclusion of Mills's twelve-year mission to convert the Jews of London, he
travelled east again in 1860, intending to visit poor Jewish communities in
Yemen, India and Iraq – for which effort, he asserts, 'the signs are that
Divine Providence is opening the way to do good for them'.[79] The account
of this second visit appeared in 1864 under the title *Three Months'
Residence at Nablus and an Account of the Modern Samaritans*.

In the preface to this second book on Palestine, he remarks that
'several eminent travellers have given brief notices of the Samaritans,
but no full account of them, so far as I am aware, has ever been
attempted . . . In eliciting information from [Amram, the priest], I made
Jewish life my stand-point, so as to be able to compare the Samaritans
and Jews, to know in what they agreed and in what they differed'.[80] This
proto-ethnographic book became an important source for the period –
for example Besharan Doumani's 1995 study *Rediscovering Palestine:
Merchants and Peasants in Jabal Nablus, 1700–1900* relies on this
work.[81] It also became a source for fictional treatment of the Samaritans:
Lily Tobias's book, *The Samaritan. An Anglo-Palestinian Novel*, is
clearly informed by Mills's viewpoint, and offers a counterpoint to his
Welsh observation of Samaritan culture, by presenting a Samaritan's
observations of Welsh culture.[82]

That Mills's approach is informed by a close comparison with British
Judaism is perhaps not in itself problematic, as it is acknowledged and the
comparative intent made explicit. More problematic in this account is the
now covert conversionism by which his interest and his enquiry is

informed, and more problematic yet are his attitudes to non-Jews and non-Samaritans.

While proximity with Jews in London led to a modification of his prejudices and an interest that, according to some of his Welsh Calvinist Methodist sponsors, bordered on conversion, proximity to the natives of Nablus, with the exception of Samaritans, does not occasion desire for greater contact; nor does he let it challenge his prejudices. Although he rather disingenuously claims, 'I have purposely refrained from advancing any of my own speculations, or making any comments, but have confined myself to merely recording as faithfully as I could just what I saw and heard', what comes across in his account is, on the one hand, an idealisation of the Samaritans as a purer repository than Jews of the source of his own religious beliefs, and, on the other, an unthinking reaction to Muslims similar to his response to notional Catholics.[83] For all his sensitivity to Jews, honed by prolonged exposure, and reinforced by a belief in the radical liberalism of Calvinistic Methodism, Mills's encounter with 'Oriental' cultural difference in Palestine proves difficult.

His book on the Samaritans begins with a description of the geography, the archaeological remains and the history of Nablus/Shechem, and he speculates that the Israelites, who used Shechem as a resting place, 'had, probably, to endure taunts, ridicule, cursing and perhaps something even worse . . . And such has been the character of the city in all ages: its inhabitants have always been domineering and insulting, from the time of the Ephraimites, through the Samaritan period, down to the present Mussulman bigots' (p. 71). Curiously, this characterisation of the inhabitants of Nablus is echoed by that rather more well-known nineteenth-century visitor to Palestine, H. B. Tristram, one of the Palestine Exploration Fund's naturalists.[84] Perhaps biblical precedent determined what both saw to some degree.

Mills juxtaposes evocative description of topography, antiquities and natural history, such as the jackals' 'nocturnal concerts' of 'antiphonal hideous music', with unremittingly hostile rhetoric about 'bigoted' Muslims. 'Nablus being one of the strongholds of Islamism in Palestine,' he observes, 'the inhabitants have been too bigoted hitherto to allow any antiquarian research to be made by Europeans' (p. 90). Former churches, now mosques, are 'jealously guarded by the bigoted Mohammedans from intrusion by any unbeliever' (p. 92). With slightly more sympathy, he acknowledges the 'spirit of independence and bravery from the earliest ages' of the people of Nablus, and remarks that 'no district in Syria has been more turbulent and less manageable to the Turkish Government' (pp.

94–5). But then comes the qualification: 'and no people in Palestine are so deeply imbued with the fanaticism of Islam ... There is a mixture of bigotry and gruffness in all the inhabitants; and even in their highest officials, with one or two exceptions, you miss that grace which characterizes the better class of Mussulmans elsewhere' (p. 95). Echoing his earlier designation of the Jew as childlike native, Mills describes Arabs as 'passionately fond of singing. All things are done by them singing, except quarrelling; and they would even quarrel singing, were it possible, quarrelling and singing being to them a second nature' (p. 96).[85]

Three Months' Residence at Nablus constitutes an invaluable study of domestic life, from food preparation to sleeping arrangements, from the division of labour to modes of greeting and grieving, but Mills shifts register when describing national character. Despite a statement that 'the whole people of Palestine, and of the East generally, are very much alike' (p. 165), when he comes to list the faults of the natives, it is Arabs who are specified, although there is a slippage throughout between Arab and Muslim that makes it unclear whether Christian Arabs are also included. In summary – for he elaborates on each of these faults at length – the flaws are as follows: Arabs are guilty of a pathological untruthfulness; of deceit; of irreligion; of cruelty and vainglory, and a love of money – 'never', according to Mills, 'did the eyes of a Jew or Gentile glisten more brightly when receiving the idol coin than do [the Arab's]' (p. 166). But, he adds,

> The Arabs, notwithstanding, have some redeeming qualities. There is a gentleness of manner strangely mixed with their character not found among persons of the same class in Europe; and, when their confidence is won, they exhibit no little kindness and hospitality. No one can fail to observe their sobriety; and in this they give an example most worthy to be followed. 'When God,' as Girius said, 'shall give them a better nature,' the Arabs will be a fine race of people. (pp. 172–3)

In *The British Jews*, in contrast, Mills's list of Jewish virtues is longer than his list of Jewish faults: the Jews are industrious, abstinent, clean, decent, hospitable, and Sabbath-keeping. These fine qualities are moderated by an intense love of amusements, a love of finery, pride and self-approval, passion and intolerance of each other, and superstition.

It is not so much the case that Mills has transferred those traits traditionally attributed to Jews wholesale onto Arabs, but that he saw both groups as sharing something of the same semitic or Oriental character. These Oriental traits are ones from which, for Mills, the British Jews are somewhat redeemed. In contrast, the Samaritans are idealised. Only one individual proves an exception: the ageing priest, who died shortly after Mills met him, and who possessed 'that sinister glance of the eye so common in his country' (p. 182). The remainder are, in Mills's opinion, very fine people:

> In appearance the Samaritans are far superior to their circumstances, as also to all others around them. I had seen individuals, among Arabs and Jews, of as noble aspect as any *one* of them; but as a community, there is nothing in Palestine to compare with them. (pp. 179–80)

The new priest, Amram, particularly impresses him: 'He was decidedly the most favourable specimen of all the natives I met with, of any creed, with the exception of two or three who had been deeply impressed by the truths of the Gospel', he remarks approvingly (p. 185).

While at every turn Mills compares Samaritan religious belief and practice with what he knows about Judaism, he also repeatedly situates it in the context of Samaritan and Jewish beliefs as they are depicted in the Christian Bible, so that one might infer from this idealisation that he is searching in Samaritan religion for the pure roots of his own. The only holy text the Samaritans recognise is their own version of the Pentateuch, whereas Judaism is, in the nonconformist view, sullied by such deviations as the Talmud, which makes it akin, as Mills observes in an early article in *Y Drysorfa*, to Catholic neglect of scripture.[86]

'Popish' as a term of contempt, and 'bigoted' as an inseparable qualifier of 'Mohammedan', carry religious meanings in the period (concerning 'obstinate' resistance to 'truth') that are quite different from present-day secular usage, according to which we are more likely to see Mills as the bigot. Nevertheless, the use of these terms by Mills constitutes a limitation to his self-styled enlightened liberalism. So too does Mills's mission to convert the Jews, although in a different fashion: these conversionist endeavours qualify the purported support for liberty of conscience that was central to Welsh nonconformity, though only belatedly to Welsh Calvinistic Methodism. In the campaign for emancipation, the disestablishment of the Church of England, and the lifting of religious disabilities that pertained to members of the Welsh chapels, the religious disabilities of Jews was a source of concern in Wales. However, such concern does not appear to have moderated this conversionism, whether overt, as in the case of Mills's missions in London and Jerusalem, or more covert, as in early twentieth-century literature that was almost certainly influenced by his accounts of Jews and Palestine.

'Y GYMRAES O GANAAN'

Though Mills was a prolific writer, and evidently enjoyed a wide readership, his accounts of Palestine competed in Wales with those contained in
a collection of letters published in 1869 under the title *Llythyrau Cymraes
o Wlad Canaan* (A Welshwoman's Letters from the Land of Canaan).
Margaret Jones, author of the letters, had left Wales to go into service with
a family of converted Jews in England, and had travelled with them to
Palestine, where her employer was engaged in missionary work. The
letters, written to her parents, were collected and published in book form
after they had first appeared in *Y Tyst Cymreig*, a journal of the
Independents. Within four years of the book's appearance, her accounts,
which had been published without her knowledge, had gone into five
editions.[87] Jones became well known as 'y Gymraes o Ganaan' (the
Welshwoman from Canaan) and on her return from Palestine she engaged
in a fund-raising lecture tour for missionary work, before leaving, in 1879,
for Morocco, again with the same family and for the same purpose. She
returned in 1882, and published an account, in part concerning the Jewish
community in Morocco, under the title *Morocco a'r hyn a welais yno*
(Morocco and what I saw there).

Jones's observations have little of the detail offered by Mills, nor the
knowledge, but there is a directness and simplicity in her descriptions that
is striking. She observes the grinding poverty and oppression of Jews in
Jerusalem with acute and strongly-felt concern, but this is coupled always
with her intolerance of their adherence to Judaism. Nevertheless, her
spontaneous exclamations of pity, and then self-criticism for her presumptuousness, differs rather from an expression of ideological distaste.

Her first letter opens in biblical fashion: 'Dyma ni fel yr Israeliaid gynt,
wedi cychwyn ar ein taith o'r Aipht i Ganaan' (Here we are, like the first
Israelites, having started on our journey from Egypt to Canaan).[88] She
describes their arrival in Jaffa, her first sight of Muslims at prayer, a visit to
the Tombs of the Kings, and an outbreak of cholera. The keening of
mourners over numerous deaths in the epidemic sounds to her as if the
destruction of Jerusalem were imminent. Her observations of women in
relation to men complements the kind of domestic detail that Mills
provides: she comments on a wife's obligation to kiss her husband's hand
whenever he comes into the house, and on how men show their wives no
respect or love. In somewhat self-congratulatory style she describes an
Arab woman's response to the European treatment of women:

Pan aeth un o ferched y wlad hon i dalu ymweliad ag un o'r cenhadon a'i deulu, gofynnodd i wraig y tŷ ar ddiwedd ei hymweliad, mewn syndod mawr, 'A ydyw y gwŷr o Ewrop yn gyffredinol yn ymddwyn tuag at eu gwragedd fel hyn?' Pan atebwyd eu bod, 'O' ebai yr Arabes, 'na'm ganesid yn ngwlad y Cristionogion, lle yr ymddygir at ferched fel creaduriaid yn meddiannu eneidiau, ac nid fel anifeiliaid y maes.' (p. 31)

(When a woman of this country went to pay a visit to one of the missionaries and his family, she asked the lady of the house at the end of her visit, in great surprise, 'Do the men of Europe generally treat their wives in this way?' When the answer came that they did, 'Oh!' said the Arab woman, 'that I had been born in the land of Christians, where women are treated as creatures with souls, and not as lowly beasts'.)

Jones is more direct in her account of the cholera outbreak, when, unfiltered by Christian grandstanding, she describes seeing a group coming towards her, 'grasping their front teeth with their fingers as though they were about to pull them from their gums, which is, with the Arabs, a sign of destitution'.[89] When she comes to describe Jews at the Western Wall, most of whom are 'poor and pitiable', she is spontaneous:

Tybia yr Iuddewon mai dyma yr unig *fan* y gall Duw eu clywed; felly maent yn myned i wylo a gweddio ar i Dduw eu hen dadau Abraham, Isaac, a Jacob, i adferu eu hen wlad a'r ddinas sanctaidd iddynt eto; ac, yn wir, yr oedd rhai o'r hen bobl yn wylo fel pe buasai eu calonau bron a thori. Oh! [*sic*] fel yr oeddwn yn hiraethu am ddeall eu hiaith fel y gallwn ddweyd wrthynt am y Jerusalem newydd, a'r Brenin sydd yn barod i'w derbyn hwy yno ond iddynt gredu fod eu Messiah wedi dyfod a hwnw yn Mherson Iesu Grist. Ond pan ystyriais, a meddwl pwy oeddwn i i fyned i ddysgu henuriaid Israel, yr oedd bron yn gywilydd genyf fod y fath feddwl wedi dyfod i fy mhen; ond os nad oeddwn yn gymhwys i'w dysgu, y lleiaf a allaswn wneud oedd gweddio drostynt, yr hyn a wnaethum a'm holl galon. Yn wir, byddai yn rhaid cael calon bur galed i beidio, wrth edrych ar y fath olygfa.[90]

(The Jews think that this is the only *place* that God can hear them; so they come and weep and pray to the God of their fathers Abraham, Isaac, and Jacob to return their old land and their sacred city to them; and, truly, some of the old people were weeping as if their hearts were about to break. Oh! how I longed to understand their language so that I could tell them about the new Jerusalem, and the King who is ready to receive them there, if they only believe that the Messiah has come, and he in the Person of Jesus Christ. But when I considered, and thought who was I to go and teach the elders of Israel, I was almost ashamed that such a thought had entered my mind; but if I was not qualified to teach them, the least I could do was to pray for them, which I did with all my heart. In truth, one would have to be completely hard-hearted not to, seeing such a sight.)

Here she expresses a sympathy and respect, but elsewhere she cites the sins of the Jews, in particular 'their chief sin, namely refusing the welcome of the Lord of the World', and regrets how the former 'lords of the land' have, through sin, been brought so low.[91]

Despite her direct encounter with Jewish subjects of conversionist attention, Margaret Jones's account of the 1860s does not greatly differ in its larger sentiment from the rather more hypothetical response of Daniel Evans in his 1826 poem, nor that of Elfed in his 1930s poem. Although her writing, like that of John Mills, is tempered by a very immediate and genuine sense of interest in and sympathy with living individuals and groups, that sympathy is irredeemably conditional and edged with a kind of knowing impatience. But in her case, perhaps in part because of her social status and class as much as her sex and her age, there is a self-questioning and an awareness of presumptuousness that is entirely absent from these other examples of conversionist discourse.[92]

CONVERSIONISM AS ETHNOGRAPHY

Like conversionism in many contexts, Welsh interest in the conversion of the Jews constitutes an internally and externally colonising and culturally homogenising force. At the same time, Welsh practical and hypothetical (or perhaps 'rhetorical') conversionism evidently springs from a number of interests and attitudes. Firstly, as is clear in Mills and other conversionist writers, no matter the degree of sympathy, there exists an apprehension of 'the Jew' as a categorically Oriental other. Secondly, the millenarian desire to fulfil preconditions for the return of the Christian Messiah took a particular form in Wales. For example, the confluence of meanings in 'dychweliad', the word for 'conversion' and for 'return' (the 'return' or 'restoration' of the Jews to Zion), suggests how this millenarian interest in the conversion of the Jews and their return to Ottoman Palestine existed in a linguistically heightened register in Welsh. Thirdly, the Welsh-Israelite tradition of identification as biblical Jews, as the new elect, and the separation this created between biblical and historical Jews, might well have made the Jews themselves of particular conversionist interest. But the living reality of Jews, and the abject condition of Jews (and of Samaritans-as-original-Jews) in Palestine, does not appear to have troubled the implicit elision that such a self-identification created.

Mills, in the Middle East as in London, was interested, on the one hand, in Jewish souls and, on the other, in the possibilities of an independent

Welsh colonial enterprise in Palestine that would further the harvesting of such souls. His *British Jews* is certainly a sympathetic account of Jewish culture, and it also constitutes an important and progressive proto-ethnographic text. His other English-language work, *Three Months in Nablus*, is perhaps less progressive, but it too constitutes an important ethnographic survey, as does Margaret Jones's *Llythyrau*. This ethnographic function is a reminder that some conversionist activity, notwithstanding its dubious intent, may have valuable outcomes. Nevertheless, despite such a caveat, it is difficult to compress the contradictions in Mills's interest and activities into some idea of philosemitism, no matter how 'kindly', in that ambiguous conversionist sense, his intentions might be. Nor does Margaret Jones's apprehension of the Jews as labouring under the consequences of their own sins, or the voyeuristic interest in the 'condition of the Jews' expressed by poets, fit comfortably or usefully within this term – and they also cannot be measured for 'virulence' or antisemitism in any particularly useful or meaningful way.

3

Welsh semitic discourse

'Vales for the Velsh! I believe in Vales for the Velsh. . . but you can have too much Vales for the Velsh.'

— Geraint Goodwin, *The Heyday in the Blood*

CRITICAL APPROACHES: ANTISEMITISM/PHILOSEMITISM AND SEMITIC DISCOURSE

An approach to Welsh attitudes to Jews that takes as its framework an opposition between 'antisemitism' and 'philosemitism' permits the notion of a predominantly tolerant Wales to remain intact and largely unexamined, notwithstanding isolated incidents, over which contrite breast-beating occurs. Expressions of hostility are isolated and rendered exceptional, and friendly, 'affectionate' or 'tolerant' and loving attitudes are presented as the default. This tendency in Welsh literary criticism and historiography to isolate hostility as an exception from the mainstream follows a wider British norm. In the English context, Bryan Cheyette argues that 'prevalent constructions of Semitic "difference" . . . dispute the humanizing pretensions of the Anglo-American literary canon and liberal culture in general', but the historiography of antisemitism and philosemitism 'continues to essentialize Jews as uniquely timeless, unchanging victims and therefore positions the history of antisemitism outside of the social, political, and historical processes that gave rise to this history in the first place'.[1] This is certainly true of the Welsh situation, too, although these parallel 'constructions of Semitic "difference"', while sharing features with such constructions internationally, nevertheless express meanings specific to the Welsh cultural context.

The aim of challenging the antisemitism/philosemitism polarisation that pertains in Wales, which permits comparable 'humanising pretensions' of Welsh literature to persist unchallenged, is not to excavate some unrecognised intolerance, or the victimisation of Jews in the particularity of the Welsh context. On the contrary, the aim is to look at how the imaging of Jews in Wales expresses, on the one hand, a distinctive cultural response to Jews and, on the other, derives from and shares features with a broader 'semitic discourse' – a discourse in which Jews serve as a malleable but representative cultural other (the term 'semitic discourse' is discussed more fully below).

The literary construction of the self – individual, social, or national – in terms of differentiation from what is other, is, in the Welsh case, often a differentiation from the notional primary other, 'the English'. Therefore the ambiguities and inherent contradictions in Welsh imaging of Jews in this context are difficult to see, let alone discuss, if the framework of the analysis is one of reductive binary opposites, or one that measures 'virulence', to invoke the model used by Matthew Biberman.[2]

While the stereotyped imaging of 'the Jew' in any particular place and time might share motifs and references with such stereotyped representations worldwide (in ways that often bear little relationship to the presence or size of a Jewish population), its deployment is nevertheless likely to be culturally specific.[3] Given the strength of the Welsh-Israelite tradition discussed in chapter 1, and the dominance of the cultural and political relationship with England (such that, according to Gwyn A. Williams, the Welsh, 'from birth . . . lived with the threat of extinction'), it would seem inevitable that the way in which Jews are imagined in Welsh literature is often caught up with how Welshness and Wales are imagined – which is to say, often in relation to (and differentiation from) Englishness.[4] Indeed, it is frequently the case – as in the example of D. Wynne Evans – that the use of Jewish imaging and reference is a constituent part of such differentiation of Welshness from Englishness, albeit in ambiguous and ambivalent terms.

The limitations of an antisemitism/philosemitism opposition are best shown by W. D. and Hilary L. Rubinstein, who define philosemitism as 'support and admiration for the Jewish people by non-Jews', and who regard it 'as the other side of the coin of antisemitism (hostility to, or dislike of, Jews)'.[5] In the Welsh context – specifically in his article in the *Welsh History Review* that re-examines the Tredegar riots – W. D. Rubinstein defines philosemitism as 'support and admiration for Jews, *both* ancient and modern'. He suggests that 'the very concept of *philo*-semitism – in contrast to anti-semitism – will possibly be unfamiliar to most readers'.[6] These readers are, one may presume, those of *Welsh History Review*, though if that is the case Rubinstein appears to present something of a contradiction if, as he claims, philosemitism was pervasive in Welsh culture until the late twentieth century. The term 'philosemitism', after all, is not of recent coinage.

These simple definitions of antisemitism and philosemitism, deployed in the context of Wales, point to the limited utility of these mutually exclusive terms. They do not admit much possibility of ambiguity or contradiction – and yet discourse about Jews is usually characterised by ambiguity and contradiction, as the conversionist texts examined so far illustrate. To situate these two sets of attitudes at opposite poles, or on reverse sides of a coin, is to separate the closely interwoven and often simultaneously contradictory responses to Jews as a distinct and different group; consequently these terms, used in this way, can limit rather than elucidate. Indeed, such 'philosemitism' in its most benign form of 'admiration for the Jews' can be as problematic as covert hostility: admiration can still position the Jews as different and alien in essentialist ways, no matter how much such difference is admired, as statements by David Lloyd George, discussed below, reveal (and as Harri Webb's poem 'Israel', discussed in the next chapter, illustrates acutely). For example, expressions of so-called philosemitic admiration for Jewish financial or musical ability – or, again, particularly in Wales, for national survival – are ambivalent: the racial essentialism that characterises this 'admiration' can hardly be deemed an unambiguous social good, for 'the Jew' is still categorically and unchangingly other, no matter whether this otherness is positive or not.

Such a definition as the one given by Rubinstein also evades the conversionist meanings in early deployments of the term 'philosemitism', in which it was used to describe the persuasive and 'loving' approach to converting Jews, as distinct from a coercive approach – indicated, for example, by D. Wynne Evans's discussion of Oliver Cromwell and Morgan Llwyd, and expressed in the *Punch Cymraeg* cartoons satirising the Calvinistic Methodists' dismissal of John Mills. While Rubinstein is perhaps attempting to reclaim the term or broaden its scope beyond such conversionist and millenarian associations, the problematic relationship that he implicitly and sometimes explicitly draws between statements about Jews in the abstract, and attitudes that might predict behaviour towards Jews in the particular, is elided. Some scholars have recognised these limitations and have instead engaged in a consideration of 'semitic discourse', an approach that permits a more subtle and complex understanding. David Cesarani, for example, remarks:

> It is preferable to speak of a discourse about the Jews which operates through stereotypes that can be either positive or negative depending upon the intention of the agent employing them, something which can be deduced by careful attention to the context in which they are used. Hence the very same Jews can be either ruthlessly selfish, capitalist exploiters or thrusting individualistic entrepreneurs. The point is not what such Jews are actually supposed to be or what they do, but how they are constructed in language and culture . . . So-called philosemitism is part of this stereotypical system.[7]

Indeed, common to many analyses of semitic discourse is this observation of its inherent binary contradictions, which points to its fluidity and malleability.[8]

In its treatment of Jewish minority experience, both Jewish historiography and British historiography might seem to have been interested in an antisemitism/philosemitism axis (an interest that has been reinforced in the first decade of the twenty-first century by the increasingly heated argument over the relationship between antisemitism and anti-Zionism).[9] In literary criticism, in contrast, the canonical literary imaging of 'the Jew' has been isolated from the actual experience of Jews: 'the Jew' in literature is treated as notional, a metaphor, as if such imaging is divorced from how the culture views or treats living, contemporary Jews. As Bryan Cheyette puts it:

> the privileged cultural realm of literature remains essentially unthreatened by the naturalized construction of an eternal mythical 'Jew'. The mythic 'Jew', that is, exists quite comfortably in the realm of culture which is, supposedly, above and beyond the messy contingencies of history.[10]

While an antisemitism/philosemitism opposition cannot usefully accommodate the contradictions in Welsh conversionist discourse, it also cannot very usefully account for the reasons behind the deployment, by authors, of positive or negative Jewish stereotypes, whose presence, as in Anglo-American literature, has been glossed over or marginalised. It is too simplistic to conclude from stereotypical imaging in work by Geraint Goodwin or Saunders Lewis, for example, that either author was 'antisemitic' (whatever precisely might be meant by the term in this context); or, in similar isolation, to infer from Lloyd George's apparently positive statements (or apparently pro-Zionist actions) that he was 'philosemitic' (again, whatever the possible meanings of the term). Nor, again, can Caradoc Evans's often-quoted and highly stylised statement on Jews be construed as evidence in itself of his attitude to actual Jews. Discussion of such

Jewish imaging, when it does occur in Welsh criticism, has been overly reductive and perhaps insufficiently analytical.[11] For example, to preface the word antisemitism with the qualifier 'virulent', which is often used in this context, evokes psychological infection rather than a widely-shared set of literary or cultural references.[12] Characterised as a virus, antisemitism is cast as an invasive, alien contamination that can and should be extirpated. On the one hand, it suggests a kind of helpless passivity on the part of its host who is infected; on the other, it leaves 'philosemitism' as the uncontaminated natural *default* state. By implication, consequently, philosemitism becomes an essentialist, unqualified and unanalysed social good. But stereotypically positive imaging of Jews is also problematic. If, as David Cesarani claims, antisemitism exists 'within the framework of a complex discourse about Jews fraught with ambiguities', so too does the much less frequently analysed set of attitudes that constitute philosemitism, no matter whether the term denotes the more common meanings associated in large part with conversionism, or the one side of Rubinstein's rather plain and problematic coin.[13]

The characterisation of antisemitism as something 'virulent' has also allowed ambivalent imaging that is not overtly hostile to be downplayed, but to downplay or marginalise the significance of such imaging by Geraint Goodwin and Saunders Lewis, for example, or to fail to contextualise Lloyd George's actions or comments in a wider consideration of his published statements, is to indulge in an apologia for, and in some cases a denial of, attitudes that should be situated and acknowledged carefully in the wider context in which they occur. In addition, negative stereotyped imaging of 'the Jew' as a representative in the literature is too quickly identified as evidence of an author's attitudes to Jews, and so the use to which such imaging is put is overlooked, as are the patterns of semitic discourse that exist more widely in the culture. Such complexity cannot be accommodated in the approach that has been taken so far to Jewish imaging in Welsh literature.

In a broad examination of English literature, Bryan Cheyette traces the modern construction of 'the Jew' back to Matthew Arnold's exploration of 'Hellenism and Hebraism' in *Culture and Anarchy* (1869), arguing that

> within an increasingly exclusivist nation-state . . . Jews are constructed in equivocal terms as both the embodiment of a transformable cultural Hebraism and, at the same time, as an unchanging racial 'other'. The stark doubleness of a semitic discourse will, in general terms, thus be seen to constitute 'the Jew' as encompassing the possibility of a new redemptive order, as well as the degeneration of an untransformed past.[14]

However, as some of the examples examined below suggest, such constructions of 'the Jew' identified by Cheyette in an English literary context can take a different form in Welsh literature in both languages.[15]

One of the figures whose purported attitudes towards Jews lend themselves conveniently to the argument both for and against the existence of a general Welsh tolerance is Lloyd George. However, the subtlety of his published statement on the matter gets overlooked. His repudiation of antisemitism, which appears as a chapter in his 1925 book *Is it Peace?*, suggests very close familiarity with the full spectrum of semitic discourse. As it also functions as a most elegantly succinct and representative synopsis of such discourse, it is worth quoting at length:

> Of all the bigotries that savage the human temper there is none so stupid as the anti-Semitic. It has no basis in reason; it is not rooted in faith; it aspires to no ideal; it is just one of those dank and unwholesome weeds that grow in the morass of racial hatred. How utterly devoid of reason it is may be gathered from the fact that it is almost entirely confined to nations who worship Jewish prophets and apostles, revere the national literature of the Hebrews . . . and whose only hope of salvation rests on the precepts and promises of the great teachers of Judah. Yet in the sight of these fanatics the Jews of to-day can do nothing right. If they are rich they are birds of prey. If they are poor they are vermin. If they are in favour of a war it is because they want to exploit the bloody feuds of the Gentiles to their own profit. If they are anxious for peace they are either instinctive cowards or traitors. If they give generously – and there are no more liberal givers than the Jews – they are doing it for some selfish purpose of their own. If they do not give – then what could one expect of a Jew but avarice? If labour is oppressed by great capital, the greed of the Jew is held responsible. If labour revolts against capital . . . the Jew is blamed for that also. If he lives in a strange land he must be persecuted and pogrommed out of it. If he wants to go back to his own he must be prevented . . . The Jews alone can redeem [Palestine] from the wilderness and restore its ancient glory. The Arabs have neither the means, the energy, nor the ambition to discharge this duty . . . The Jewish race with its genius, its resourcefulness, its tenacity, and not least its wealth, can alone perform this essential task.[16]

When viewed in the light of Cesarani's recommendation, it becomes apparent that Lloyd George was particularly *au fait* with the nuances of this discourse. Nevertheless, it is easy to see how this whole chapter in support of a Jewish 'national home' in Palestine might be seen as constituting some kind of 'philosemitism': after all, it expresses, on the surface of it, admiration and support for Jews. On closer examination, however, it serves as an exemplar of Cesarani's argument, for even in the positive stereotypes, the Jew is still constructed as other, and these positive attributes carry echoes all the time of their negative twins. Shylock resonates in the stereotype of the wealthy Jew, and in Jewish genius and resourcefulness lies the deracinated, materialistic cosmopolitan whom, among others, Saunders Lewis invoked – embodied in the person of Welsh Jewish MP and industrialist Alfred Mond. In tenacity as a positive attribute lies its negative shadow, stubbornness – stubbornness, amongst other forms, against seeing the 'truth' of Christianity, as expressed by Daniel Evans in *Golwg ar gyflwr yr Iuddewon*: 'Gwargaled, O Israel, gwargaled yn wir' ('Obstinate, Oh Israel, truly obstinate').

This statement by Lloyd George was dismissed as 'sugary political cant' by local historian Ivor Wynne Jones in an address to the Friends of the Lloyd George Museum in 1999, and Geoffrey Alderman is perhaps correct when, in his rebuttal of W. D. Rubinstein's claims about the Tredegar riots, he observes that 'Lloyd George was philo-Semitic only when it suited him'.[17] Nevertheless those assessments overlook the rich material that Lloyd George offers in this extended passage, with its delineation of essentialist racial attributes and twinning of hostile opposites – bloodthirsty capitalist versus labour agitator; deracinated cosmopolitan versus unassimilable national other; coward versus international warmonger; abject primitive versus powerful predator. This stereotyped imaging sounds in both major and minor keys throughout Welsh literature in both languages, and Lloyd George's synopsis of it provides a useful reference point.

Notoriously, Lloyd George had rather different things to say about Jews in other contexts, such as his observation about Minister of Munitions Edwin Montagu, who, he said, 'sought cover, as was the manner of his race'.[18] Biographer and historian John Grigg claims that Lloyd George 'shared the popular Gentile belief that the Jews were natural cowards',[19] but curiously Lloyd George himself chose to invert that charge of cowardice and redeploy it in rather overcompensating 'muscular' rhetoric against those who persecuted Jews:

> No good has ever come of nations that crucified Jews. It is poor and pusillanimous sport, lacking all the true qualities of manliness, and those who indulge in it would be the first to run away were there any element of danger in it. Jew-baiters are generally of the type that found good reasons for evading military service when their own country was in danger.[20]

Such protest of course betrays him, and would have done even if he had not been on record for his comment about Montagu – or for his exclamation, in Wales, about Jews in the context of the Boer War: 'The people we are fighting for, those Uitlanders, are German Jews – 15,000 to 20,000 of them . . . Pah! fighting for men of that type!'[21] Importantly, considering what it reflects about his assessment of his audience's receptivity to such sentiment, this latter comment was made in a speech in Carmarthen in 1899, a detail that seems to get overlooked when claims are made that his purported immersion in the Welsh-Israelite tradition would have predisposed him to have positive attitudes to Jews (as, by implication, would have been the case for others who experienced such immersion).

On the other hand, in the account given by David Berry about the discovery and restoration of the film *The Life Story of David Lloyd George*, it is clear that the suppression of the film in 1918 was not attributable simply to Lloyd George's hostile attitudes to Jews, which might have surfaced when the Jewish identity of the film's sponsors belatedly emerged. Whatever his views on Jews, Berry suggests, these and Horatio Bottomly's rantings about 'Huns' were probably of less concern to Lloyd George than 'the vote-losing possibilities, on the election eve, of making a film for a Jewish concern in such xenophobic and racist times'.[22]

SEMITIC DISCOURSE IN TWENTIETH-CENTURY FICTION: GERAINT GOODWIN

Poets and fiction writers are likely to be less overtly polemical than a politician such as Lloyd George, of course, and the depiction of Jews in literature is therefore often very much more ambiguous. Here a comparison of the use of Jewish imaging can be revealing. In Ron Berry's 1970 novel *So Long, Hector Bebb*, for example, Jewish imaging is intrinsic and incidental, rather than representative.[23] The novel follows the rise and fall of the eponymous protagonist, a boxer, and the boxing world is portrayed unapologetically, as is Hector's manager, Abe. Abe is a slob. Fat, pale and bald, he suffers from perpetual indigestion, eats midnight fry-ups, and is interested in making money on Hector. He 'waddles' out of his office, and speaks in inverted word order: "'Such things I got to know'", he says.[24] In a characteristic interaction, when he asks Hector a question, and the trainer, Sammy, answers for him, 'Abe did Shylock with both palms. "I'm enquiring off the boy, Sammy'", he protests.[25]

The character of Abe might be based on Jack Solomons, the well-known boxing manager of the 1950s, the period in which *So Long, Hector Bebb* is set; alternatively, he might be written as a Jewish manager because so many of the boxing managers and promoters in the period were indeed

Jewish. That he 'did Shylock' with his hands is the only overt reference
to his Jewishness, however. He is coded not by his appearance (which
is to say in essentialised terms) but by his intonation and gestures: he is
not a stereotype, who represents a notion of a Jew and who, as such, is
intended to indicate something about Jews in general, or something
which, by comparison, non-Jews are not. On the contrary, he is a
well-written, credible and rather unpleasant though understandable character who happens to be Jewish, and who happens to use recognisable
Jewish gesture.

The Jewish 'cheap-jack' in Geraint Goodwin's 1937 story 'Come
Michaelmas' is a somewhat different matter. This figure, using the same
stage Jewish gestures, is an outsider. In the story, Annie has arrived at
market to sell her geese, but, hard-faced and intractable on price, she has
failed to sell any, and at the end of the day she is made a poor offer:

> The cheap-jack had waddled through in a last saunter. He was a round Jew,
> with a set smirking face, wet like a toad, and the same bulge in the eyes . . .
> 'sixteen pence,' he said, spreading out his hands.[26]

Later, after a melee in which Annie's geese get scattered, a crowd gathers.
'The moochers were picking her geese up and rubbing the dirt off them;
the Jew was gesticulating among them, telling them how it had all
happened. "Vent off like that," he said, bringing his hands together in a
clap. "Just like that!"'[27]

The Jew selling cheap goods at town markets features in several of
Goodwin's stories, which are set in the border country. Unlike Abe, who is
unambiguously a member of the community in Berry's *So Long, Hector
Bebb*, the cheap-jacks come from over the border.[28] In 'Janet Ifans'
Donkey', which precedes 'Come Michaelmas' in Goodwin's collection
The White Farm, the cheap-jacks are identified as 'the Salford Jews'. In
this story the setting is again a market, with 'all the china laid about, from
the best Staffordshire sets to the ordinary things in every day use – a cheap-
jack among them like a hen among the eggs'.[29] Again there is a
confrontation. Janet Ifans's donkey, provoked by malicious boys, runs
amok and smashes the china:

> That was how she came to be summoned. It was the cheap-jacks who kept the
> Sergeant up to it, and he had no choice. She was charged with creating, or
> causing to be created, a breach of the peace and word of it went round. The
> whole town was behind Janet, who was a Welshwoman, and had never done
> any harm, and why should the Salford Jews go and make trouble? No one had
> asked them to come.[30]

Again the cheap-jacks or Salford Jews represent an intrusion from across the border – and an across-the-border *cultural* disruption to the unchanging pace and manner of life in a Welsh community.

This Jewish outsider from across the border with England also works as a motif in Goodwin's novel, *The Heyday in the Blood*, which had been published a year earlier, in 1936. The novel is set in a border village full of natural, 'very Welsh' (and problematically reductive) characters, and centres on the Red Lion where there is a constellation of people around the owner, Twmi, and his daughter Beti. Every year, 'jentlemens' come to stay for fishing in the spring and grouse shooting in the summer, and at least one of these, Birbaum, is Jewish:

> Beti disliked them for many reasons. They caused needless work . . . occupied the best part of her own home . . . spoke with a funny accent, and their faces were white and puffy, with lined blue rings under their eyes . . . Mr Birbaum and Mr Shufflebotham came from Manchester. They were something big in business, but what it was no one knew.[31]

On one occasion, the 'jentlemens' bring a younger partner with them, 'a young sprig of a man in brown suede riding-breeches' (p. 23), and he makes a pass at Beti. Though as a country girl she knows the 'facts of life', she knows them in an earthy, wholesome way, 'not dressed up and embellished and made dirty', and after the young man makes his suggestive move on her, she has to go 'up on to the mountain to clean herself' (pp. 24–5). The young man is not himself identified as Jewish, but by association all of the 'jentlemens' carry the threat of worldly contamination – contamination of Beti in particular:

> Those men assailed her like a foul breath: they brought with them something foul and dirty and smoke-fretted. They spoke another language . . . these men brought with them a knowledge of the world, and every fresh discovery was like a smudge across a clean page. (p. 25)

Suggestively, in a curious parallel to 'the Jewess' as an insidiously double object of conversion (conversion through religion and through her body), Beti as a *woman* is subject to that outside influence in a way that neither the place itself nor its men are:

> Whether the 'jentlemens' came or not, the life of the Red Lion went on just the same . . . For nothing changed; the old place defied change . . . But it was not the same to Beti. The whole place changed with the 'jentlemens'. They were there or they were not there; life was one thing or the other. And yet she had no reason to dislike them – not the elder men – except that they made life different. She could not forget them as her father did, they were too big a part of her world for that.

And now Mr Birbaum, warming his back against the fire, had spoken to her
when she was clearing away the dinner things. (pp. 40–1)

Mr Birbaum has asked her age, and expressed a wish to talk to her father.
Beti knows it concerns her, but not how. Birbaum talks to her father,
though obliquely:

'You think it over,' said Mr Birbaum. He had come to the end before he had
begun . . . He would have liked to say what was on his mind and got done with
it – that his sister in Golders Green had written him to find a country girl when
he was next in Wales. Country girls were cheaper than town girls, were not so
flighty, and were satisfied with half the time off. (p. 51)

For Beti, the idea of going into service is unthinkable. 'Mr Birbaum and
the other English "jentlemens" were just like the smoke: they made the air
smell. They took something away from it all' (p. 55). Earlier, her disgust is
described as a reaction against the men's unnaturalness: 'their dressing
tables were loaded with pomades and grease and hair-oil, which gave her
an actual sense of physical revulsion. That a man should scent himself,
even his hair, was something totally beyond her: that a man should have
anything but that sweat-smelling, earthy odour of the fields was something
wrong and even wicked' (p. 23). This emasculating characterisation,
hinting at the common trope of the feminised Jew, further underscores the
visiting men's otherness and unnaturalness.

However, it is not through Beti's reaction but through the response of
local people in the bar that Goodwin hints at the layered complexity of his
Mr Birbaum, who is the only one of the visitors identified clearly as a Jew.
Birbaum is 'other', and from across the border with England, but his
Englishness is also in question:

'Whist; whist,' broke in Dici in alarm. 'Remember the jentlemens.'
    'Nice man, Mr Birbaum,' said Moses unctuously.
    'But what I can't see, now,' said Dici in his inquiring way, 'iss as how a Jew
iss an Englishman.' He paused and scratched his head. 'For an Englishman
can't be a Jew, now. Iesgyrn . . . it hass me beat, it hass.'
    'They are the chosen race,' answered Moses. 'They can pick and choose,
like.' (p. 49)

Birbaum's 'something big in business' Jewishness is highlighted by the
feelings he expresses towards the unspoiled natural world – he sees its
value in terms of its untapped commercial potential (one can almost see
the stage Jewish hand-rubbing gesture, though Goodwin is more subtle on
this occasion):

'Vell, vell,' answered Mr Birbaum. 'It is all the same to me. The countryside is so beau-tiful.'

'Not pad,' said Dici modestly . . .

'Not bad!' answered Mr Birbaum coming alight. 'You vant to put it on the map, make it go, like the Sviss do. Nobody knows about it! Vales for the Velsh! I believe in Vales for the Velsh . . . but you can have too much Vales for the Velsh.'

'Yes: yes,' said Wili breaking in, in his best voice. 'Too insulated we arr . . . and that's straight.'

'Vhat is business vidout Nature . . . especially in the spring,' went on Mr Birbaum. (p. 50)

While the young man, identified only by his 'brown suede riding breeches', is the one to make a sexual move on Beti, and, with the foulness of Manchester commerce, threatens what Goodwin depicts as her unsullied, wild Welshness, he himself is not identified as Jewish, except, perhaps, by association with Birbaum. The only developed character of the three 'jentlemens' is Birbaum, who is identified as 'the Jew wan' by Beti's father (p. 52). Nevertheless, in a less overtly sexual way, he is the personification of the threat to the wild, untouched (unanglicised) Wales by way of commerce and 'development'; at the same time, he more deeply troubles Beti's status by offering her a position as a maid in his sister's house in Golders Green.

The world from across the border – simultaneously England, the metropolis, and contaminating modernity – has broken in, and Mr Birbaum is its embodiment: he is the precursor to the inevitable and implacable process of change to and destruction of this borderland Welsh idyll. The threat builds through the novel, in ways very similar to the ominous advance of the opencast mine in Ed Thomas's play, *House of America*, written decades later, in 1988. At the close of Goodwin's *The Heyday in the Blood*, workmen arrive to begin digging Twmi's property for the new 'arterial road' that will pass right by the pub, and Beti has left for England.

In Sam Adams's monograph on Goodwin in the Writers of Wales series, there is not even a passing mention of the use of Jewish images to embody that contaminating and destructive world across the border. Goodwin's writing is powerful, vibrant, intensely sensual and broodingly sexual, and there is plenty of complex material to deal with, not least his difficult and stereotyped depiction of the Welsh. But if Adams does not discuss the Jewish imaging, his recognition of it is implicit in a way that effectively reinforces rather than challenges its stereotypes. 'The novel still has a relevant point to make in the continuing controversy about tourism,' he writes.

The developer's instinct to exploit that which is beautiful resides in Birbaum. We see the same false, money-centred motivation behind the unsuccessful plan to get Beti into service for his sister in Golders Green . . . however the book as a whole is an elegy on the passing of an old and distinctively Welsh order.[32]

By contrast, in his survey *A Hundred Years of Fiction*, Stephen Knight does make a small acknowledgement of this Jewish imaging. However, here, too, the extra load carried by such Jewish characterisation of outsiders is glossed over. Knight's rather pointed gesture of deploying, in an otherwise Anglophone text, the word 'Cymraeg' in place of the English word 'Welsh', signals his sensitivity to the highly politicised situation of the Welsh language. But his gesture in this direction, which includes identifying Welsh writing in English as first-contact literature, goes hand-in-hand with this glossing over, to sometimes odd effect. According to Knight, Goodwin's Jewish characterisation in *The Heyday in the Blood* is 'not, especially in the period, an antisemitic presentation' – which, of course, it isn't, though this is hardly the point.[33] Instead, he observes that the novel 'starts with a standard first-contact scene . . . [whose] characters invite the gaze, even embrace, of an appropriating Englishman, but Goodwin shapes his account of the hybrid experiences of colonization from the Welsh side' (p. 45). Beti, the native, invited by the Manchester Jew, Mr Birbaum, to join his family in Golders Green, 'is able with her father's support to refuse this diasporic servitude' (p. 45).

Knight's identification of Birbaum as an 'appropriating Englishman' rather adds weight to Bryan Cheyette's objections that postcolonial theory has failed to grapple with the ambivalent figure of 'the Jew' in Anglophone literature. Postcolonial theorists Henry Louis Gates and Edward Said both speak 'consistently of a homogenous and dominant white "Western Judeo-Christian" culture', Cheyette observes, and he asks: 'Where within this supposed "common culture" does "the Jew" – other than as an aspect of dominant "white" oppression – fit?'[34] Knight apologises for and thus exculpates Goodwin's stereotyped depiction, which he is able to downplay by measuring its lack of 'virulence'. At the same time he overlooks the significance of Goodwin's choice here and elsewhere to use a Jewish character to represent 'English' colonial appropriation, and the nuance of how a Jew as an Englishman is seen as incongruous and unassimilable by the puzzled 'native' Welshman, Dici.

Katie Gramich offers a useful approach to Goodwin's deployment of Jewish stereotype in her foreword to the reissued *Heyday in the Blood*, when she describes the 'jentlemens' as being 'caricatured in the unsettling terms which are all too prevalent in Anglophone writing of the 1930s'.[35] But though she finds it interesting that 'Jewishness is perceived by the Welsh locals in the Red Lion as a problematic identity not dissimilar to Welshness', she doesn't comment on how this characterisation heightens the register of Birbaum's arguably colonising 'otherness'.[36]

Both Ron Berry and Geraint Goodwin use images of Jews that exist within a web of familiar, popular tropes, both positive and negative. However, to categorise Goodwin's depiction of cheap-jacks as antisemitic (and therefore explicitly or implicitly to characterise Goodwin himself as antisemitic) would reduce this imaging, and would isolate it both from the context in which it is used and from the reasons for its deployment. Such a designation precludes a consideration of the associations that such imaging evokes in that particular time and place, and its relationship with the image of 'the Jew' in literature more generally.

SEMITIC DISCOURSE IN SAUNDERS LEWIS

It is of course not Geraint Goodwin but Saunders Lewis who has become something of the representative figure of Welsh antisemitism – rather as Lloyd George is put forward as the showpiece for Welsh philosemitism. Saunders Lewis was one of the most important and influential Welsh-language writers in the twentieth century, and a great deal has been made of the fact that he was a Catholic with, in the 1930s and 1940s, protectionist and xenophobic overtones, whose intellectual roots lay in the Action Française; these were shared to some degree by his co-founder of Plaid Genedlaethol Cymru, Ambrose Bebb. Lewis is less well-known for his later repudiation of his early overtly hostile comments on and images of Jews. Author Judith Maro, for example, claims that this early attitude was an aberration, and believes that he changed his mind, and regretted his mistakes.[37] W. D. Rubinstein also acknowledges the shift in Lewis's attitude, and locates the original source for his antisemitism in his Catholicism, a religious affiliation that Rubinstein is quick to emphasise as being largely alien to Wales (and as largely responsible for the worst persecutions of Jews). He thus separates Lewis from the purportedly philosemitic nonconformist mainstream in Wales, and isolates him and his attitudes as exceptional.

In a similar vein to the established view of Geraint Goodwin reinforced in the Writers of Wales series, the entry on Saunders Lewis in *The New Companion to the Literature of Wales* (published in 1998) contains no hint of his considerably more prominent and problematic views on Jews, even though as late as 1949 he expressed a continued discomfort with Jewish otherness (the *Companion* is similarly silent on the problematic imaging of Jews by Goodwin).[38]

Curiously, perhaps Lewis's most overtly 'semitic' text is his 1960 play *Esther*, which situates the biblical story of the Jewish queen in a contemporary post-Holocaust and suggestively Welsh setting.[39] However, examining its implicit comparison of Welsh and Jewish experience, one might recall Dorian Llywelyn's discussion of Gildas and Charles Edwards, or again Derec Llwyd Morgan's description of Charles Edwards: Gildas and Edwards draw parallels between the biblical Jews and the Welsh or Proto-Welsh labouring under Assyrian or English oppression. In the biblical account of Esther, of course, the Jews are labouring under Persian oppression. In fact Lewis's *Esther* belongs more overtly to the twentieth-century political comparisons made between Wales and Israel (discussed in the next chapter) than to discourse on Jews as such.

In contrast, Lewis's hostile statements about Jews seem particularly to concern the stereotype of the international Jewish financier; these occur in his political comments, his editorial direction of *Y Ddraig Goch* (the Plaid Genedlaethol Cymru party newspaper in the 1920s and 1930s), and in his poetry.[40] In this he is very much within a tradition in Wales, from O. M. Edwards in the 1880s, Lloyd George at the turn of the century, Crwys in 1918, through to his near contemporary, Geraint Goodwin. Such stereotyped imaging partakes of the international financier paranoia of *The Protocols of the Elders of Zion* and its offshoots and legacy, but it would seem that Alfred Mond, the Clydach works industrialist, in particular embodied the 'cosmopolitan' Jew of Lewis's disaffections (Mond was the Liberal MP for Swansea from 1910 to 1923, and first Liberal and then Conservative MP for Carmarthen from 1924 to 1928).

It is in his play *Buchedd Garmon* (The Life of Germanus), for example, that Lewis imagines Wales as a refuge from the threatening modernity that someone like Mond represented.[41] That imaging of Wales as a refuge, as a pure holdout unsullied by materialism, is a powerful trope in Welsh literature in both languages, whether or not it is informed by the Welsh-Israelite tradition discussed by Dorian Llywelyn (one might recall again Gwenallt's imaging in this regard); but it also appears in inverted form in the imaging of Wales as a fortress, as in Gwyn Thomas's *The Keep*, or, redacted again in somewhat different form, as already mentioned, in Ed Thomas's play and screenplay *House of America*.

Ned Thomas describes Lewis's play *Buchedd Garmon*, which was
written for St David's Day in 1937, as showing how 'cherishing and positive Saunders Lewis's attitude to Wales is', and he suggests that it 'can
stand as the motto and explanation of the whole national movement in
Wales, which came into being not to assert a political ambition but to
defend a human and precious heritage'.[42] He reproduces in translation a
key passage that has become an icon of this movement and its culture of
resistance:

> A certain man planted on a fruitful hillside
> A vineyard in which he set the best vines;
> He built a wall around it, raised a tower in the centre
> And gave it to his son as an inheritance
> To bear his name from generation to generation.
> But a herd of pigs broke down the wall of the vineyard,
> Rushed in to trample and eat up the vines.
> Is it not right that the son should stand in the breach now,
> And call his friends to him, and protect his inheritance?
> My country of Wales is a vineyard, given into my keeping
> . . .
> And look, the pigs are rushing in to despoil it . . . (pp. 64–5)

In his study of Lewis in *Sacred Place, Chosen People*, Dorian Llywelyn
explains that in *Buchedd Garmon* 'the land of Wales is . . . described by
Lewis as a sanctuary', and suggests that 'in the image of Wales as a vine-
yard, Lewis is stressing the need for boundaries, proposing a strict
separation'.[43] He concludes:

> Lewis's writings are the latest layer of a palimpsest: the struggle of Naboth
> against Jezebel, of the Britons against the Saxons, of culture against igno-
> rance, salvation against damnation, Welsh pacifism against English
> imperialism, are all part of the same pattern, in which the whole is visible
> through the various strata.[44]

The description of the play as a palimpsest suggests the depth in time
and cultural reference of this protective motif used by Lewis, and suggests
a similar resonance in Geraint Goodwin's construction of the dangerous
intrusion of the 'cosmopolitan' Jew in his novel *The Heyday in the Blood*,
which was published a year earlier, in 1936. While Katie Gramich is
undoubtedly right to situate Goodwin's depictions in the 'unsettling'
imaging prevalent in the 1930s, nevertheless in some cases this rhetoric,
while partaking of discourse that lies far beyond the boundaries of Welsh
Anglophone writing, is put to a particular Welsh use.[45] Though the imagined Welsh borderlands of Goodwin's fiction may not obviously share

much with Saunders Lewis's Catholic sanctuary, his Jewish Mr Birbaum and his Jewish cheap-jacks from Salford do share something with the characterisation by Saunders Lewis of Jewish financiers with 'their Hebrew snouts in the quarter's statistics' – namely the trope of the cosmopolitan Jewish capitalist.[46] Both authors' versions of Wales imaginatively come into being in part through the depiction of an opposing, threatening and conjoined Jewish-English contaminating modernity: both writers' invocation of familiar Jewish stereotype adds an anxiety about an insidious 'otherness' which an image of an appropriating Englishness alone might not so successfully achieve.

MY PEOPLE AS JEWS: CARADOC EVANS AND THE WELSH-ISRAELITE TRADITION

If there is one writer whose work could be said to be imbued with a Welsh Old Testament idiom, it is Caradoc Evans. His collections of stories *My People* and *Capel Sion*, published respectively in 1915 and 1916, introduced a unique modernist literary voice, and his work, his intent and his reception have been widely analysed, though almost exclusively within a Welsh scholarly framework.[47] That neither Dorian Llywelyn nor Derec Llwyd Morgan makes even a passing reference to Welsh literature in English is suggestive of the now much-diluted hostility to the competing claim that it made with Welsh-language literature to represent Welshness. However, their omission of Caradoc Evans in particular is also suggestive of the selective and romanticised assessment of the biblical influence on Welsh literature, or, in Llywelyn's case, of the influence of the Welsh-Israelite tradition.[48]

Background: Evans and Jews
In seeking to develop a dialect that could convey the heavily biblicised language and reference of his rural Welsh characters, and the manner in which such biblical allusion was twisted for hypocritical purposes, Evans incorporated biblical image, reference and rhetoric along with preaching cadence in a combination of literal translation of Welsh idiom, an exaggerated Welsh sentence structure, and phonetic translation of Welsh pronunciation of English. Suggestively, Eryn M. White describes a 'pulpit language' created by revivalist preachers that 'combined the spoken word with scriptural language to create a common religious dialect' for an audience that did not speak any 'one particular dialect', and this effectively describes the register of Evans's work too.[49]

Both the narrative sections and the dialogue that is written in this idiom reveal the narrow horizons of Evans's characters, and the abuse of power by the 'elect' of the chapels. Arguably, this is the Welsh-Israelite spiritual tradition par excellence, but in a wholly different register to that argued by Derec Llwyd Morgan and Dorian Llywelyn. The former, in Llywelyn's translation, comments on how 'the totalising Biblical influence has been very great in our literature. In the modern period, it is religious literature from root to branch, and it is not surprising that its main readers should see themselves as a spiritual Israel living in Bethlehem and Carmel, whether in Carmarthenshire or in Caernarfonshire.'[50] Clearly, to include Caradoc Evans's excoriating fiction in that 'Biblical' literature would subtly change the positive and uplifting spectacle that Llwyd Morgan intends to convey here.

In an essay in *The Welsh Anvil*, Aneirin Talfan Davies positions Evans as an inheritor of Gildas and Charles Edwards, depicting him as a sulphurous Mount Sinai, an 'Old Testament prophet' (as against Dylan Thomas, whom he describes as a religious poet – and, implicitly a Christian poet – 'the mount where the vine-entwined tree drops sacrificial blood').[51] In a now-dated view (definitively corrected by Jane Aaron and others), he claims that Evans was the progenitor of Welsh writing in English:

> There is hardly a writer who does not show some sign of his influence. He is the product of the Welsh Sunday-school, brought up on the Bible – the Welsh Bible, and the eloquence of the pulpit. His prose, in a subtle way, is moulded on the rhythms of the Bible. He reacted violently to what he considered the pharisaism of the chapel-going nonconformists. His blistering invective was directed against his own people . . . but his prophetic message was no more acceptable to his own people than was that of the Hebrew prophets of old to the Jews.[52]

That Caradoc Evans has not been co-opted into an English modernist canon the way several Irish authors have been (and, indeed, as Dylan Thomas has been), suggests that opposition to him has been oddly, and surprisingly, successful. The reasons why Dorian Llywelyn and Derec Llwyd Morgan should avoid Evans are not simply rooted in a focus on Welsh-language literature, but perhaps are more attributable to the reputation Evans still suffers in some circles as a 'traitor'. A review of Evans's *My People* in *The Welsh Outlook* in 1916 is indicative; it acknowledges that 'unquestionably there is shown in these stories a great, almost uncanny power of squeezing the last dregs of sordidness out of a sordid tale', and adds: 'When we have said this we have said everything that can be urged in extenuation of a book which in conception and in detail is artistically and ethically repulsive.'[53]

The challenge to idealised notions of rural nonconformist culture by Evans continues to rankle, as indicated, for example, in the irritation expressed energetically by Hywel Teifi Edwards in his survey of the literary image of the village as repository of unsullied romanticised national life (in both English and Welsh contexts).[54] This is a tradition in which one might usefully, if troublingly, situate *Buchedd Garmon* by Saunders Lewis, and Geraint Goodwin's fiction, including the latter's fictional treatment of Jews. Hywel Teifi Edwards describes the descent of Evans's satire 'fel barcud ar gyw' ('like a hawk on a chicken'), but in characterising 'ei dresbasu ysbrydoledig ar arddull y Beibl' ('his inspired trespass on the style of the Bible') he misses the evidence of Evans's Welsh-Israelite inheritance.[55] His dismissal of a letter by Evans to the *Sunday Express* as the production of 'pwll o grawn' ('a pool of pus') invokes antisemitism as virulent infection, but in assuming this letter by Evans to be antisemitic (and therefore further support for Evans's *persona non grata* status), he overlooks the significance of Evans's statement about the Welsh and the Jews, which, I believe, holds a key to the author's intent and to his influences.[56] In the letter in question, which was published in the *Sunday Express* in 1923, Evans had written:

> The trouble with the Welsh is that they are not Welsh. Our place of origin is somewhere on the Red Sea. I believe that our ways were so abominable – leading astray the loose women of Egypt and tricking the House of Israel – that Egyptian and Jew combined to rid the land of us. We wandered hither and thither and found ourselves in Wales. But our mentality is Oriental, hence our friendliness with the Jews. This is a byword; wherever two or three Welshmen are gathered together, there is also a Jew.[57]

This is an intriguingly layered observation by Evans, for he appears to have taken the Welsh-Israelite tradition to its logical conclusion: in this letter, as in his powerful fiction, the rural chapel-going Welsh *are* the biblical Jews of that Welsh-Israelite equation. The Welsh are inserted not only into the biblical text, but into Wales-as-Zion – or, to use Evans's imagined Welsh Palestine, into 'Sion'. Here the legacy of the Welsh-Israelite tradition is illuminated from a very different angle than the rather romanticising light cast on the biblical literary tradition by Derec Llwyd Morgan, for example, because in Evans's work a belief in divine election, the purity of the Welsh language, and the moral superiority of the Welsh are turned in on themselves and reflected as small-mindedness, bigotry, and moral degeneration.

If, in the nineteenth century, Welsh literature was imbued with the imagery of biblical Palestine such that, as Derec Llwyd Morgan suggests, religious readers saw themselves 'as a spiritual Israel living in Bethlehem and Carmel, whether in Carmarthenshire or in Caernarfonshire', biblical Palestine had also been mapped topographically onto nonconformist Wales: the numerous Hebrew place-names in Wales in the present derive from villages and settlements that grew up around nonconformist chapels whose names denoted that Welsh-Israelite self-image.[58] Therefore I would argue that when Caradoc Evans uses 'A Mighty Man in Sion' or 'Three Men From Horeb' as titles of stories, he is playing both on that self-perception and at the same time re-imagining (and re-presenting) his rural Welsh as *Jews*. Innovatively, and I believe uniquely, however, he re-imagines his *gwerin* or 'rural folk' as simultaneously notional *and* historical Jews – and that, perhaps, is one of the disturbing undercurrents to which many of his critics responded so vehemently, if not necessarily consciously.

A tradition of an imagined Welsh nation of biblical 'Israel' may be celebrated as an uplifting religiosity, but to take that self-image of the Welsh as biblical inheritors and join it to the Bible's living descendants is to pull the Welsh down into what was, at the time, and probably still would be, a deeply troubling *ethnic* association. This, as much as allegedly selling out his people (and his soul) to the English, might be Caradoc Evans's sin. The response to his work suggests rather disturbingly the boundaries and delimits of that twentieth-century idea of a tradition of identification with Jews, as much as of the Welsh-Israelite tradition.

Biblical place-names in Evans's work reflect a reality in Wales in the period, as do biblical personal names, which provided a similar mapping in the nineteenth and early twentieth centuries (indeed the proliferation of Hebrew personal names in Wales has led to some confusion about ethnic identity, as Ursula Henriques observed).[59] In *My People* these names are mostly, though not exclusively, from the Hebrew scriptures rather than the Christian Bible, and perhaps this streak of apparent realism in his portrayal of Welsh nonconformity obscures a more complex semitic undercurrent that is at work.

An overt comparison to biblical Jews occurs in the story 'A Mighty Man in Sion', in which Lias, trying to seduce Ellen, and suggesting that she should have children, remarks in typical Evans inverted word order: 'Large the families Boys Israel had' – but, with one exception, Jews qua Jews make no appearance in his short stories.[60] However, the meanness, avarice, lechery and false piety of his biblically-named characters are redolent of Jewish stereotype, particularly for English readers unfamiliar with the insider view of Welsh nonconformity that this work so challenged. If *My People* and the work that followed it was written, as Evans stands accused, for English delectation, it is also with English prejudices in mind that he presents the Welsh as biblical Jews. The characterisation, naming, and particular contorted speech, I would suggest, are simultaneously a play on Welsh stereotypes got up for English consumption, and a sign of Evans's quite conscious and deliberate deployment of a widely familiar set of Jewish stereotypes.

Evans was, by all appearances, a little obsessed with Jews. His letter to the *Sunday Express*, the sustained commentary on Jews in his novels, and the published excerpts from his journal all suggest considerably more than passing interest, but his widow, Oliver Sandys, is more explicit: 'Caradoc was always looking for and seeing the gipsy or the Jew in so many people,' she remarks in her biography.[61] In a way, this is no surprise, given how his immersion in a chapel culture saturated with stories of biblical Jews must have been cast in a new light by his encounter in London with the very sizeable, prominent and alien Jewish community when he arrived there from Cardiff in 1899. At that time, Jews and Jewish immigration were also a matter of obsessive interest in the wider culture, as Jewish immigration from eastern Europe provoked a fearful (and still familiar) rhetoric of tidal waves and exodus, of England being 'swamped' by diseased masses, scum and residue – even if 'Jewish' was often elided rhetorically, though not semantically with the terms 'foreign' and 'alien', as Lara Trubowitz has shown.[62] Such an 'interest' led to the anti-immigration Aliens Acts of 1904 and 1905. These fierce debates around immigration (which were about Jewish immigration) were ones to which Caradoc Evans would have been exposed.

Sources old and new

The influence on Evans's unique prose style and dialogue by a number of writers, and by the King James version of the Bible, has been much discussed, as has the influence of the satirical publication, *The Perfidious Welshman*.[63] But there is an element in this latter work that has been overlooked – namely the author's close comparison, and in places equation, of the Welsh and the Jews.

The Perfidious Welshman, by 'Draig Glas' (Arthur Tyssilio Johnson), was published in 1910.[64] Addressed to the English visitor to Wales, it promulgates and expands upon anti-Welsh stereotype in a way that will be familiar to anyone examining semitic discourse (indeed it and its fellow travellers in works by G. K. Chesterton and Evelyn Waugh suggest the need for a comparative study of Welsh and semitic discourse in English literature).

The stereotype of avarice and meanness are as much semitic as Welsh, and to reinforce the association, in the portrayal of the untrustworthy Welsh landlady, they are conflated: 'you or some one else will be expected to pay with interest by-and-by for every halfpenny Mrs. Taffy has expended on you', Draig Glas writes. 'The average Welsh landlady is never at a loss for some deceitful ruse by which she can entrap the unwary to her advantage . . . and while she is telling you her family history your general appearance and probable worth are being estimated by her Jewish eye' (p. 15). In Draig Glas's warning about Welsh shopkeepers, the Welsh and the Jews are set apart even from the stereotyped legendary meanness of the Scots – who are here generously folded into Englishness in comparison:

> It makes little difference . . . whether the Englishman is fleeced by his land-lady or by the equally astute shopkeeper – for by one or the other, or both, fleeced he certainly is, even though he be a Scotsman. Even a Jew finds it diffi-cult to avoid being 'done' by a Taffy – but then it is a matter of 'when Greek meets Greek'. It is well known that Wales is the only country in which a Jew cannot live. (p. 74)

A grotesque fascination with funerals attributed to the Welsh cannot simi-larly be attributed to Jews, though the Welsh, 'this clod of humanity', are still portrayed as Jews by place of worship, claiming, as they do for them-selves 'the front seat in the synagogue of righteousness'. Instead, the comparison – unfavourable to the Welsh – is with 'the grossest nigger', who, Draig Glas speculates, 'would surely behave in a more seemly manner' (p. 88). Fairs follow funerals in the hierarchy of important matters for 'Jones', he goes on – even small mean fairs, which 'would appear to have an eternal fascination for Taffy, who has a Jew's regard for anything pertaining to barter' (p. 88). Cheating and the expectation of being cheated is also in the Welshman's blood; indeed 'the only difference between the Welshman and the Jew in this matter is that the former drinks and the latter does not – at least, not while he's "on the make"' (p. 89). Draig Glas's concluding statement (and what it offered) must surely have been noted by Caradoc Evans:

> No man covets his neighbour's goods with a more Jewish eye than does Taffy – more particularly if his neighbour is an Englishman. The remarkable simi-larity which exists between him and the Israelite no visitor to Wales has failed to observe. (p. 147)

If Evans was attuned to the Jewish imaging and comparisons in *The Perfidious Welshman*, he would also almost certainly have been aware of the work of Israel Zangwill, the high-profile Anglo-Jewish writer whose portrait of East End Jews, *Children of the Ghetto*, had been published at the end of the nineteenth century. Though I have not found evidence of contact (and nor has Caradoc Evans's biographer, John Harris), Zangwill is unlikely to have passed unnoticed by Evans in his early years in London.[65] Zangwill has been largely forgotten outside Jewish scholarly writing (except occasionally, and inaccurately, as originator of the contested description of Palestine as 'a land without a people for a people without a land'), but between the 1890s and the 1920s he was, as Meri-Jane Rochelson, Joseph H. Udelson and others have shown, a prominent, celebrated, highly regarded and very widely-read English author.[66] Indeed, he enjoyed high status in Wales, too, as suggested by the notices about his doings that appeared regularly in the *Western Mail*.[67]

In Zangwill's and Evans's subject matter – which included false piety, marriage matchmaking for economic gain, and the depiction of a closed and unsophisticated world – there are strong correlations, even if in style Zangwill is verbose where Evans is condensed and contracted; and there are strong comparisons to be made between Zangwill's rendering of Yiddish and of a new Anglo-Yiddish, and Evans's rendering of Welsh and anglicised Welsh. But even if these were not direct influences on Evans, Zangwill's reinforcement of Oriental Jewish stereotype would have provided powerful material: though Jews make little appearance in Evans's stories, they feature prominently in two of his novels – and they are Oriental in their every aspect.

Semitic discourse in the overlooked novels
When viewed in isolation, the depiction of Jews by Evans in these novels might seem particularly hostile and stereotyped, which may account in part for the silence on the subject (this despite the quite extensive critical material on other aspects of Evans's work). On the other hand, it may have more to do with the struggle that literary scholars have to engage in with the long memory of the outrage Evans caused. Against the background of this hostility (and the still-current sensitivity of his pandering to English stereotyping of Welsh character), any argument for the excellence of Evans as a modernist writer will be troubled by this Jewish imaging, which poses some difficult critical challenges. At a basic level his imaging offers rich material for those who in reductive manner might seek to undermine arguments about Evans's importance: according to the prevailing approach in Wales, such imaging – and the writer who produces it – can be seen in the simplistic terms of a 'virulent' antisemitism. In fact Evans, even more

than other writers such as Saunders Lewis, is not well served by a critical approach that sees Jewish material or imaging in terms of its virulence or affection, for, as I hope to demonstrate, a consideration of this particular example of semitic discourse shows Evans engaged in a portrayal not of Jews but of the Welsh.

Evans's collections of stories and a novella have been republished and remain in print, but his novels, plays and a posthumous collection of stories have been long out of print. Critical attention has therefore focused disproportionately on Evans as a short-fiction writer. The two novels in question are *This Way to Heaven*, published in 1934, and *Mother's Marvel*, commissioned and written in 1934, but not published until 1949. The most sustained material occurs in *Mother's Marvel*, which is passed over by Evans's literary critics, at least in part because of its structural and narrative flaws. Nevertheless, perhaps the comment by T. L. Williams, that he preferred 'to say nothing about the two disastrous novels of 1934, *This Way to Heaven* and (what came to be called) *Mother's Marvel*', derives as much from a reaction to its content as its style.[68]

In *This Way to Heaven*, one of the shaping characters of the novel, Simon Moreland, is only gradually revealed to be a Jew, an 'accusation' he denies but finally accedes to when fellow Jewish businessmen corner him in order to exact retribution for his shady dealings. The Jewish figures here are representative financial ones: moneylenders, property dealers and theatre producers, but Simon Moreland's Jewishness is largely incidental in a novel in which every major character is avaricious, licentious and deeply self-interested and corrupt. The paternity of most of the characters is unclear: the novel opens in a home for illegitimate boys born in prison, and one of these, Ben, characterised by 'animality', is both suggestively named and suggestively described. When, as a test to see if he's employable, he is asked by Moreland to calculate a daily rent if the weekly rent is two-and-six, 'an ancestor awoke in Ben and gave him this answer: "He ought to pay the whole week, please, sir."'[69]

Of course Moreland's name itself is suggestive, and this is expanded on in one brief passage in which Evans describes him in terms of 'Jewish' traits that might at first appear to suggest that familiar, highly ambivalent sympathy expressed, in similar form, by Lloyd George:

> Simon was a great Jew. His was the wisdom of a people who raised the ancient tales of persecution and God's chosen children and the world-wide ramble, the humility of a people who thrive by the jibe and scorn of the Christian, the

dexterity of a people whose fingers are more skilled than the fabled fires of the alchemists. (p. 282)

Evans leaves little room for ambiguity, however, when he concludes that Moreland's wisdom is also 'the subtlety of a people who fit themselves into every condition and who rule every land in which they sojourn' (pp. 282–3).

In his superficial portrayal of a group of unnamed Jewish businessmen who support a production of *The Merchant of Venice*, Evans satirises a Jewish willingness to profit even from hostile depictions of Jews, and this is greatly expanded in the other novel of 1934, *Mother's Marvel*. Originally entitled *Kitty Shore's Magic Cake*, the novel was commissioned and written in 1934, but was rejected as obscene; it was published posthumously, in 1949, and is described in an unattributed quotation in *The New Companion to the Literature of Wales* as '"dangerous and pornographic"', but, the entry continues, 'more obviously claustrophobic and tedious'.[70] It is curious that this 'dangerous' should not have intrigued scholars. As with Geraint Goodwin, there is nothing on Evans's Jewish imaging in the *Companion*, nor in the Evans monograph in the Writers of Wales series.

Mother's Marvel opens with a description of Kitty Shore that owes more to Evans's stories than the novel form, and of Griff, a hunchback who, among the grotesques of the book, emerges as the only character with anything approaching sympathy or integrity. The son of the union between Griff and Kitty is equally grotesque – in fact the Jews, despite the roughness of their depiction, are, by comparison, considerably more credible as characters, which suggests that Evans might have needed to rely on an identifiable ethnicity for effective, if problematic, characterisation.

Soon the novel is peopled by a proliferation of characters whose complex double-crossings, failed business deals, thefts and corruption become difficult to navigate. Evans's sparse, hyper-condensed style, which works to such strong effect in the short-story form, in places causes near-incoherence in the novel, and the convoluted plot suggests one of the reasons for the book's neglect by critics and literary historians. Its interest lies more in its extended imaging of Jews, in particular in the portrait of Lam Ach, who is perhaps something of the writer's self-image as a man divided against himself.

The first Jewish character to appear, however, is one Sam Gordon, 'a yellow man' (p. 81), but it takes some sixty pages before he is clearly identified as Jewish, and this sets the tone for much of the discourse on Jews in the rest of the novel:

'You're after Peter's money, Miriam,' said Sam, 'and bumming him for the price of your dress is not the right way of getting it. You've got the fault of our people, Miriam. You show your hand too much. We Jews are not greedier than any other people. We lend a pound and we want it back and as much more as we can get. That's true of every Christian, but the Christian keeps it dark.' (p. 144)

Evans's imaging of Jewish women in particular is overtly Oriental: his 'Jewesses' are sensual, vengeful, voluptuous and eastern – and dangerously emasculating. Miriam, for example, who has 'the silky insolence of the East' (p. 152), and 'whose olive skin paint did not entirely hide, whose face was a smile of peace, and whose eyes were smoky cells', is an actress: 'if she was encased in the chastity of Zion, she went through the scenes of her brother's play with the abandonment of one born under a passionate star' (p. 150). Another actress, Eve, deprived by Miriam of her lover Tony, plots vengeance, and when she reveals Miriam's behaviour to Miriam's mother, whose 'fatness' is 'clothed most voluptuously', the mother responds: 'You will have him . . . Hoi, yes, I'll give you the Christian bit' (p. 181). The outcome is predictable, but still surprisingly shocking and crude: the mother proceeds into Tony's house and circumcises him, and returns to Eve with the evidence. The 'Jewess . . . giving her a portion of flesh, said: "Here's your bit of Christian flesh"' (p. 181).

Where Shylock is arguably humanised by having to forego his claim to a payment of flesh, this dangerously sexualised 'Jewess' enacts the desire not only to castrate, but to doubly feminise her victim by rendering him Jewish (if there is any doubt about Evans's depiction of circumcision as a symbolic emasculation, his use, elsewhere in the novel, of 'an incomplete' as a term of abuse for a Jew, and its association with not needing to shave, might lay that doubt to rest). This forced circumcision is no re-gendered hint of Shylock, but perhaps a literary actualisation of the fear that lies behind the perpetuation of the Shylock stereotype. Here Evans follows through from suggestion to deed, where another less driven writer might hang back, and there is little need to look further for the startling evidence of what others have argued is his tormented attitude to female sexuality.

Curiously, and suggestively, although Evans's Welsh women and men are equally sexually driven, the frank sexuality of his Jewish characters is considerably less contorted than the repressed and hypocritical sexual antics of the populations of Sion or Manteg in his early short stories, or of his London Welsh in *My Neighbours*.

There is a more complicated portrayal of Jews in *Mother's Marvel* that suggests if not realism (Evans is hardly a realist) then at least familiarity with the underworld of film production, dominated, in this portrayal, by Jewish businessmen and 'Jewess' actresses.[71] One of the former is Guy Bernard, 'who bossed over ninety cinema theatres, and loud-speakers only he could tell how many, and who was a famous judge of a film-picture' (p. 154). He is described as 'an unpleasing man, grunting like a swine at the trough, dribbling, and dipping his hairy snout in soup' (p. 158). The main-stay of the second half of the novel, however, is Lam Ach, who is described, rather unoriginally, as being 'greasy' (p. 155). He is a nominal and expe-dient convert to Christianity, whose moving towards and away from some form of Judaism provides the vehicle for Evans's discourse on Jewishness – and, by projection, also perhaps on Welshness, and on his own 'apostasy'.[72]

It seems highly suggestive that, as is the case with *This Way to Heaven*, there is a proliferation of Jewish characters in a novel in which there is no hint of Welsh character or caricature, which is otherwise the sustained subject matter of Evans's writing life. But if his Jews are in this way a substitute Welsh nation (in an inversion of that self-image of the Welsh as substitute Jews), they are racially essentialised in a way that is less clear with his Welsh characters. Indeed, though he reinforces in his stories and other work the Welsh stereotypes so caustically exaggerated in *The Perfidious Welshman*, and though his Welsh people are caricatured and scorned, he perhaps has insufficient distance from them to portray them as 'other': they are too close to him, too familiar, and too real.

In contrast, in *Mother's Marvel* the signifier 'Jew' and 'Jewess' allows him distance from his characters – or, perhaps, makes it impossible for him to get close, to get beyond writing a representation to creating a living, credible characterisation. Indeed, the words 'Jew' and 'Jewess' recur so frequently as to become absurd, and this is, perhaps, in part Evans's intent: the characters, like all those of the novel – from the hunchback Griff, to the mummy's boy Peter, to the 'Jewess' Miriam – are closer to caricature. There is no question that the figure of the Jew is, for him, here, irredeem-ably 'other', but at the same time this is a source of fascination and familiarity.

The exception is in the figure of Lam Ach, through whom he appears to explore his own situation, for while other Jews in the novel constitute superficial and stereotyped sketches, in the reprehensible Lam Ach there is an attempt to elucidate what motivates him – a motivation located in his familiar but other Jewishness:

> Lam Ach was a bald-headed Jew. In his youth . . . he was that Boy Earl who in choirboy robe stirred music-halls with songs his father made for him . . . The

father fell sick and, nearing death, prayed to be delivered to Father Abraham according to the law. The son cavilled, saying that if it became known he were no Christian lad but a Jew-boy, pit and gallery would drive him from his occupation. (p. 124)

Lam Ach does not honour his father's request for a Jewish burial, but instead 'lightened his hair and curled it and he whitened his face and . . . sang a Christian song at his father's Christian grave. He was not punished immediately' (p. 124). Ten years later it gets about that 'he was an incomplete, that he was a Yid, and that a razor had never touched his face' (p. 125). He does not come out as Jewish, but decides to do so only 'when he would be well armoured with Christian money', at which point he would give his father a Jewish reburial 'and so gain for himself a place on Abraham's bosom' (p. 125).

Lam Ach moves from performance to teaching, and then to directing cheap, bad 'film-plays'. Throughout, he is a man divided against himself, and he switches back and forth between his identities and affiliations with increasing anxiety:

> 'I've been too long among Christians,' said Lam, 'to know Jew tactics. I must become a Jew. Now I am a Jew.' He spread his hands and spoke Jew-like. 'My right side has been inside and is now the right side and the inside that was my outside I put inside.' (p. 155)

At a late stage Evans introduces his own, known subject matter, and in the synopsis of one of Lam Ach's scripts, situates a hidden Jew in the Welsh landscape, and ridicules those who write about Wales. The screenplay is called 'Little People, Where Are You Now?', and is set in a Welsh town called Holy City (curiously, according to John Harris, Evans began and abandoned a novel about Aberystwyth entitled 'Holy City', suggesting that he had tried to take this material a bit further).[73] The new 'film-play' is intended to show Jews in a positive light, with the 'hidden' Jew revealing himself, and declaring that 'the Jewish mission is peace on earth'.[74] The film is shown to exhibitors, and 'maybe five hundred Jewish exhibitors and renters . . . applauded this picture which showed the loving-kindness of a persecuted race', but Lam Ach remarks that this means it's a flop, because 'the Jews never praise a thing they want to buy' (p. 166). Guy Bernard, judge of what will sell, agrees, saying 'nobody's going to believe we're as good as your film Jew' (p. 166).

Lam, disappointed, abandons his new Jewishness, buries his Talmud, his *talith* and the failure of a film, and gets drunk. He drinks away the autumn, surrounded by labour-saving devices, because, as he observes, faithful to stereotype, 'his own hands were alabaster as are the hands of the Jews. The Jews do not toil. Christians break the earth and sow and reap and harvest and the Jew takes the harvest. "What I mean to convey," said Lam, "is this. A Christian killed the first bear and a Jew wore the first fur-coat"' (p. 167).

Although he is now determined to 'remain forever a Jew', he wonders why he is 'not like his people who heap up wealth not only to enslave other [*sic*], but also to armour themselves' (p. 168). On Christmas Day, he switches back again, saying, '"I must get rid of my Jewish ways"', and he begins, absurdly, to wash himself Christian in cold baths (p. 168). He starts a new film, offering the part of 'A Jewess. An old Jewess. The real sort who'd steal a crucifix from a dying man's hand' (pp. 172–3). This echoes the proposal by the actress Mary, in the other novel *This Way to Heaven*, to portray Shylock as 'what he is – a swine of an old Jew who'd take a baby's rattle for a debt'.[75]

Lam is intent on making a profit, whatever the ethical cost, but he becomes increasingly irresolute:

> Lam was Christian and Jew and one overlooked the other. The Christian rehearsed scenes which exposed Judaism to scorn and contempt and the Jew tamed such scenes before they were photographed . . . Lam, his two selves bickering each other [*sic*], could not sleep and spent his nights in restless preambles on the floor. (pp. 173–4)

Eventually the one wins out over the other: 'the Jew was vanquished from Lam and the Christian in him notified the Jewish characters in the play with the emblems of greed, deceit, cowardice, violence and suchlike' (p. 174), and he makes a film 'of Jewish treachery, corruption, knavery, seduction, sadism, and greed', which he shows to exhibitors (p. 176). Proclaiming it 'a sure winner', Guy (waddling, like Geraint Goodwin's cheap-jacks and Ron Berry's Abe) buys the film, and it does indeed turn out a success (p. 176). Lam, dismayed that no Jew speaks against it, and stricken with guilt, gives the profits away.

One wonders how much Evans is commenting on his own work when he writes, 'So spoke the Jew who was brought to shame that he was of the race that profited by contumely of its own make' (p. 178). Just as suggestively, as Lam once again dithers between his two inclinations, his comments might be those of Evans when he tells Eve that 'it was folly for an artist to let the hate-bug possess him entirely. In creative work, he said, love and hate should be blended if the artist is to produce the mean that is like life' (p. 179), but after another (Christianising) bath, he asks:

'But what can you do with the Jews who on one hand claim to be God's chosen and on the other are the smartest Christian propagandists in the world? . . . Who Christianises the blacks to pinch their oil-wells? The Jews. Who are the biggest printers and binders and distributors of the New Testament? The Jews. Who has the monopoly in church furniture? The Jews . . . Who make a bargain sale of Christmas? The Jews. What comics we are!' (p. 179)

Despite the vulgarity and the crude humour, there is a certain sympathy for Lam in his confusion and equivocation. This builds by the end into tragicomedy, as, feeling responsible for the violent and very bloody circumcision of Tony, among other misdeeds, he tries in a befuddled way to make amends. But atonement sits on him lightly and he determines to make a film out of the story, 'done biblically with Eastern costumes' (p. 182), and sympathetic to the 'Jewess' misused by a Christian lover. Guy Bernard won't support it, and for reasons which, again, may reflect more on Evans's view of Welsh failure than Jewish failure:

'I thought, Mr. Bernard,' said Lam, 'you'd do this for the Jews.'
'There's no money in it, Lam Ach.'
'There's a fortune in it, Mr. Bernard.'
'Okay, big boy, get on with it and if I like it, I'll buy it.'
'I want to do it for the good of the Jews.'
'You won't do the Jews any good by losing money on them. We get respect because we're winners, not losers. Waste isn't patriotism.' (pp. 182–3)

This sustained use of Jewish material by Evans is quite unlike anything else in Welsh literature. Despite its difficulties and many narrative and character flaws, the novel deserves closer study. On the face of it, it is riddled with familiar stereotypes, whether it is the 'greasy' Jew who is always on the make, the oversexualised emasculating Oriental 'Jewess', or the avaricious amoral business Jew who will sell out his own people. There are 'chequered people' generalisations and film-underworld specifics; universal tropes and detailed characterisation; representative signifiers of 'the Jew' (and more so 'the Jewess'), and developed character. Such Jewish imaging invites an easy and convenient interpretation: Evans deploys here in his invective style attitudes to Jews that were simultaneously current in the culture and internalised in him; these are hostile, stereotyped portrayals of the 'Jew' as other. But to claim that this portrayal is antisemitic and Evans an antisemite would require a selective reading, a deliberate neglect of the complexity and subtlety of his discourse, and a marginalisation of the dominant themes in his work. It would be difficult also to place his untitled late story about Joshua, a third-generation Jewish Baptist who suffers a midlife crisis of Christian doubt, but is reprieved. Published posthumously, this portrayal of a Jewish pedlar in the Aberystwyth area carries no hint of stereotype either in attitude or appearance; on the contrary, it is, for Evans, a remarkably gentle and affectionate story.[76]

If the Jewish imaging in the novels is 'typical' semitic discourse in its detail, it appears far from typical in its intent. The portrait is made very much more layered and complex when considered in the context of other work by Evans. If I am right that his depiction of a rural chapel Welsh in *My People* and *Capel Sion* is a conjoining of notional and historical Jew as an embodiment of the Welsh-Israelite spiritual tradition, then perhaps it is also true that his representative Jews in *Mother's Marvel* are, in parallel, another way of imaging the Welsh. Taken together with *This Way to Heaven* – the other novel from which Welsh discourse is absent and in which Jews proliferate – the correlation between his depiction of Jews and his depiction of the Welsh becomes stronger yet. It is worth recalling his letter to the *Sunday Express*, in which he provocatively stated that 'the trouble with the Welsh is that they are not Welsh . . . I believe that our ways were so abominable – leading astray the loose women of Egypt and tricking the House of Israel – that Egyptian and Jew combined to rid the land of us'. The ways of these London Jews is surely no more abominable than the ways of his Cardigan Welsh. If, as he states in the letter, the mentality of the Welsh is Oriental, at the close of *Nothing to Pay*, written the same year as *Mother's Marvel*, and perhaps something of a companion piece, there occurs a scene that could not be more redolent of the Jewish miser: the dying Amos 'groaned dismally, as if he were parting from money' and is comforted: '"It's o-rait," said Sara. "There's nothing to pay for death."'[77]

Evans's observation that 'wherever two or three Welshmen are gathered together, there is also a Jew' is reversed in *Mother's Marvel*, and where two or three Jews are gathered together, there perhaps also is a Welshman – a particular Welshman: Caradoc Evans himself.

4

Twentieth-century political comparisons

'The mountains are red with their blood
The deserts are green with their seed.
Listen, Wales.'
         – Harri Webb, 'Israel'

POLITICAL DEVELOPMENTS AND PALESTINE

Where two or three Jews are gathered together, there is also a Welshman, Caradoc Evans claims, and for better or for worse, this was arguably true in Palestine between 1916 and 1948. When the British Army fought its way from Gaza to Jerusalem in December 1916, it included a disproportionate number of Welsh conscripts, and left in Be'er Sheva a cemetery full of young dead Welshmen. Likewise, Welsh military and civil service personnel were numerous in Palestine during Britain's military occupation and the ensuing twenty-eight years of the British Mandate period.

For some twentieth-century Welsh writers, the question of Jewish 'return' to Palestine was the basis for national and political comparisons between Zionist hopes (and their subsequent realisation) and Welsh aspirations towards self-determination. These parallels took a cultural nationalist expression in the early Edwardian period, but this was challenged by the reality of conflict in Palestine, first during the 1914–18 war and then during the conflict between Jews and Arabs, and the struggle of both groups against British Mandate rule.

Although the work of some Welsh authors, particularly poets, was influenced by the imagined or actual experience of a geographical Palestine and the Jewish struggle for autonomy, this was not always a positive encounter. Indeed, poet Harri Webb's exquisitely throwaway line of the mid-1940s, realised in 1948 when the British withdrew, might be seen as more representative of Welsh (and more generally British) attitudes by the end of the Mandate period: 'let the fuckers fight it out themselves, we said.'[1]

Political comparisons between the Welsh and the Jews, and between Welsh and Jewish national aspirations, constitute a distinct strand of the Welsh engagement with historical Jews that was identified in chapter 1. This political discourse – which one might characterise as a 'Wales-Israel tradition', as it pertains largely to Zionism, the Israeli state and its implications and opportunities – is also inevitably informed by the long history of conversionist interest in Jews (whose echoes may still be found in Gwenallt's poems about Israel in the late 1960s), by twentieth-century semitic discourse (one sees this in Harri Webb's poems, for example, and in Saunders Lewis's play *Esther*), and by the Welsh-Israelite tradition (echoes of which appear in writing by Gwynfor Evans, the first Plaid Cymru Member of Parliament and, later, an influential popular historian).[2] All of this combined with a stronger sense of Palestine as a real place rather than an imagined geography, as so many Welsh people were present there during the Mandate.

At the turn of the century, and into the interwar period, *Y Traethodydd*, a leading philosophical, religious and cultural journal, included a considerable amount of material dealing with Jews, although the majority of this work was in the form of religious enquiry.[3] In the 1940s, this interest by the periodical widened to include contemporary accounts of travels in Palestine, which are consistent with Christian tourist accounts of the preceding century: the place and people are seen largely through the filter of the imaginatively reconstructed biblical landscape. An early article on Zionism, in 1903, was entitled 'Seioniaeth (Zionism)', the translation in the title perhaps indicating the unfamiliarity of the term. This article is rooted in a view of the deep biblical past, and sees the Jewish 'return', in the present, as a fulfilment of prophecy (the author identifies 'arwyddion arwyddocaol' – significant signs – of Providence at work). But it also covers the early political Zionist movement in some detail, and discusses John Mills's proposals for a Welsh colony in Palestine. Curiously, the author explicitly equates the purpose of the East India Company and the Palestine Exploration Fund, in a clear identification of British imperial aspirations in Palestine in the nineteenth century. Given the ambivalence about Israel that emerges later in the political nationalist movement in Wales, the author's conclusion about Zionism at this early point, that 'ein gweddi ydyw am i'r mudiad gyrraedd ei amcan' (our prayer is that the movement will achieve its aim) is of particular interest.[4] Another article, published in 1918, not long after the Balfour Declaration, examines Jewish involvement in the war (as financiers and soldiers), describes in detail the corporate organisation of the Zionist movement, and – as is the case with the earlier article – makes an inevitable association between Jews and wealth. On the other hand, the author of this later article makes a more explicit comparison with Wales, though again it is within a religious-cultural frame of reference, rather than a political one:

> A pha Gymro sydd nad yw y wlad, ei phobl a'i phethau, yn llawn o swyn iddo? Gwlad yr Addewid, Gwlad y Proffwydi, gwlad ag y bu Duw mewn cnawd yn rhodio ei daear hi. Mor debyg i Gymru fechan ydyw.[5]

> (What Welshman is there for whom the land, her people and attributes aren't full of magic? The Promised Land, Land of the Prophets, the land where God made flesh walked the earth. It is so like a little Wales.)

Like his predecessor in 1903, the author concludes with an expression of hope: 'Hyderwn fod gwawr gobaith wedi torri arni, ac y bydd eto fel cynt yn gyfrwng bendith i'r byd' (let us trust that the dawn of hope has broken upon her, and that she will be again, as she was before, a vehicle of blessing for the world).[6]

These articles are in the main consistent with D. Wynne Evans in how they draw Welsh parallels with Jewish national aspirations in Palestine in largely cultural and religious terms, and thus reinforce the legitimacy of both national movements. Such comparisons are largely absent from the early political nationalist movement in the 1920s and 1930s, however. More overtly political comparisons only began to emerge and then become widespread in the 1960s and into the 1970s. This political development occurred in conjunction with the emergence of the Welsh language movement, the growth of political nationalism, and the electoral successes of Plaid Cymru, but it also grew out of the proliferation of small groups engaged in direct action, such as Mudiad Amddiffyn Cymru and the Free Wales Army (in the 1960s and 1970s), as well as Meibion Glyndŵr in the 1980s.

When Plaid Cymru was struggling with new political legitimacy after the election in 1966 of Gwynfor Evans as its first MP, it found in the example of Israel a model of cultural and language revival, and of national feeling translated into action, rather than a method of achieving independence. But for the Republican movement, and writers associated with it such as Harri Webb, and for some of the small shadowy underground groups with whom its membership crossed (like that of Plaid Cymru), Israel offered a model of direct armed action against the British. The Free Wales Army, for example, tiny as it was (and dismissed by some as mere public gesture), looked for inspiration to the acts of the young Menachem Begin, the Irgun, and the Stern Gang, rather than to the revival of Hebrew as a national language.[7]

Notwithstanding the interest in Israel and in the revival of Hebrew that prominent Plaid Cymru members took in the 1960s, it was an interest always qualified by ambivalence – an ambivalence about armed nationalism, and a continued ambivalence about Jews. It would be a mistake, therefore, to see such interest in Israel as constituting some form of identification with Jews qua Jews. Equally it would be a mistake to infer from the interest in Hebrew and Israel on the part of Plaid Cymru members during the 1960s some kind of long-standing tradition within the party of such modelling, or a continuity in any kind of 'identification' or sympathy, for in its early years in the 1920s and 1930s, the attitudes among party members and followers differed markedly.

When founded as Plaid Genedlaethol Cymru in 1925 by Saunders Lewis, Ambrose Bebb and others, the party was small and largely cultural, and initially attracted low levels of support and high levels of suspicion. Although from 1945 it was transformed under the leadership of Gwynfor Evans into a viable political force that fought successful elections, even at the height of its electoral prominence between 1966 and the Referendum on Devolution in 1979, it was still very much a minority party. The attitudes to Jews, to Israel, and to Hebrew expressed in its publications are not therefore representative of Wales in a broad sense; indeed Leo Abse argues that a very different set of attitudes pertained among 'internationalists' in the Welsh Labour Party at the same time.[8] Nevertheless, according to D. Hywel Davies, Plaid Cymru attracted increasing support from most Welsh-language writers from the 1930s onwards, even if not all of them became members.[9] More importantly, it was through the nationalist movement – and specifically through the related organised language movement from 1962 – that the most overt, sustained and practical connection was made between Wales and Israel. This was the adoption of the Hebrew revival method in Israel as a model for the rescue and revival of the Welsh language. (The relationship was an important one to Israel, too, it would seem: the Ministry of Foreign Affairs published an article on the subject entitled 'Learning from Hebrew' in 2001, in which Amnon Schapiro argues that '"Welsh is the language most influenced by the Hebrew experience"'.)[10]

Although this model took concrete expression in the early 1970s with the adaptation of the Hebrew *ulpan* into the Welsh *wlpan*, its possibilities as an inspiring example had been admiringly noted decades earlier, in 1934, by Mallt Williams in *The Welsh Nationalist*, and subsequently by a young Gwynfor Evans in *Y Ddraig Goch* in 1946. This latter paper was the official Welsh-language publication of Plaid Cymru, and it provides one of the most interesting documentary trails of changing attitudes to Jews – and changing semitic discourse in the context of the national movement – in the twentieth century. Predictably, in *Y Ddraig Goch*, and subsequently also in its sister publication in English, *The Welsh Nationalist* (later renamed *Welsh Nation*), neither the apparently negative nor the positive discourse on Jews employed by some contributors is quite as simple as it first appears. On the contrary, when considered in a wider context, it shows itself to be complex and contingent.

JEWS IN *Y DDRAIG GOCH*, *THE WELSH NATIONALIST* AND *WELSH NATION*

As indicated in the previous chapter, a great deal of inflamed argument has taken place over the depiction of Jews in Saunders Lewis's poetry, and over the statements about Jews in his political writing. The threats to Wales identified in the early years of *Y Ddraig Goch*, which began monthly publication in 1926, echo with the image of Jews both as rootless cosmopolitan capitalists and as international Marxists. The imminent war, in the thirties, was seen by the paper and the party as a war between imperial powers and international capital, facilitated by a press controlled by Jews. Some locate the source of Lewis's anti-modernism and his hostility to Jews in his 'unWelsh' Catholicism, which thus separates him and his beliefs from 'normal' tolerant Welsh Protestantism, and places them in the context of continental antisemitism.[11] However, the contribution of J. Arthur Price, an Anglican, breaks down that isolation of hostile stereotype, for in 1926 he describes Sir Alfred Mond in terms that chime with Lewis's anxieties.

Mond, an industrialist, the son of a German Jew, and the Liberal MP first for Swansea and then Carmarthen, changed parties from Liberal to

Conservative in 1926 and, according to Price, 'would be a laughing stock' as a Welsh Member of Parliament, 'were he not one of the most sinister and dangerous characters in the politics of the age'.[12] As this article is, like the statement made by Lloyd George, illustrative of a common attitude, I reproduce the relevant passages in full:

Mond yw'r cymeriad tebycaf i Lenin a welodd Prydain hyd yn hyn. Iddewon yw'r ddau . . . Cryfder yr Iddewon napoleanaidd hyn yw eu bod yn gwbl rhydd oddiwrth draddodiadau culion gwlad a bro. Nid oes un darn o ddaear yn llyffethair arnynt, nac un genedl yn glawdd terfyn iddynt. Y byd yw eu plwyf, ac ar raddfa gydwladol yn unig y symud eu meddyliadau. Megis nad oedd Rwsia ond man cychwyn i syniadau Lenin orchfygu Ewrop ac Asia, felly nid yw Lloegr i Mond, nac Ymerodraeth Loegr, ond cyfle i'w gynlluniau econo-maidd ef i orchfygu'r byd.

(Mond is the closest in character to Lenin that Britain has ever seen. The two are Jews . . . The strength of these Napoleonic Jews is that they are completely free of narrow national or regional traditions. There is not a strip of land that constrains them, or any nation that presents a barrier to them. The world is their parish, and their minds move entirely on an international scale. Just as Russia was only the starting place for Lenin's ideas of conquering Europe and Asia, so for Mond England and the English Empire are merely opportunities for the world domination of his economic plans.)

In a rather convoluted act of disingenuousness, Price suggests that 'Peth gwael a thaeogaidd yw ceisio maeddu dyn drwy ei alw yn Iddew' (It is a low, churlish thing to try to slur someone by calling him a Jew). But, he goes on:

Ni fynnem ni wneud hynny ond am resymau arbennig iawn, ac am gredu ohonom mai Iddewiaeth Mond sy'n esbonio ei amcanion. Sylwer mai Iddewon sy'n llunio syniadau economaidd y byd modern, gwŷr fel Marx, Lenin a Mond, gwŷr nad etifeddasant un traddodiad gwlad a bro, a gwŷr hefyd – a phwysicach hyn – nad etifeddasant draddodiadau Cristnogaeth. Mewn byd a drefnwyd ar sail gydwladol, yn ôl syniadau Marx, neu Mond, yr Iddewon a reolai. Dyna'r ffaith gyfrin sy'n egluro dyheadau Mond, a dyna sy'n berigl ynddo. Iddo ef nid yw rhwygo Prydain oddiwrth gyfathrach Ewrop yn ddrwg o gwbl os bydd i hynny effeithiau masnachol cymwys. Ni ŵyr ef guriad calon y Gorllewin, na thraddodiadau gwareiddiad Lladin Ewrop, na rhan Prydain yn y traddodiad Cristnogol. Ni falia ef os bydd y rhwygo hwnnw'n dinistrio etifeddiaeth ysbrydol Lloegr a Chymru ac Iwerddon. Ni falia ef ychwaith os arwain ei bolisi i dranc Seiat y Cenhedloedd, a pharatoi ar gyfer rhyfel mor eang fel na byddai'r rhyfel diwethaf ond cweryl bychan o'i gymharu ag ef. Fe gyrraedd ef ei nod pan welir diorseddu'n llwyr egwyddorion Cristnogol yng nghyfathrach y gwledydd, a choroni syniadau cenedl a fu'n ffoadur drwy'r byd ac yn ddirmygedig drwy'r oesoedd. Nid cyfoeth yw chwant Alfred Mond, ond gallu ac awdurdod. A hwn yw un o aelodau seneddol gwlad nad oes iddi hanes o gwbl ar wahan i Gristnogaeth. Cook, Mond, — wele dy wŷr di, Gymru!

(We would not do this but for very special reasons, and because of our belief that it is Mond's Jewishness that explains his intentions. It should be noted that it is Jews who formulate the economic ideas of the modern world, men such as Marx, Lenin and Mond, men who have not inherited a single tradition of country or region, and men also – and this is most important – who have not inherited Christian traditions. In a world organised on an international foundation along the ideas of Marx or Mond, it is the Jews who would run things. That is the hidden truth that explains Mond's aspirations, and this is what is dangerous about him. For him, severing Britain from its relationship with Europe would not be a bad thing at all if it were to result in appropriate market conditions. He does not know the heartbeat of the West, nor the Latin traditions of European civilisation, nor the part Britain plays in the Christian tradition. It would not trouble him if this rupture were to destroy the spiritual inheritance of England and Wales and Ireland. It would not trouble him either if his policy led to the death of the League of Nations and prepared for a war so extensive that by comparison the last war would look like a little quarrel. His aim will have been achieved when we see Christian principles in the relationship between nations deposed completely, and see crowned the ideas of a nation that has been fugitive throughout the world and despised through the ages. Alfred Mond's lust is not for wealth, but for power and authority. And this is a Member of Parliament of a country that has no history at all apart from Christianity. Cook, Mond – behold your people, Wales!)[13]

That concluding warning continues through the 1930s overtly and covertly in relation to international capital and the press, as though *The Protocols of the Elders of Zion* had never been debunked.[14] There is little in the pages of the paper about the situation of Jews in Germany, or about Zionism, or events in Palestine. The exception is a short article by Mallt Williams in 1934 in *The Welsh Nationalist*, where she discusses Eliezer Ben Yehuda as a shining example of commitment to language revival, and concludes: 'If one man has been able to resurrect a dead language, the many thousands of Welsh people, still speaking a living tongue, can surely hope to establish it on a firm foundation.'[15] But in the pre-war period it is Ireland, not Palestine, that serves as the chief country for comparison with Wales.

Indeed, where Jewish national aspirations in Palestine are commented on, in 1938, it is in comparison with England's struggles with Ireland. Here, in an article by J. E. Daniel, the identification, if there is one, is with an Arab population that is being 'swamped' by Jewish immigration. One might infer that the author sees a parallel threat to Wales in the horribly swelling 'flood' of Jewish immigration into Palestine.[16] These 'swamping' and 'flooding' terms of reference echo those of the anti-immigrant debates at the turn of the century: although figures for Jewish immigrants are given, Daniel does not explain why they jump from 9,553 in 1933 to 42,359 by 1934, when Germany's Jews had been subjected to intensified persecution.

J. E. Daniel was at the time acting president of Plaid Cymru, and W. J. Gruffydd was vice-president: even as late as 1942, Gruffydd was still recycling Jewish conspiracy theory in *Y Llenor* – not, as Grahame Davies suggests, in an isolated or exceptional fashion, but as part of a widely accepted discourse that was firmly established in the thirties among leading nationalists, which these articles by J. Arthur Price and J. E. Daniel indicate.

The fear of world Jewish power and Jewish capital that runs like a thread through the paper in the thirties is explicit in Daniel's interpretation of the reasons behind the Balfour Declaration:

> Yn Nhachwedd 1917, er mwyn cael help Iddewon y byd yn y Rhyfel cyhoeddodd Lloegr Ddeclarasiwn Balfour, yn addo sefydlu ym Mhalesteina 'Gartref Cenedlaethol' (O amwyster bendigedig na ŵyr neb ei ystyr!) i'r Iddewon. Ni soniwyd gair wrth yr Iddewon am addewidion McMahon i'r Arabiaid . . . Y mae llif ymfudwyr Iddewig wedi chwyddo'n aruthrol ers 1933 . . . nes y mae'r Iddewon bellach ymhell dros draean y boblogaeth. Oherwydd y gallu economaidd sydd tu cefn iddynt, gallant brynu tir a 'datblygu''r wlad yn ystyr gyfalafol y gair, a gwêl yr Arabiaid y dydd yn nesáu pan na fyddant ond proletariat dieiddo yn gweithio i'r meistri estron hyn.[17]

> (In November 1917, in order to secure the help of world Jewry in the War, England published the Balfour Declaration, promising to establish in Palestine a 'National Home' (Oh wonderful ambiguity whose meaning nobody knows!) for the Jews. Not a word was said to the Jews about McMahon's assurances to the Arabs . . . The flood of Jewish immigrants has swelled terribly since 1933 . . . so that now the Jews constitute more than a third of the population. Because of the economic power that lies behind them, they can buy land and 'develop' the country in the capitalist sense of the word, and the Arabs see the day approaching when they will be nothing but a property-less proletariat working for these foreign masters.)

Nevertheless it is England that suffers his greatest opprobrium, for, as he concludes: 'as long as Jews continue to cling to a country like England, which is only interested in its imperial gains in Palestine, peace will not be seen there.'[18]

Between 1937 and 1939, the paper publishes Lewis Valentine's diary excerpts, which include occasional comments on the Jews he encounters in Wormwood Scrubs, where he was imprisoned with Saunders Lewis and D. J. Williams for their symbolic arson attack on the bombing school at Penyberth in 1936. Although in many ways these express sympathy for the hostility Jews experience from English prisoners and the English more widely (and include, interestingly, a brief portrait of a fellow prisoner who appears to be the German-Jewish novelist Robert Neumann), Valentine sees his fellow prisoners in the typically essentialist terms of the period: the Jews are clumsy with gardening tools, and are obviously not 'men of the soil' ('yr oedd yn amlwg nad gwŷr y pridd mo'r Iddewon'), and are acquiescent.[19] In addition, their desperate royalism is seen as an extreme form of servility.[20]

There is another attack on Mond in 1941 (although this does not constitute a specific attack on him as a Jew, but as an exploiter), and then at the end of the war matters shift, no doubt due in part to the growing realisation of the genocide that had been perpetrated by the Nazis, but also, perhaps, reflecting the new editorial direction of Gwynfor Evans, who was subsequently elected as president of the party in 1945.

Welsh soldiers returning from active service reported on attitudes to the use of the Welsh language in the army, and on attitudes of the English to Welsh people, to Jews, and to Arabs. In January 1945, under the heading 'Profiad Milwr' (A Soldier's Experience), an anonymous soldier recalls 'the treatment by the Englishman of the natives – the "bloody wops" as they call every Arab from Casablanca to Tehran, and the "bloody Yids"'.[21] He continues:

> Y dyn mwyaf creulon a didrugaredd a welais yn fy mywyd oedd y plisman Prydeinig ym Mhalestina. Y mae'n debyg fod 63% o'r bechgyn hyn, cyn y rhyfel, yn gyn-ddrwgweithredwyr. Oddi ar hynny, chwyddwyd eu rhengoedd gan lanciau yn ceisio osgoi ymuno â'r lluoedd. Y mae gennyf brawf y'u hyfforddir i fod yn wrth-Semitig.[22]

> (The most cruel and merciless man I ever saw in my life was the British policeman in Palestine. It seems that before the war 63% of these boys were former criminals. Since then, their ranks have been swollen by lads trying to avoid joining the armed forces. I have proof that they are trained to be antisemitic.)

It is noteworthy that as the English become the object of deepest suspicion, and of intemperate and sometimes self-righteous criticism, the renewed sense of embattled Welshness relies in part on the enlistment of the victimised Jew as a brother target of English hatred. Once again this indicates how semitic discourse in Wales is often an integral part of discourse on the English as the prime 'other':

> Ni chredais erioed cyn hynny fod y Sais yn gallu ar y fath gasineb. Ac yr wyf yn argyhoeddedig fod y casineb hwnnw oedd yn ei fron at y 'bloody Jew' yno hefyd at y 'bloody Welshman.'[23]

> (I had not ever believed before this that the Englishman could harbour that kind of hatred. And I am convinced that this hatred he had in his breast for the 'bloody Jew' he also had for the 'bloody Welshman.')

In 1945 an echo of this sympathetic comparison appears in an article about Scottish hostility to the Welsh (and to the Jews), which concludes that the English, 'bungling' things 'with their devilish imperial spirit' ('â'u hysbryd imperialaidd cythreulig'), are responsible for setting Arab against Jew in Palestine as they had set Hindu against Muslim in India, and Protestant against Catholic in Ireland.[24] 'But the best of Jews are far beyond the Scots or the Welsh, and the worst are to the same degree lower than the lowest of the Scots or Welsh, because they have suffered more heavily', the author claims, before concluding: 'We will build our Jerusalem in our own land, wherever it may be, because *this* is our Sacred Land.'[25]

This is a sharp turn from attacking Mond as the personification of sinister Jewish intent, or bewailing the control of the British press by Jewish financiers; indeed, there is the suggestion of a guilty overcompensation in some of the rhetoric that follows. This is particularly apparent in article titles, for example 'Gwyrthiau yr Iddewon' (The Miracles of the Jews), which reports on a note about reviving the language that appeared in an English publication, and, most importantly, Gwynfor Evans's article in 1946, entitled 'Neges Palesteina i Gymru: Camp Iddewon Heddiw' (The message of Palestine for Wales: the achievements of the Jews of today).

This is Evans's first call for an adoption in Wales of the model of Hebrew language immersion, although it wasn't until 1949, after Israeli independence, that the Hebrew *ulpan* was formally instituted as a state-supported language system. 'Gwnaeth y rhai a ddychwelodd i Balesteina,' he begins, 'ddigon eisoes i ddangos bod ynddynt yr ynni a'r gallu i arwain unwaith eto ymhlith y cenedloedd' (Those who returned to Palestine have already done enough to show that they have the energy and the will to once more lead among the nations).[26] This is not the flood of capitalist Jews forcing Arabs into landless servitude of J. E. Daniel's assessment; on the contrary, in this remarkably apologist article, Evans claims that fewer than five hundred Arabs were displaced from their land by Jewish immigration and land purchases. There is nothing but admiration for Jewish achievement – in particular for the revival of Hebrew, which, as he suggests, is perhaps the most interesting and relevant for Welsh people: 'mae darllen amdano yn symbyliad ac ysbrydiaeth i'r Cymro a ddymuna weld Cymru oll yn siarad Cymraeg unwaith eto' (reading about it is an incentive and inspiration for the Welshman who wishes to see all of Wales speaking Welsh once again).[27] Following a detailed account of Eliezer Ben Yehuda's efforts to revive the language, the development of Hebrew-language institutions, and the emergence of new generations of Hebrew-speaking children, he wonders whether in Wales something similar can be done. This is repeated twenty-five years later in an article by him in *Barn* in 1969, as well as in an article by the assistant editor in *Welsh Nation*, also in 1969.[28]

Gwynfor Evans aside, the 'admiration' beginning to emerge in the 1940s is still qualified by older suspicions and a strong continuing ambivalence about Jewish actions in Palestine. In a brief note in October 1947, for example, a reader comments on a proposal in Palestine that Arabs who sell land to Jews be excommunicated, whether they are Muslim or Christian, and he asks: 'Could this plan be made to work here in Wales in connection with selling land to the English?'[29] In contrast, in the following issue, in November 1947, Wyn Jones suggests that Jewish land-buying and communal land ownership holds a lesson for Wales: Saunders Lewis had called for a fund to buy farms and retain Welsh land in Welsh ownership, and to keep it from falling into the hands of foreigners, and he goes on to describe the *moshav* system (although as yet there was no use either of the word 'moshav' or 'kibbutz'). Nevertheless, although he recommends this communal land ownership for Wales, his description of the background to Jewish settlement in Palestine harks back to the capitalist development of the land described by J. E. Daniel in 1938:

> Pan ymfudodd yr Iddewon cyntaf i Balestina yn chwarter olaf y ganrif diwethaf, o Rwsia yn bennaf, nid oeddynt yn rhy barod i weithio â'u dwylo. Cyflogi gweision – Arabiaid gan mwyaf – a wnaent, a rheoli'r ffermydd eu hunain heb weithio â'u dwylo. O'r herwydd, codai helynt byth a beunydd rhwng y perchnogion a'u gweithwyr. A gwelwyd yn fuan bod raid wrth rhyw gynllun gwell na hwn er mwyn gwladychu Palestinia yn llwyddiannus.[30]

> (When the Jews first emigrated to Palestine in the closing quarter of the last century, mainly from Russia, they weren't too willing to work with their hands. They employed men – mostly Arabs – and managed the farms without working with their hands themselves. Consequently continual trouble arose between the owners and their workers. And it was soon clear that there was a need for a better plan than this for the successful settlement of Palestine.)

Efforts to educate Jewish settlers in the necessity of physical labour leads to a change in settlement and land ownership, Wyn Jones explains, quoting Aaron Gordon on Jewish labour, as Gwynfor Evans also does. However, there is no acknowledgement that the calls for Jewish labour were also calls for a boycott of Arab labour, with its complex political and economic implications. As D. Hywel Davies observes:

> the analyses published in *Y Ddraig Goch* and the *Welsh Nationalist* were inevitably amateur, arm-chair exercises inspired not by an unique 'Welsh view', though Lewis's group clearly thought this to be the case, but by attitudes that were commonplace in a variety of political circles, albeit heavily spiced with criticism of England and the Empire.[31]

From 1945, under Evans's leadership and editorial guidance, and then from 1948 under the editorship of J. Gwyn Griffiths (husband of Kate Bosse-Griffiths, a German-Jewish refugee), attitudes to Jewish success in creating a national language out of Hebrew, and then the achievement of independence, also reflect the wider view, heavily coloured by post-genocide dismay and guilt.

It may well have been the influence of Gwynfor Evans in nationalist circles more widely in the 1960s and 1970s that directed thoughts to Israel and to Hebrew, but in his autobiography Evans does not discuss this and, in an early 1937 article in *Y Ddraig Goch*, he compares the situation of Welsh with that of several other languages without mentioning Hebrew.[32] Nevertheless, as early as 1946 he had seen a political parallel between the situation of Jews in Palestine and the Welsh in Wales – specifically those threatened by the British War Office's plans for taking over vast tracts of land at the heart of Welsh-speaking communities.[33] According to his biographer, Rhys Evans, he remarked at the time that 'the Welsh will have no land left – they will be like the Jews, scattered and lost in their own country'.[34] Three years later, a year after Israeli statehood was declared, and not long after the final ceasefire in the 1947–9 war, he began his 'Parliament for Wales' campaign, a campaign, according to Rhys Evans, whose 'undoubted inspiration was reading the Israeli President Chaim Weizman's *Trial and Error*. The book, he told Pennar Davies in May 1949, was "loaded with lessons and inspiration", and the clearest lesson was that the Welsh language could not be protected without a state.'[35] This is in sharp contrast to Saunders Lewis, who comes to the opposite conclusion in his iconic 1962 Radio Wales lecture 'Tynged yr Iaith' (The Fate of the Language):

> The language is more important than self-government. In my opinion, if we were to have any sort of self-government for Wales before the Welsh language

is recognised and used as an official language in all the administration of state and local authority in the Welsh areas of our country, it would never attain official status, and the doom of the language would come more quickly than it will come under English Government.[36]

Yet Lewis himself cites the example of The Hebrew University of Jerusalem, where the medium of instruction is Hebrew, and compares it (and other examples) to the lack of Welsh-language provision in the University of Wales.[37]

How much a close association with German-Jewish refugees influenced Gwynfor Evans is not possible to say, but it seems likely that their experience was a factor in his attitudes: Pennar Davies's wife, Rosemarie Wolff, was a Jewish refugee, as was another prominent associate, Kate Bosse-Griffiths, who was already establishing herself as a Welsh-language writer of note. They were members of Cylch Cadwgan, a pacifist internationalist group of writers who met in the Rhondda in the 1930s and 1940s.

Nationalist politics, closely interwoven with the struggle for the language, became the focus of cultural production from the early 1960s until the 1979 Referendum and beyond, in both languages. Indeed, the newly articulated threat to the Welsh language stimulated a renaissance in the literature in both languages that was closely allied to the national movement, and although certainly not all writers were Plaid Cymru members, or even sympathetic with the party's electoral efforts, many of the most prominent were.

The trigger was, arguably, Saunders Lewis's 'Tynged yr Iaith' – 'the most important lecture in the history of the Welsh language and also the most misinterpreted', as Rhys Evans puts it.[38] His biography of Gwynfor Evans situates the two formative figures of Plaid Cymru at fundamental and vindictive odds, and he proposes that Saunders Lewis's lecture was 'a calculated attempt to undermine Gwynfor's whole political strategy'.[39]

But if 'Tynged Yr Iaith' – and Cymdeithas yr Iaith Gymraeg (The Welsh Language Society) that was formed in response to it – focused on the issue of the language, in the same period there emerged a proliferation of small direct-action underground groups: Mudiad Amddiffyn Cymru (MAC), the Free Wales Army and, later, Meibion Glyndŵr. References to the Haganah and to Israel were often made about and by these groups, particularly the Free Wales Army, which was mocked for being the fantasy of a handful of overgrown boys playing military games.[40] One supporter, Keith Griffiths, reported that he 'believed basically as did the Israelis in the Haganah, that the nationalist movement had to have a military wing to act as a threat'.[41]

Rhys Evans claims that 'it is difficult to overestimate the profound effect' of Gwynfor Evans's 'continual message' to the Welsh to think of themselves as Welsh rather than British: 'Gradually, he, and a handful of others, were beginning to convince thousands of people in Wales that Britishness was rotten to the core and that they should look to countries like Denmark and Israel for inspiration.'[42] Despite widespread use of such models (at least anecdotally, if not so statistically dominant in the documentary record), Israel is only one of several countries used for comparison. When looked at in the context of more widespread admiring (and guilty) attitudes towards Israel in the post-Holocaust period, it is difficult to see such comparisons as necessarily constituting an overt political 'identification' that had roots in much older Welsh attitudes to Jews (though such echoes were evidently present for figures such as Gwynfor Evans and Cynog Dafis).[43] In other words, with the exception of language comparisons specifically, the evidence of Plaid Cymru's publications suggests that Welsh semitic discourse between the twenties and the sixties in many ways reflected attitudes that were held more widely in Britain, as much as it reflected Welsh particularity. Attitudes to Israel and attitudes to Jews are not necessarily consistent, either, though these are often conflated. Indeed, some of these distinctions emerge in responses to two prominent Jewish figures in Wales: Judith Maro, who moved from Israel to Wales in the early 1950s and who wrote extensively on Israel, on Hebrew, and on Wales-Israel resonances; and Leo Abse, the Labour MP for Pontypool, who was a vigorous and vituperative anti-nationalist.[44]

JUDITH MARO'S *ALTNEULAND*

In 1974, Welsh-language publisher Y Lolfa brought out Judith Maro's collection of articles entitled *Hen Wlad Newydd*.[45] The name is a translation of Theodor Herzl's Utopian Zionist novel, *Altneuland*, 'Old New Land', while the cover shows biblical place-names scattered across a map of Wales juxtaposed with a map of Israel and the West Bank. Visually it is a parallel to the Sunday School movement map published in John Harvey's book *Image of the Invisible* and reproduced in this volume as a frontispiece; culturally and politically it diverges from that in resonance, because the book constitutes the response of an Israeli to the Welsh situation, but without an awareness of the deeper roots and tropes of the Welsh-Israelite biblical tradition.

Hen Wlad Newydd brought together diverse pieces of journalism by Maro that had appeared in English and Welsh in numerous journals and papers between 1959 and 1974, including Welsh-language periodicals *Taliesin*, *Llais Llyfrau*, *Tafod y Ddraig* and *Barn*, and English-language publications *Planet*, *The Anglo-Welsh Review*, the *Cambrian News*, and the Plaid Cymru paper *Welsh Nation* (formerly *The Welsh Nationalist*).[46] Maro also published articles and reviews in *The Jewish Quarterly* and in various UK broadsheet newspapers, and did some broadcasting for the BBC World Service.

Maro had grown up in Palestine and met her husband, the artist Jonah Jones, when he was stationed in Palestine during the British Mandate. Maro herself served in the Haganah, and recounted these experiences in her prose nonfiction account, *Atgofion Haganah* (Memories of the Haganah), which was published in 1973. The couple moved to the heart of a Welsh-speaking community in north Wales in the early 1950s and, though Maro did not write in Welsh, she had her work translated and published in Welsh out of sympathy with the political and cultural atmosphere in which she found herself. She commented on how she felt 'a resonance between my own country and the country I had gone to live in ... I was home – almost', but she also wrote extensively about Israel, about Hebrew literature, Jewish history, the Haganah and, importantly, about the revival of Hebrew.[47] Indeed, two articles on Hebrew were perhaps her most influential contributions: one appeared under the title 'Adfer yr Hebraeg' (The Revival of Hebrew) in 1971 in *Taliesin*; the other, a two-part article on the *ulpan* system, which used a great deal of material from its predecessor, appeared in 1973, under the title 'The Hebrew revival – a lesson for Wales', and the following week, 'Welsh "Ulpans": the way for a major linguistic breakthrough?'[48] These constitute polemical accounts of the 'miracle' of Hebrew's rebirth, the miracle of Jewish 'return', and the dedication of one man, Eliezer Ben Yehuda, to the revival of the language. The whole is presented as a model for Wales to follow.

Taken together with her repeated celebration of the peacefulness of Wales (and the unfamiliar but deeply welcome peacefulness of Israel in 1959, when she returned for a two-month visit), it is no surprise to find that the introduction to her collection of essays *Hen Wlad Newydd* is by Gwynfor Evans. 'Bu'n genedlaetholwraig yn Israel ymhell cyn iddi ddod i fyw i'n plith. Yn awr y mae'n genedlaetholwraig o Gymraes' (She was a nationalist in Israel long before she came to live in our midst. Now she's a nationalist Welshwoman), he remarks. 'Beth bynnag yw ein barn am rai agweddau ar ei pholisïau cyfoes, rhaid inni oll edmygu camp anghymarol Israel yn adfer yr Hebraeg' (Whatever our opinion on some aspects of its recent policies, we must all admire the incomparable achievement of Israel in reviving Hebrew).[49]

Evans goes on to repeat from his 1946 article, which he had published again in new form in 1969, the details of how Hebrew had become a genuinely national language of work, daily life, politics, industry, literature, culture and education.[50] In cultural and language terms, at least, Israel is an inspiring example and a model: 'Dengys bywyd Israel y grym moesol difesur sydd mewn cenedlaetholdeb. Gwnaeth hyn yr amhosibl yn bosibl' (The life of Israel shows the immeasurable moral strength of nationalism. It made the impossible possible). Nevertheless, the qualification about Israeli policy points to an unease that goes back to 1938 and earlier in *Y Ddraig Goch*. It is an unease about military violence as much as about Israel's post-1967 policy.

A similar discomfort makes Ned Thomas question the whole comparison when he interviews Maro the following year in *Planet*. His own highly influential collection of essays, *The Welsh Extremist*, had been published by Gollancz in 1971, and had been issued in paperback in 1973 by Y Lolfa, the press that published Maro's *Hen Wlad Newydd*.[51] In *The Welsh Extremist* Thomas expresses a profound ambivalence about how to respond to the violence of the direct action groups such as MAC and the Free Wales Army, which were causing dissension among nationalists in the late 1960s and early 1970s. Although he identifies 'the moral corruption that is introduced into the situation by violence', and suggests that 'the most hopeful course for an honest Welsh person ... is to back the non-violent civil disobedience campaigns of the Welsh Language Society', he nevertheless acknowledges: 'I should find it impossible to hand over to the police a Welsh bomb-layer.'[52]

The question of violence and morality recurs in his interview with Maro just three years later – though he does not express the same ambivalence about Israel that he does about Wales:

> There are things that worry me in the comparison, and while some of these are merely doubts about the logical appropriateness of the comparison, others ... appear to be doubts about the direction taken by the Israeli state ... I do feel that the moral idea which Israel represented to so many people, has suffered badly.[53]

To this suggestion, Maro responds, apparently rather resentfully, 'First, let me clear the air on Welsh/Israeli affinities. They *do* exist, and I have pointed them out. If others take it too far, why blame me?'[54] But Thomas continues in critical vein, questioning whether the development of the kibbutz movement, the language revival and the violence of Israel as an armed state are good points of comparison for the Welsh situation in the 1970s:

Don't you sometimes think that perhaps the Israeli comparison is a danger-ously delusory one for Welsh people, allowing us to combine our Biblical tradition – the place-names that appear on the cover of your book, with the dream of power that lurks at the back of the mind of every suppressed minority?[55]

Ned Thomas was at the time editor of *Planet*, and was therefore respon-sible for juxtaposing with this discussion the poem 'Roll Call', by Raymond Garlick. Perhaps this is in order to ameliorate in part the harsher criticisms in the interview, for in 'Roll Call' Garlick, recalling his time teaching poetry to Israeli and Welsh students in Holland, reiterates some of the Wales-Israel connections that Thomas is querying, and invokes a collective international blame for the violence that Thomas condemns. In the poem he commemorates an Israeli killed in the 1973 Yom Kippur war, a Welsh man imprisoned for actions in support of the language, and a Welsh girl who has died. The poem concludes:

> At least, thank God
> no blood's shed here – except the odd
> policeman's fistful, in a cell
> where no eye sees, no tongue can tell.
> But in those sun-glazed rocks and sands
> the blood dries brown on the world's hands,
> and Cardiff and Caersalem* both
> give deep-dug ground for grief's sharp growth.[56]

In 1971, when Thomas commissioned and published the translation of Saunders Lewis's lecture 'Tynged yr Iaith' in *Planet*, he had included in the same issue an article on the revival of Hebrew entitled 'This is not a Fairytale', by S. Ariel. This article was prefaced by an introduction that noted: 'Modern Israeli Hebrew is the supreme example of a language being raised from the dead. It was a question of national will, but also of the special circumstances in which the state of Israel came into being.'[57] In *The Welsh Extremist*, Thomas acknowledges some of the connections to which Maro responds and which make him uneasy about her book. Interestingly (and unusually), he compares this to the African American identification with Jewish experience:

> Like American Blacks, the Welsh have identified themselves with the Jewish people. In both cases this stems from a Protestant, Biblical culture. But while that explains what made the identification *possible*, the depth of feeling comes from the common experience of exiled or rejected groups. Listening to our hymn-singing, who can doubt that like that of the American Black it expresses

* The Welsh name for Jerusalem.

the yearning of a group whose identity has been suppressed, and the same internal triumph over external circumstances.[58]

Thomas, like Gwynfor Evans, identifies the deep pacifist tradition of Welsh-speaking Wales, claiming that 'the Welsh-speaker, even when a political nationalist, has hitherto been a natural pacifist' (p. 18), but the unease he expresses about 'the dream of power that lurks at the back of the mind of every suppressed minority' takes on a somewhat suggestive undertone when considered in the context of his observation elsewhere in *The Welsh Extremist* that 'even as a pressure group, Welsh-speakers lack power in places where it is really useful – for example in the business community and inside the English communications media. Jews in Britain present a very marked contrast in these respects.'[59] This echoes uncomfortably, if perhaps accidentally, with the characterisation of Alfred Mond in *Y Ddraig Goch* in 1926, and the widespread (but by the 1970s very much more muted) discourse on Jewish control of money and media; it usefully highlights how sympathy with the Jewish experience of oppression can nevertheless be expressed in terms that evoke stereotypes of Jewish power. As with the most overt expressions of sympathy, motifs prevalent in the broader discourse on Jews can creep in without the author necessarily being conscious of their historical resonance.[60]

Erroneously, I believe, Thomas claims that 'the identification with the Jews was carried to its furthest and most explicit' in Saunders Lewis's comments on his play *Esther*.[61] Again, this term 'identification' requires closer attention. The source for Lewis's play, which was televised by the BBC, was Racine's *Esther* rather than the biblical story, and Lewis explained, according to Thomas: '"Between my time and Racine's there lay Hitler's attempt in Germany, Poland and Austria, to destroy the Jewish nation utterly . . . And I could not forget that my own nation too was being wiped out, just as efficiently, though not in such obviously diabolical ways"' (p. 123).

Thomas points out that there is a great difference 'between physical annihilation and cultural annihilation, which is what makes Saunders Lewis's formulation appear so extreme. But it is a formulation to which a Welsh person can respond' (p. 123). Yet this relationship created by Lewis is a deeply troubling one. Even without his earlier depiction of Jewish capitalists and his position of neutrality during the war (and whatever his expressed and reported statements about revised post-Holocaust attitudes to Jews), this comparison is rather more than 'extreme'.[62] The play itself contains references to villages under water, which evidently invokes

Tryweryn, the galvanising political issue of the late 1950s and early 1960s, when, despite universal Welsh objection, the Welsh-speaking community of Capel Celyn was destroyed by the building of the Tryweryn dam to serve the needs of Liverpool. With the text of the play, and his comments on it, Lewis takes an ancient Jewish story and the recent Nazi genocide and maps them onto a present-day Welsh situation. Drawing a parallel between the threat of destruction by Haman and the actual destruction by the Nazis is a common enough Jewish tendency to see history as one of repeated oppression – what has come to be called the 'lachrymose conception of Jewish history', after Salo Baron, or arising out of an 'ideology of afflic- tion', as Bernard Susser describes it.[63] Lewis is not equating the Jewish experience of oppression and genocide with the Welsh experience, but nevertheless this use of a terrible recent past to make a point about an entirely unrelated present suggests not so much identification as co-option.[64] According to Judith Maro, *Esther* was an allegory on the Jewish genocide perpetrated by the Nazis, and this is how it has been widely viewed, even though Lewis's own comment, published by Ned Thomas, suggests rather more that it is an allegory of the threat to Wales.[65]

As discussed in the context of ambiguous attitudes in conversionist discourse, the word 'identification' often contains these kinds of elisions. Maro herself provides an inverse identification that similarly elides certain complexities in Wales: in a 1960 article in the *Anglo-Welsh Review*, enti- tled 'Wisdom Be Thy Chief Thought', she observes that 'intrinsically, the Welsh too are "the people of the book"'.[66] This reverse 'identification' served a mutually productive relationship. Maro was embraced and promoted by the Welsh-speaking literary establishment, and Gwynfor Evans's characterisation of her as a '[c]enedlaetholwraig o Gymraes' was high praise indeed. But that embrace of Maro as a Jew and an Israeli is a product of her credentials as a 'good' nationalist. A more insidious under- current may be seen in this 'identification' on the other side of the debate of the 1960s and 1970s, particularly in letters to Gwynfor Evans's evil twin, the MP Leo Abse.

LEO ABSE AND JEWISH ANTI-NATIONALISM

The increased electoral profile of Plaid Cymru in the 1960s occurred during a period of political and social ferment that included the direct action of the Welsh Language Society, the imprisonment of many of its members for civil disobedience, the emergence of MAC and the Free

Wales Army, and the violent response to the investiture of Charles Windsor
as Prince of Wales in 1969. All of this was viewed with dismay by members
of the Welsh Labour Party, and among the most outspoken was Leo Abse,
who saw the 'Nats' (the Nationalists) as an increasing challenge and then,
following Plaid Cymru's electoral gains, as a genuine threat. Abse's position as a prominent and usually confrontational anti-nationalist and
anti-Zionist Labour MP, was, as he revealed in an interview in 2002,
deeply informed by his understandings as a Jew. A prolific
'psycho-biographer' and autobiographer, Abse tended to repeat himself on
his attitudes to 'parish-pump' and 'xenophobic' nationalists, and his rhetoric was intemperate and on occasion vindictively personal, particularly
when it came to his chief bugbear, Gwynfor Evans, who, he claimed
repeatedly, was 'a bore'. In Abse's own calculated flamboyance and his
harping on Evans's political focus one might detect the very great fear of
the vain man: the fear of being thought *himself* a bore. In the interview in
2002, he recalled his first encounter with Gwynfor Evans:

> I can remember in a building in Cardiff, the British Council had set up a
> debate. I was still in my teens – I remember then the whole issue between us.
> It really was between a virulent nationalism and internationalism, and he
> never changed. Of course I expect the speech he made then was the same
> speech he made when he came into the House of Commons. Because he only
> had one speech. In his autobiography he talks about how he was persecuted by
> the Speaker, and he names me. Well, he wasn't persecuted by the House of
> Commons as an outsider – it's a myth. He *bored* the House of Commons. And
> what the House of Commons can't stand is not somebody who is an individual
> with eccentric views, but they couldn't stand a bore. And he was a crashing
> bore; a humourless bore.[67]

In fact, in his memoirs Evans doesn't claim, as such, to have been persecuted as an outsider or by the Speaker, though he does describe the Labour
MPs as 'particularly hostile' and in rather melodramatic terms identifies
the Speaker, George Thomas, who was then leader of the Welsh Labour
group, as 'savage in his readiness . . . to cudgel a Nationalist about the
head and stab him in the chest or from behind. He was the very scourge of
Welsh Nationalism and the Welsh language. Leo Abse,' he adds, 'was
tender-hearted in comparison'.[68]

Much of Abse's anti-nationalist invective occurred in the 1970s, particularly in the lead-up to the 1979 Devolution Referendum, when, by his
own admission, he used 'every stratagem' first to derail the planned
Devolution Bill by instituting the Referendum, and subsequently to
achieve a 'No' majority in the Referendum itself. But his political papers

reveal that as early as 1966 members of the public in Wales were writing to him with a kind of hostile incomprehension of his views, apparently drawing conclusions about how a Jew should naturally feel about the nationalist aspirations of Welsh people. Abse vehemently opposed demands for the legal recognition of the Welsh language, for the legal rights of Welsh speakers, for the right to be tried in Welsh, and for the institution of bilingual road signs, and he was also extremely hostile to the Welsh-medium nature of the National Eisteddfod, as a letter to a Monmouthshire County Councillor reveals in 1966. In this letter, Abse enquires whether the council makes grant money available to the Eisteddfod, suggesting that, if so, further action should be taken, for it is 'iniquitous that the Welsh Nationalists should regard Monmouthshire County Council as a good County to be marked for the Eisteddfod and not in anybway [sic] be accommodated for its own people'.[69] In 1968, a correspondent asks how it can be that, as a Jew, he does not have more sympathy with the language:

> Do you honestly think that this is fair in view of the fact that the nation from which you have sprung, has in a period of less than two decades, succeeded in reviving the Hebrew speech from centuries of slumber into a vital, living language of modern times. . .? Remember that the Welsh through the medium of their Bible have always identified themselves with the shepherds and fishermen of Canaan, and that Welsh culture and society are largely based on the Biblical teachings of the Hebrews.

In 1978, another correspondent, who had served in Gaza, writes to Abse in a somewhat threatening tone. He argues that there would be no Israel had there not been a Welsh Division, reminds Abse that Lord Melchett (Alfred Mond, the Jewish Liberal MP for Swansea) used to proclaim 'Wales for the Welsh', and concludes: 'Out of racial gratitude it is my belief that most Jews would hesitate to oppose those claims.' In an earlier letter, a correspondent enquires after the sources of Abse's hostility to the language, equates Wales and Israel, cites 'your people', the Hebrew language, Jewish dignity, and trilingual road signs in Israel, and asks: 'if you agree and accept what is happening to your own people Israel today it should follow that you should at least appreciate the aspirations of the Welsh nation. If not you are unworthy and disloyal to Israel – the principle is the same.'

    Abse was as hostile to Zionism as he was to nationalism in Wales, and he responds to the letter accordingly, arguing, as he also does in his book *Wotan, My Enemy: Can Britain Live with the Germans in the European Union?*, that it was only in the last resort that Jews yielded to 'the outmoded concept of a nation-state'.[70] He reminds his correspondent that Babel was a divine punishment for man's sins, and concludes:

> The views that I hold, therefore, about Israel, are informed by the same atti-
> tudes as I hold towards the country of my birth . . . It is because I do not wish
> the same confusion as fell upon Babel to come about in our Wales, that I take
> the view . . . wholly in opposition to the Welsh Language Society. For me, like
> four out of five of those living in Wales, the Welsh language is not the carrier
> of the specific positive values that have grown out of the unusual socio-cultural
> race of industrial Wales in this century: and to protect those values is one of
> the tasks I set myself in my public life.[71]

Abse denies that he was hostile to the language, claiming in the interview in 2002: 'of course they established myths that I'm so anti-Welsh
language. It was my mother's language! I didn't have that attitude at all.'
Nevertheless, in the 1979 Referendum, he recalled, 'one was . . . meeting
the language question. Because the Nats had politicised the language at
that time totally.' This 'politicisation' (assigning an urgent primacy to
Welsh) was as objectionable to him as the primacy accorded to Hebrew in
Israel.[72] Given his strong anti-Zionist position, the identification with the
resuscitation of Hebrew as a national language by some members of Plaid
Cymru no doubt reinforced his suspicions about the Welsh nationalist
movement as a whole.

Abse's repeated characterisation of nationalism as 'virulent' invokes
rhetorically if not explicitly 'virulent' antisemitism, and indeed the two are
never far apart. In the interview conducted in 2002, he explained his
response to Plaid Cymru:

> The picture I had of the Welsh national movement when I was young,
> remember, was influenced by my picture of Saunders Lewis – who was
> drenched in antisemitism. One forgets the Catholic – the right-wing Catholic
> – mood of the early Welsh nationalists. Saunders Lewis was linked with
> Action Française in France . . .

His response to Catholicism as antisemitic colours his whole understanding of the party, both at the time in the 1960s and 1970s, and
subsequently. When asked about Lewis Valentine, one of Saunders Lewis's
two co-arsonists, a nonconformist, not a Catholic, and the pacifist who had
written rather sympathetically about Jews in Wormwood Scrubs, Abse
simply said:

> 'I don't know, I don't know . . . What I do know is we saw them as a right-wing
> movement: a typical nationalist movement – who during the time when Hitler
> was building up his power, and when there was the anguish within the Labour
> movement because of its pacifism as to how it should respond to the Hitlerian
> threat – the anguish between those of us who had been brought up in a pacifist

tradition at the same time finding that we are confronted with somebody who wouldn't respond to pacifism as a method of overcoming – at that time, Saunders Lewis was burning down the RAF aerodrome, or attempting to.

Leo Abse identified deeply with industrial, English-speaking south Wales, and he describes a nonconformist-infused south Wales Labour internationalism that is utterly at odds with Welsh nationalism, which he associates repeatedly with Catholicism, fascism and antisemitism. In a review article criticising the focus of the 1993 book *The Jews of South Wales: Historical Studies* edited by Ursula Henriques, he claims that the story of Jews in Wales was one 'more of collaboration than conflict', and he describes a 'fruitful bond between many Welsh Nonconformists and the more learned of religious immigrants'.[73] He is dismissive of the way in which the much-cited conversionist tale of the 'abduction' of Esther Lyons is treated, arguing that

> Henriques makes heavy weather of it, seeming to believe it did serious and lasting damage to the relationship between Welsh Nonconformists and the Jewish community; but, in fact, it lacked such significance. The Nonconformists esteemed the Jews as 'People of the Book' and very often had a special regard for them.[74]

Abse presents the experience of his own 'Talmudic' grandfather who was often invited to speak in chapels, where he was made welcome, and he argues that 'it was, moreover, the Nonconformist tradition which infused the thinking of early Labour activists and the first Welsh Labour MPs, causing them to be sympathetic to the Zionist movement'.[75] George Thomas was one of the most important of these Labour MPs, and indeed W. D. Rubinstein also cites Thomas as a 'philosemite', although Dannie Abse is more cautious: Thomas, who taught him as a child, 'unashamedly favoured the Jewish boys in his class', he claims, and adds: 'Probably his pleasant bias had a complex aetiology.'[76]

The link that Leo Abse makes between antisemitism and Catholicism, and between a love of the Jews and Protestant nonconformity, may in part be informed by his experience of standing for council elections in the pre- and post-war period, which exposed him to rancorous divisions between the dominant Conservative Catholic and somewhat abject Labour noncon-formist sections of Cardiff.[77] However, it may also be traceable to his childhood, for as he claimed in 2002:

> I never encountered antisemitism when I was a child, at the beginning, and even [when I was] much older, except from the deraciné Catholic section of Wales, the Irish, who are still carrying the 'you killed Christ' story. As a child in the playground in a working-class elementary school – where of course

ours was the only Jewish family in the school – being taunted 'you killed Christ' used to lead me into innumerable fights. The Welsh Nonconformist teachers would look through the window: if I was winning the fight, they'd leave it alone; if I was losing, they'd intervene and haul the other boy always off to be caned. And that was because I had Welsh Nonconformist teachers . . . Nonconformist Wales believed that the Jews were the chosen people.[78]

That monolithic 'Welsh Nonconformist' and 'Nonconformist Wales' designation of Abse's is, of course, a strongly bounded one: insofar as it represents a cultural and religious tradition that informed the internationalism of industrial south Wales, it is an unqualified good, and one that by its nature produced 'a fruitful bond' between the Welsh and the Jews. This is something that is inimical to nationalism and to the Catholicism by which, for Abse, such nationalism is always tainted, despite the overpowering influence on Welsh nationalism of that same nonconformist religious tradition.[79]

If this interview and Abse's publications suggest attitudes to the language that were, at best, slightly more nuanced than some of his public pronouncements, he is remembered nevertheless as being irredeemably hostile to the claims made for Welsh. The letters he received at the time, which ranged from incomprehension to a demand that he be racially grateful, suggest how widely a connection between the revival of Welsh and Hebrew had spread.

Subsequent to Judith Maro's articles in 1960, 1971 and 1973, and Gwynfor Evans's repeat, in 1969, in *Barn*, of his call for an adoption of the Hebrew model, a version of the Hebrew *ulpan* was introduced in 1973 by Chris Rees, vice-president of Plaid Cymru.[80] This practical outcome, the Welsh *wlpan* system of adult language immersion, enjoyed a relatively undisturbed life of forty years, during which the word *wlpan* carried with it to all learners and those involved in Welsh-language adult education the legacy of that Hebrew model. Indeed, radio and television producer Ali Yassine, for example, a Muslim from Cardiff of Egyptian and Somali descent, initially found this association so objectionable that he felt he could not learn the language, though he later put aside his discomfort and became a fluent Welsh speaker.[81]

Since the profound shift in attitudes to Israel from about 2002 onwards, however, the word has been gradually replaced by other terms, and many county councils, universities and other Welsh-learning providers for adults no longer offer a Welsh 'wlpan' at all. The word is dropping from use, and may well soon become a linguistic relic.

That shift in attitudes, and the loss of what was a ubiquitous daily reminder of a powerful association, has also resulted in a rapid cultural amnesia. Among some Welsh-speakers, and particularly those who learned Welsh or those involved in cultural or political activity in relation to the language, the long association with Hebrew and the more circumscribed association with Israel is a familiar, if troubling one. For a younger generation, however, it is now largely unknown.

'LISTEN, WALES' – A POST-ZIONIST ASSESSMENT

Returning, however, to the earlier period when this linguistic and political association was strong, one poem stands as exemplar of the comparisons made between Welsh aspirations and Israeli realities, and of the ambiguities this entailed. Harri Webb's poem 'Israel' was written, or so Meic Stephens speculates, in 1966, but in tone it belongs more to 1967, after the brief but decisive Arab-Israeli Six Day War of that year.[82] It appeared in Webb's collection, *The Green Desert*, in 1969, and is reproduced here in full:

> Listen, Wales.
> Here was a people
> Whom even you could afford to despise,
> Growing nothing, making nothing,
> Belonging nowhere, a people
> Whose sweat-glands had atrophied,
> Who lived by their wits,
>
> Who lived by playing the violin
> (A lot better, incidentally
> Than you ever played the harp).
> And because they were such a people
> They went like lambs to the slaughter.
>
> But some survived (yes, listen closer, now),
> And these are a different people;
> They have switched off Mendelssohn,
> And tuned in to Maccabeus.
> The mountains are red with their blood
> The deserts are green with their seed.
> Listen, Wales.[83]

This 'Listen, Wales' address by Webb is a long way from the 'Wele dy wŷr di, Gymru' of *Y Ddraig Goch* in 1926. And yet there are elements that connect the two exhortations. One may see in this poem an inversion, perhaps, of Saunders Lewis's play *Esther*: instead of Jewish experience being mapped onto Wales, Welsh experience is here mapped onto Israel, and Israel, in the last stanza, is held up as an inspiring example of empowerment.[84] Nevertheless, throughout the poem, common tropes and essentialist traits reappear. Apparently positive recognition for musical and intellectual ability, for example, constitutes immediately recognisable essentialised 'Jewishness'. The Jews, 'a people/ Whom even you could afford to despise', are abject: in going 'like lambs to the slaughter', that trope of Holocaust victimhood controversially articulated by Bruno Bettelheim in *The Informed Heart*, they are not just passive or weak and victimised, but also, by implication, degenerate and less than human.[85] The line 'Growing nothing, making nothing', echoes the early articles in *Y Ddraig Goch*, including Lewis Valentine's prison diary notes, in which Jews cannot work with their hands: it is another widespread motif that presents Jews as being not only incapable of physical labour, but also, again by implication, as exploiting the labour of others. Finally, the Jews belong nowhere and live 'by their wits' – an echo of the characterisation of Jews as landless cosmopolitan intellectuals.

All of this is part of a wider discourse on Jews, but Webb is deploying these images in order to set up a dramatic transformation in the last stanza, in which the 'remnant' who survived are redeemed through armed nationalism, through bloodshed, and the conquest of land. A very great deal in the poem hinges on one phrase – 'a people / Whom *even you* could afford to despise' (the emphasis is mine). In this formulation, the Welsh are only slightly less abject than the pre-statehood Jews. The comparison weaves in and out of the poem, but the message of parallel contempt is clear, as is the message of its solution: Webb's conclusion, 'Listen, Wales', constitutes something like a call to arms.[86]

This poem is perhaps less interesting for the stereotypes of degeneracy in its first two stanzas than for the way this degeneracy is deployed in counterpoint to the final stanza, in which the Jews are Maccabeans, mounting a courageous resistance. Webb's characterisation of the Jew as simultaneously abject and powerful is thus, if not ameliorated, then glossed over by the depiction of redemption through armed and militant statehood.

Harri Webb's presentation of Israel as a model for Wales to follow is considerably less equivocal than that presented by Gwynfor Evans, and there is none of Ned Thomas's ambivalence. Consequently, more than any other text of post-1948 political 'identification', the poem lends itself to assessment in terms of so-called post-Zionist analysis. Indeed, the ways in which post-Zionist analysis examines the tension between ethnic or cultural (and language) preservation and multicultural liberal democracy might have a great deal to offer the Welsh situation, and to an analysis of Welsh writing in both languages.

The term 'post-Zionism' is rather broad: it can include, at one pole, anti-Zionism and, at the other, revisionist work by a range of the 'new historians' in Israel. However, there is a developing body of historiography and social science which shares particular concerns, concerns that set its enquiry apart from that of some of the so-called 'new historians', such as Benny Morris, whose amended historical narrative of Israel nevertheless does not challenge the foundational Zionist framework or ideology. By contrast, Shlomo Sand's *The Invention of the Jewish People* examines the way in which modern Jewish identity is constructed, and the way in which a notional continuity between pre-Diaspora Jews in Palestine and modern Jews in Europe was used to validate the idea of Jewish homeland in Palestine. By questioning the unbroken continuity of Jewish ethnicity, and consequently the continuity of a relationship of Jews to the physical place of Israel/Palestine, Sand challenges the whole Zionist narrative and the basis of Jewish statehood itself.

In his introduction to the collection of essays *The Challenge of Post-Zionism*, Ephraim Nimni claims that 'the debate around post-Zionism paradoxically tackles, with unusual clarity and vigour, the tensions and difficulties in the question whether Israel should be a Jewish state or a democratic state, and the actual and potential contradictions in pursuing these two goals at once', although he acknowledges that the term 'is itself far from consensual or clear among its users and detractors'.[87] Among others, post-Zionism constitutes those historical reassessments of what has been done – or, to use a more rhetorically loaded term, what has been perpetrated and what is being perpetrated – in the name of Zionism; it constitutes an assessment of the costs, to others and to Jews, of the establishment of a Jewish state in Palestine; it reassesses the validity and dominance of the traditional national, which is to say Zionist, narrative. As well as incorporating anti-colonial and post-colonial arguments put forward by radical anti-Zionist groups in Israel, and examining the position of minority groups and women within the traditional Zionist view, post-Zionist scholarship re-examines the relationship between Jewish nationalism, Judaism and ethnicity. As Nimni observes, 'post-Zionist' is also, of course, a term of abuse, an epithet used by Zionism's defenders.[88]

Examining Harri Webb's poem 'Israel' in the light of some of these concerns is instructive. By its invocation, Webb reinforces the vulnerability of 'the Jew', and, juxtaposing this with heroic redemption in Israel, reinforces the legitimacy of the Zionist narrative, and the necessity of the Zionist project. Armed independence lends new muscularity: it relieves the Jews of their degenerate vulnerability.[89] Much of this is typical of nation-alist discourse quite broadly (and, indeed, of Zionist ideology), but here Webb legitimises in the Welsh context not only the Zionist goal and its achievements, but also its method. In doing so, he glosses over its costs.

This lacuna is most striking in the line 'The mountains are red with their blood': the land is red with the blood of Jews, but this conveniently over-looks the blood of Arabs. The following line, 'The deserts are green with their seed', contains a more complex elision. Here, seed operates as a duality, both of whose elements are troubling, for the so-called 'deserts' are green through cultivation of land newly divested of its Arab population (whether through purchases by the Jewish National Fund, or through war, or, if one takes Ilan Pappe's view, through ethnic cleansing), and they are also green with the seed of active (Jewish) re-population of places depopu-lated between 1947 and 1949.[90]

It might be possible to argue that Webb is writing out of a genuine igno-rance of what occurred in the lead-up to and during the course of the 1947–9 war, as a great deal of the historiography that introduced the Palestinian 'Nakba' into common parlance in the UK in the first decade of the twenty-first century had not yet been published. But Webb served as a soldier in British Mandate Palestine in the 1940s, and he was therefore witness to some of the conflict. Perhaps quite unknowingly he replays the political intentions, in landscape, of the Jewish National Fund, whose motto is 'For Israel, forever', and whose forestation conceals, renames or co-opts depopulated or destroyed Palestinian settlements in what some describe as an act of deliberate cultural, linguistic and topographical rubbing out.[91] Whether or not he is familiar with the aims and acts of the Jewish National Fund, Webb is nevertheless complicit: in a similar way, the entire Arab population of Palestine is absent from his poem, and the Jew is empowered subject.

The 'green desert' in this poem also operates more widely in Webb's work as a motif for the harsh lands above Tregaron, which stand in for a remnant of Wales. Inaccessible, uncorrupted but also redeemable, this 'green desert' works in a similar register to that of the Jewish 'redemption' of 'Eretz Israel', the 'Land of Israel'.[92] But if Webb's 'green desert' is both difficult landscape and cultural vestige, in this context it is also an ethni-cally 'clean' one.

Webb not only presents a dubious model for Wales, but in the process re-situates the Zionist narrative, the Zionist project, with all that it entails, in Wales, and in so doing validates and reinforces it. In turn, Israeli writer Judith Maro validates and reinforces him, for she reproduces extracts of the poem in her 1971 article 'Adfer yr Hebraeg' (The Revival of Hebrew), which was then republished in 1973 in *Hen Wlad Newydd*. Of the poem she writes:

> Yn ei gerdd deimladwy, *Israel*, mae'n ceryddu ei bobl . . . I mi, mae'r gerdd hon yn un gyffrous, ond hefyd yn un sy'n rhy agos at yr asgwrn imi deimlo'n gysurus wrth ei darllen. Nid wyf yn siwr fod gan Gymru'r amser i wrando, neu faint o amser.[93]

> (In his sensitive poem, *Israel*, he chastises his people . . . This poem is exciting to me, but it's also too close to the bone for me to feel comfortable reading it. I am not sure that Wales has time to listen, or how much time.)

Maro's discomfort is not a response to the uneasy mix of admiration and negative, essentialised stereotype in this poem, but to its urgency: she takes Webb's call to arms further, and suggests that Wales is running out of time. That she is able to overlook the implicit contempt in the first two stanzas, and promote the poem as a positive identification with Israeli experience, in part arises out of her identity as an Israeli: according to her own assessment, this has protected her from being 'over-sensitive' to what others think of Jews.[94] But perhaps the key to her being able to overlook the poem's admixture of Jewish degeneracy and Jewish power lies in her political orientation: the reinforcement of the Zionist narrative and achievement permits her to bypass the profound ambivalence in this stirringly validating poem.

Maro follows in a long tradition of Jewish writers responding to elements of Welsh semitic discourse (of which, of course, this examination itself is another example). In almost all cases, this response, from the early twentieth century onwards, downplays problems and tensions, and reinforces notions of Welsh 'tolerance' and Welsh 'philosemitism'. However, the reasons for such reinforcement vary widely. The most overt and sustained engagement with Welsh semitic discourse occurs in the work of novelist Lily Tobias, aunt of poet Dannie Abse and politician Leo Abse. By a curious historical coincidence, before she moved to Wales in the early 1950s, Judith Maro lived in the same town as Tobias, and knew both her and Leo Abse by sight. Tobias followed a reverse trajectory to that of Maro, having grown up in Wales and moving with her husband to Palestine in 1936. The next chapter examines the ways in which she and others responded to the Welsh discourse of which they were themselves the subject.

5

The Jewish response

'Why, I do love the Jews, indeed I do. You are the people of the book and the lord will show His wonders through you yet. You have got a big job in front of you my gell . . . the return to Zion.'
                                    – Lily Tobias, *The Nationalists and Other Goluth Studies*

As Judith Maro's response to Harri Webb's poem suggests, semitic discourse does not take place in isolation, but is part of a dialogue with its subject. During the sixties and seventies, Maro's contribution to the question of Hebrew as a model for Welsh would perhaps have naturally been linked, in the popular imagination, to earlier Welsh cultural and religious interest in Jews, early Zionism, and particularly the Welsh-Israelite biblical tradition. But the discussion of Israel and Hebrew, and the parallels that were made between nationalist and Zionist aspirations, was part of a mutually reinforcing dialogue between the author on the one hand, and editors of journals, newspapers and books on the other. The compliment bestowed on her by Gwynfor Evans that she was a 'Cymraes' might not have been so readily earned had she taken a more critical stance on Welsh attitudes to Israel and to Jews – had she, for example, engaged with the troubling stereotypes in Harri Webb's poem. Ned Thomas's more probing questions constituted a somewhat exceptional holding to account in a critical context that celebrated Maro's reinforcement of Welsh national aspirations.

If semitic discourse is part of a dialogue with its subject, Jews often react within the terms of that discourse (for example seeking solely to repudiate negative stereotypes). However, the response also sets its own agenda. In England, for example, as Michael Ragussis and others have shown, conversionist efforts in the nineteenth century triggered a literary

response by Jewish women writers in particular, leading to the development of a distinctive tradition of Anglo-Jewish literature.[1] Indeed, the
Anglo-Jewish answer to conversionist efforts and to nineteenth-century
literary discourse on Jews created an Anglo-Jewish cultural vitality that
has parallels in the Welsh reaction to the mid-nineteenth century 'Brad y
Llyfrau Gleision' – the 'treachery of the Blue Books': in the latter case this
was a nationalising reaction to the woundedness of 'collective humiliation', to invoke Isaiah Berlin's apposite observation.[2]

In Welsh literature, as in English literature, 'the Jewess' in particular
may be a focus of conversionist attention, whether she is a romanticised
figure, or is racialised and sexualised. In both depictions she is potentially
convertible through sexual as much as ideological conquest. The 'Jewess'
who appears or is addressed in poems by Morgan Llwyd, Henry Vaughan
or George Herbert serves as an early example of this romanticised or idealised imaging (although, occurring prior to the readmission of Jews to
Britain in the seventeenth century, this constitutes a rather hypothetical
conversionism). Caradoc Evans's castrating, sexualised 'Jewesses' are not
so convertible – which is to say redeemed of their Jewishness: their
Jewishness is essentialised and, indeed, dangerous. As Lara Trubowitz has
observed of the immigration debates in the early twentieth century: 'on the
one hand, Jewishness is presented as an ontological or essential condition
– one either is or is not Jewish – while on the other hand, Jewishness is
represented as a form of contagion, which presupposes the belief that
contact with the Jew can, in effect, make non-Jews into Jews'.[3]

While Jewish writers may seek to challenge such imaging, their work
also on occasion reinforces and consolidates stereotypical perceptions, as
is the case, for example, with Israel Zangwill's Oriental depictions in
Children of the Ghetto, or the image of the romanticised 'Jewess' in
nineteenth-century Anglo-Jewish fiction by Grace Aguilar.[4] In the Welsh
context, such reinforcement of stereotype by Jewish writers is often less
overt, but no less significant. It may occur in the process of overlooking
and thereby acquiescing to some imaging (as Judith Maro does with Harri
Webb's poem 'Israel'), or it may occur in the redeployment of the imaging
in a new political context. This can be seen in the work of Lily Tobias,
discussed below.

If Maro's work contributed to a quite long-standing popular association
between modern Hebrew and modern Welsh, and between the Zionist
'achievements' since the forties and the Welsh national movement in the
sixties, this raises the question of how much Jewish responses more widely
might have helped foster ideas of a long-standing 'tradition' of Welsh

identification with the Jews. Indeed, it raises the question of whether such an idea of a national tradition might be, in part, a Jewish 'invention'. As discussed in this chapter, writing by Jews in Wales is suggestive in this regard, though not conclusive.

THE PEOPLE OF THE BOOK: EARLY JEWISH RESPONSES

What is glossed over or marginalised is just as interesting as what is reinforced. Overt hostility to Jews, stereotyping and conversionism are all suggestively downplayed in this way in Welsh Jewish writing. Nevertheless, it is evidently the case that what writers confidently assert is sometimes precisely what is felt to be most tenuous; what is promoted as the state of relations may be an imagined possibility that a writer seeks to transform into reality. If Maro sought to defend Israel's actions, and to defend the moral legitimacy and necessity of Zionism, this would surely not have been a matter of such interest, either to her or to the editors who published her work, had such attitudes been widespread and secure. In the same way, in *The South Wales Jewish Review*, the earliest Jewish periodical in Wales, one sees an almost anxious reiteration of notions of Welsh 'tolerance', and of close Welsh and Jewish associations and parallels. This is hardly surprising, given the context. In the first few years of the twentieth century, the period during which the journal was published, there occurred three matters of grave concern for the Jewish community: the Kishinev massacres, the Aliens Acts, and, of more immediate consequence to Jews in Wales, the confrontation between Irish and Jewish workers at the Dowlais Works. It may well be, therefore, that Jewish writers sought to reinforce a cultural or political sympathy that was tenuous, in order to try to secure a support and reassurance that was not in fact felt. It would be a mistake, consequently, to view such 'reinforcements' as evidence in and of themselves of a 'tradition of identification'.

The South Wales Jewish Review
It is evidently problematic to attribute to an author an intent that might be seen in his or her writing (though this is not so much of a problem with overtly polemical work), and it is perhaps just as theoretically complicated to attribute to editorial intent an orientation that may be evident in a journal. Nevertheless, in the case of *The South Wales Jewish Review* such evidence of editorial intent seems clear – though any such attribution is, necessarily, speculative.

The South Wales Jewish Review was the first sustained Jewish publication in Wales. During its brief life between 1904 and 1905, the *Review* frequently commented upon and promoted the work of the Jewish Literary and Social Societies that had sprung up in the south Wales valleys by this time.[5] Although, as Anthony Glaser and Ursula Henriques argue, the peculiar vigour of these societies may be attributed in the first place to the uniquely scattered demographics of Jews in south Wales (exclusive of the major towns), such vigour may also be attributed to that of the wider community of which they were a part – a community whose numerous literary journals was so remarkable.[6] There was at the same time a proliferation of political newspapers, worker education institutes, public lectures and political meetings, as the Independent Labour Party and political organising more generally became widespread up to and on into the First World War. The contentiousness of the conflict between socialist and nonconformist ideologies during the rise of the Independent Labour Party has been challenged, and continuities rather than contradictions might now be emphasised; nevertheless, the social and political debate of the period was passionate and sustained, and was heightened by the suffragette movement and conscientious objection to war, particularly after the introduction of conscription in 1916.[7]

An example of the impact on Jewish social and cultural life of this political ferment in the surrounding community appears early on in Tredegar. In September 1904, the *Review* reports that the Tredegar Workman's and Literary Institute, which already subscribed to the *Jewish Encyclopaedia* and whose library contained a wealth of Jewish fiction, would now allow Jewish members to compete for scholarships to local intermediate schools.[8] Tredegar appears to have had a particularly active Jewish literary society, which is frequently mentioned in the *Review*. This includes the report of a lecture in Yiddish at the Tredegar Literary Society, which was 'altogether a new feature'.[9] The suggestion of quite positive Welsh and Jewish relations in Tredegar, although perhaps mediated by the involvement of one individual, deepens the problems raised by the 1911 riots that began in the town, whose anti-Jewish nature has been much debated.[10]

Alfred Einstein, the editor of the *Review*, echoes some of the Welsh and Jewish associations that D. Wynne Evans had made two years earlier, both through his quotation from and republication of other sources, and through the Jewish and Welsh contributions to the journal. These associations include political comparison, claims about Welsh sympathy with Jews, and parallels between the two cultural histories. Welsh 'sympathy' is first suggested in reports about the opening of the new Cardiff synagogue by

Colonel Goldsmid, the Jewish commander of the Welsh Regiment, who
was stationed in Cardiff at the time:

> The Chief Rabbi, in the course of his sermon, at the opening services of the
> Cardiff Synagogue, gracefully referred to the distinctive educational instincts
> of the Cymry. He might have also alluded to the exceptionally amicable feel-
> ings entertained by the Welsh towards the Jews. Indeed, it was stated not very
> long ago by a prominent member of the Jewish persuasion, that in no quarter
> of the globe does the Jew meet with the hospitality he receives in Christian
> Wales. In the Welsh hymn books a most popular hymn . . . commences
>
> > 'O arglwydd cofia am
> > Hiliogaeth Abraham, A dychwel hwy, etc'
> > Translation: O Lord, remember
> > The followers [sic] of Abraham, And their return, etc[11]

It is not clear whether the choice of this hymn as an example of Welsh
'hospitality' to the Jews indicates a selective or genuinely misinformed
understanding of the resonance of the word 'dychwel', which, as much as
the physical return of the Jews to Palestine, also refers to conversion (the
religious 'return' to Christ). As discussed later in the context of Tobias's
work, such selective reading of dual meaning in Christian Zionist discourse
reinforces 'amicable feelings' and 'hospitality' in the context of securing
support for a Jewish homeland in Palestine.

The *Review* is particularly cautious about giving credence to an antisemitic interpretation of violent incidents that involve Jews. The large
group of Jewish immigrants employed at the Dowlais Works caused
considerable unease in 1904, and relations with fellow workers were tense.
However, although the *Review* reports that 'further unfortunate incidents
have occurred at the Dowlais Works, in which two of our co-religionists
are alleged to have been brutally attacked by some fellow-workingmen',
and comments on the 'sorrow that such a state of things is still possible to
exist in enlightened Wales', this is followed in the next issue by a correc-
tion: 'The report of the scuffle between the Jewish and other working men
at the Dowlais Works was quite unfounded. An Irishman in an unsober
condition had, indeed, assaulted a Jewish fellow-workman, but the newspaper reports greatly exaggerated the incident.'[12]

In the same issue, the *Review* comments that *The South Wales Daily
Post* is reported to be 'sympathetic with our race', and includes a letter
from W. Ben Griffiths that refers to the need to preserve the unity and
'glorious heritage' of the Jews. 'I am always happy', Griffiths states, 'in
my name being associated with your much maligned people'.[13]

Welsh sympathy is also discerned in the composer D. Emlyn Evans, who had written 'The Captivity' to a libretto by Oliver Goldsmith. Under the heading 'A Jewish Oratorio', the *Review* reports that a Cardiff newspaper critic had said of the piece that '"The Captivity". . . gives ample scope for the genius of a versatile Welsh composer to portray the Jewish character – a task peculiarly appropriate owing to the similarity of the associations and aspirations of the national life of the Welsh and the Jews'.[14] Herbert Roberts, MP, also discussed the oratorio, according to the *Review*: he is reported to have said that 'the national life of Wales had passed through many similar phases of the experience that fell to the lot of the children of Israel, for they had been kept in isolation for many centuries; but now they had emerged with new hope, broader sympathies, and a wider outlook upon human affairs'.[15]

Despite this publication of associations between Jewish and Welsh experience and aspirations, the *Review* produces an ironic response to the tradition of Welsh descent from Gomer:

> Is there any relation between the Welsh and the Jews? Yes, there is! The daily papers have proved that Adam was a Welshman and it has been proved beyond doubt that the Jews are descended from Adam . . . Adaptability is certainly a characteristic of the Jews. The number of Jews who speak Welsh perfectly is amazing. We have not yet met one Welshman who can even stutter imperfect Yiddish.[16]

Although published without editorial comment, pieces like these promote the idea that the Jews are welcomed in Wales, and that parallel experience and cultural national aspirations lend themselves to mutual sympathies and support. Of course, the very need to argue the former point suggests the degree of insecurity that many Jews undoubtedly felt at the time in the context of the Kishinev pogrom in Bessarabia in April 1903, the disturbances at Dowlais, and the hostile discussion of Jews and calls for restriction on Jewish immigration to Britain in the lead-up to the passage of the Aliens Acts of 1904 and 1905. Indeed, even in the radical socialist newspaper, *Llais Llafur*, published in Ystalyfera where Lily Tobias was born and grew up, and possibly the paper in which she published her earliest work, a hostile image appears in 1905 (and no doubt elsewhere, too), when the paper attacks the Conservative government and its 'nest of Jewish capitalists' who were responsible for 'destroying the freedom and independence of small nations'.[17]

Lily Tobias and 'the people of the book'

Lily Tobias, growing up in that uneasy atmosphere but writing a few years later, promotes similar expressions of sympathy or support, and in her polemical fiction consistently associates hostile attitudes towards Jews with hostile English or anglicised attitudes towards the Welsh language and Welsh cultural particularity. In parallel, she presents a consistent association between 'admiration' for Jews (albeit with conversionist and millenarian overtones) and 'good' nationalist Welsh-speakers. In her work, the Welsh-speaker who seeks English assimilation and dismisses or denigrates the Welsh language is almost always hostile to Jews, and is implicitly equated with the deracinated 'treacherous' Jew who seeks assimilation. While Tobias presents a Welsh support for Jewish national self-determination grounded in desires for comparable Welsh national self-determination, she downplays or qualifies the conversionist subtext of this often millenarian discourse. Throughout her work, comparison of the two cultures is a major preoccupation, whether it is expressed in parallel political and national aspirations, in attitudes to language, in the physical geography of Wales and Palestine, or in physical similarities between the two peoples. Nevertheless, the Jewish half of this duality is privileged, and she uses Wales as a location in which to promote specifically Jewish national aspirations and social tensions.

These themes, and the redemptive necessity of both cultural and political Zionism, which are explored at length in three of her four novels of the 1930s, appear first in the short polemical sketches she wrote between 1914 and 1920, mostly for the London-based *Zionist Review* and, on occasion, the *Socialist Review*. They were collected and published together by C. W. Daniel in 1921, under the title *The Nationalists and Other Goluth Studies*. The cover of the book is embossed with the figure of a red dragon woven into a six-pointed star, an emblem of the political comparison between the Welsh and the Jews that is common to most of the stories in the collection. Although Leo Abse describes his aunt's work as seeking to 'intertwine the destinies of the Welsh and the Jews', the stories contained in the collection compare parallels and affinities, and, importantly, highlight unbridgeable differences rather than intertwined destinies.[18] The title story, written sometime between 1911 and 1914, and 'Stray Sheep', evidently written after the Balfour Declaration in 1917, in particular establish the boundaries to such parallels.

In 'The Nationalists', which is perhaps the only fictional treatment of the Tredegar riots of 1911, a young socialist and nationalist firebrand named Idris courts his Jewish schoolfriend, Leah, who is both religious and a Zionist. The setting is a fictionalised Ystalyfera, whose development from village to industrial town is described as a backdrop to their growing relationship. The parallel history of Welsh oppression, told by an old teacher, politicises Idris:

> the boy, too, burned with love for his land and people. The fire in him had been lit by a flickering brand . . . His young heart flamed at each exploit of daring, each fresh attempt at independence, and grew morosely bitter at defeat and treachery. His eyes dilated as he heard how the brave Llewellyn [sic] fell – last of a line of great warrior princes, whose crowning at London, foretold by sage and poet, was fulfilled in direst mockery.[19]

A portrait of Tobias appeared in the *Western Mail* in 1927, at the time that her dramatisation of George Eliot's *Daniel Deronda* was performed at the Q Theatre in London. Here Tobias recalls her own discovery of Llywelyn:

> When quite young, I was reading a Welsh history and came across a passage which recounted the grievances of Prince Llewelyn at the treatment of the Welsh. 'We are treated as if we were Jews,' said the Prince. That phrase stuck, and as you know, a fellow-feeling makes us wondrous kind.[20]

Contrary to Tobias's reading, the intent of Llywelyn's comparison might not have been fellow-feeling: the complaint in the thirteenth century is more likely to have been based on a view that *unfavourably* compared the Welsh and the Jews, in a way not dissimilar to the view expressed in Harri Webb's poem 'Israel' discussed in the previous chapter: 'Here was a people / Whom even you could afford to despise'.[21]

In 'The Nationalists', although Idris is deeply sympathetic with Jewish experience, Leah observes that 'while the Welsh had been deprived only of their independence, the Jews had lost land, home, and liberty'.[22] Idris, 'jealous of the suggestion that the incomparable sufferings of the Jews made insignificant the claim of the Welsh', objects that the Jews are treated well in Wales, '"just like ourselves"', to which Leah agrees. Nevertheless, she adds, this is not the same as having freedom. '"No! No!"' cries Idris enthusiastically: '"A people can only be free in its own country, with its own head and its own laws and its own soldiers. Hurrah for the freedom of the nations!"' (pp. 17–18)

Idris urges Leah to marry him, claiming that this would strengthen rather than kill their 'joint ideals', but Leah objects, asking: '"How can you think I would be false to all the ideals of my people? We are a separate race – intermarriage is death to us. And – and I thought you a true Welshman"' (pp. 22–3).

The boundaries of this sympathy between the two cultures are, consequently, clear: there is affinity but there is neither shared identity nor
shared 'blood'. Suggestively, in this regard, in Tobias's first novel, *My
Mother's House*, the marriage between a Welsh girl and a Jewish man
results in a pregnancy that miscarries.

A racialised depiction of Jewishness and ethnic separatism is more
explicit in Tobias's story 'Stray Sheep'. Here a Welsh professor, travelling
to the meeting of a nationalist society in 'Pontawe' (apparently a fictionalised Pontardawe), being a 'student of human nature' notes the
unmistakeable qualities of a family on the Fishguard train:

> It was most strongly marked in the young lady, though perhaps it was her
> general charm that caused the professor to concentrate attention on her. Her
> soft, delicious voice captivated his ear, and her handsome face, with the dark
> hair curling over roselit cheeks, drew his fascinated eye. In those luxuriant
> features lay the clue; repeated in almost similar degree in the boy . . . it was
> eloquent of a racial descent considerably older than the Saxon traits of habit
> and speech.[23]

The professor engages the father in an awkward exchange:

> 'I see . . . the prospect of Palestine for the Jews is fairly assured. This must
> be very gratifying to you.'
> 'To me?' said the old gentleman, considerable surprise in his courteous
> voice.
> 'I believe I am right in assuming that you are a—'
> 'Ah, yes, I am of the Jewish persuasion,' interposed the gentleman hastily
> . . .
> 'Then you are to be congratulated,' said the professor in his marked Welsh
> accents, 'on the realisation of your national hopes— '
> 'I am afraid, sir,' said the old gentleman, 'that you are under some misap-
> prehension. I have no national hopes of the kind you allude to.'
> 'You are not a Zionist?'
> 'Certainly not. I am an Englishman, and have no desire for any other
> nationality.'
> . . . 'But surely it is not a matter of desire. You either have or have not a
> nationality – and the Jewish nationality is a fact.'
> 'Excuse me,' said the old gentleman complacently, 'but I do not regard it
> so. There is certainly a Jewish religion, and I am not ashamed to profess it. But
> I strongly repudiate anything of a political nature. You see, my dear sir—'
> 'I see, I see,' cried the professor, becoming angry. 'Allow me to say, sir, that
> I am a Welshman who is a convinced nationalist, and engaged in the task of
> promoting the political independence of Wales . . . I have always been in
> sympathy with the Zionists, and I really cannot understand your attitude —'.[24]

When asked for his opinion, the son reiterates his father's position, claiming that they are '*thoroughly* English' and 'have been for three generations', but Tobias mocks them both: at Dawport (a word-play on Abertawe, the Welsh name of Swansea), two women, 'fashionably dressed and carrying pet dogs', approach the carriage, but the first, seeing its inhabitants, retreats, exclaiming, '"No Amelia – not in here . . . it's full of *Jews*. It's hard if we can't find Britishers to travel with—"'(pp. 83–4).

But a contrary misapprehension is to be made by the professor when he arrives at his destination in Pontawe, where he is to give a speech to the local 'nationalist' society. He compliments the young secretary, Davies, on his involvement in the society and on the evocative sound of his local Welsh. Davies, who says he was 'born and bred' in the town, explains: '"I showed my sympathies, of course . . . It was natural for me to take an interest – as a strong nationalist . . . but I must tell you, professor . . . the fact is, I'm not a Welshman – I'm a Jew"' (pp. 86–7).

Like the Zionist literature she was undoubtedly avidly reading, Tobias takes the experience of cultural rejection and puts it to work in the cause of Zionism. The politics of assimilation are presented as delusional: a Jew can never quite be an Englishman. But both in the stories and in her first novel, *My Mother's House*, a slightly different situation pertains in Wales: a Jew cannot quite be a Welshman either. However, this arises from Welsh recognition of separate Jewish nationality as a *positive* attribute. Davies, the politicised Jew in the story 'Stray Sheep', identifies this Welsh/Jewish distinction as a parallel and positive separation. In the novel *My Mother's House*, by contrast, Simon, the protagonist, is a Welsh Jew desperate to be free of both cultural inheritances; he longs to become fully an 'Englishman', and repudiates the Welsh appellation in horrified rejection. In London he is accosted by Rees, an old acquaintance from Wales, who grabs his arm:

> 'What the hell d'you mean, you young pup, passing every Welshman as if he was dirt? Wales isn't good enough, indeed, now you've been in London for a bit?. . . Once you pups get the Saesneg fog into you, you forget the way even to *swear* in Welsh! What's the matter with yr hen iath [*sic*], anyway?'*
>
> 'Let go,' said Simon. 'I suppose you've been sending me those notices of meetings? – I'm not interested. Don't you know I'm not a Welshman?'
>
> Rees let go.
>
> 'Born and bred in Wales, but not a Welshman. Ay, ay, that's it. Christ, I was forgetting.' He looked at Simon in the same ironic way that little Ieuan Richards once had done, using the same words –
>
> 'No – you're not a Welshman. You're a Jew.'[25]

* Yr hen iaith: the old language.

The irony on Rees's part (as it had been on Ieuan Richards's part in an earlier section of the book dealing with Simon's childhood) is not hostility, but bemusement at Simon's 'self-hatred' both as a Welshman and as a Jew. For his assimilationist desires, Simon is set up for one humiliation after another, and his final redemption as a British soldier dying in Palestine becomes an inevitable if ambiguous conclusion. Along the way Tobias mocks him continually, though with considerable sympathy, for his self-delusions and his attempts to 'pass' as an Englishman, and she consistently situates his attitudes to his Jewishness in close relationship to his attitudes to Welshness.

In one scene, set against the symbolically English background of Hampton Court, his inevitable later 'outing' as a Jew is foreshadowed.[26] Here Simon explains to Edith, whom he believes to be a paragon of Englishness, his desire to work in the civil service. Not realising that Edith is also Jewish, he attempts to avoid the question of his own Jewishness:

> 'You see, I always wanted it, not as a career, but because it would identify my life completely with my country. I wanted to serve England and feel myself part of her. Things around were so – different.'
> . . . 'You mean the Welsh life? Of course, not being Welsh, you wouldn't care to identify yourself with *that* —— '
> 'Good Heavens, no! You couldn't expect it, surely?'
> 'No. It wouldn't be natural. Though I've noticed that the Welsh themselves don't care to, either —— '
> '*That's* natural enough.'
> 'Oh no, it isn't. How can you say so? With all your feeling about history! It's natural that Welshmen should be conscious of their own, and wish to preserve it. I was wrong in saying that about the Welsh just now. Many of them are traitors, of course. But not all.'
> 'Traitors!' Simon was a little put out by the diversion, but he was faintly amused . . .
> 'Yes – to their past. You know as well as I do that their records go further back than this ——'
> 'To savagery,' said Simon.[27]

Edith reminds Simon that 'the Tudors had Welsh blood in them', to which he responds: '"I hope you haven't any."' But Edith protests: '"If I had, I shouldn't disown it . . . I have nothing but admiration for the Welshmen who maintain their nationality"' (pp. 164–5).

Neither Simon nor Edith know that the other is Jewish; indeed 'passing' as gentiles is the subtext of the whole discussion and of the scene that follows, when the two are joined by Edith's cousin, who also conceals his Jewishness, and a friend, a nurse, who has brought her elderly and somewhat confused patient in a wheelchair to visit Hampton Court. This woman wakes suddenly from a nap and calls tremulously: "'Nurse! There are Jews here – nasty horrid Jews! Send them away'" (p. 167).

There is a subtle distinction made by Davies and by Edith: 'sympathy' is considered natural, but 'identifying' with another culture is not. Throughout the novel the comparison of the barriers to Welsh and Jewish entry into English life is didactic. What is available to both groups – the partial, anxious status allowed them – is unsatisfactory and ultimately is not sustainable; self-realisation is only attainable through a commitment to the national project. Consciousness of difference from the dominant culture, the claim of a national past, the hope of a national future, and a racial or national sense of self is shared by both groups. Thus, like D. Wynne Evans, but for different purposes, Tobias posits a close affinity between Welsh and Jewish identity in an oppositional relation to Englishness.

The Samaritan, the sequel to *My Mother's House*, opens in Palestine, where Edith is now the widow of Simon. Edith returns to the subject of sympathy between the two cultures when she takes Musa, the Samaritan of the title, back to Wales with her. By 1938, when the book was finished, the earlier overt political comparison of Welsh and Jewish nationhood made by Tobias has been replaced by a more diffuse sensitivity to the dire social conditions in Wales in the 1930s.[28] In this novel it is Musa who notes and absorbs the distinctiveness of the place and people:

> The change of speech struck his keen ear. He had learned already that another race inhabited the British principality that was once a separate kingdom . . . he burst into a spate of questions. Had the Welsh merged into the English? Did their common tongue supersede the Celtic vernacular? Were their institutions, their system of religion and education, identical? Was there complete political equity?[29]

With the observation that Musa was 'almost disappointed that the Welsh language did not resemble Hebrew except in sounds like "ch" and the broad "a", emphasised in the ubiquitous Biblical names', it would appear that Tobias neither observed any structural similarity between the two languages, nor was aware of – or chose to ignore – the tradition that attributes to Welsh a linguistic descent from Hebrew.[30]

While Tobias does not cite any of the Welsh-Hebrew comparisons present in the turn of the century compilations by D. Wynne Evans, she does compare Wales and Palestine as physical entities. In *The Samaritan*, Edith describes Wales as "'the little country – no larger" – she quoted inversely the famous parallel – "than the Land of Israel"'.[31] She adds: "'There are many Welshmen to whom it *is* the Land of Israel, since they believe they are descended from one of the Lost Tribes."'

Musa treats this as an exaggeration, until he sees, 'in driving through the valleys, a chain of chapels called Zion, Bethel, Jerusalem, Carmel, and other familiar place-names of Palestine'.[32] Moreover, Tobias makes an ethnic comparison, for Musa expresses astonishment that 'the little dark people are just like Jews' (p. 178). In turn, the familiarity of the biblical terrain prompts Isaac Tudor, a Welsh official in Mandate Palestine, to comment:

> 'Next to dear old Wales, I always wanted to be in the Land of the Bible. When I was in Sunday School I could draw a map of the land from Dan to Beersheba, easier than I could draw the mountains of Wales . . . And the shape of the hills of Gilboa and the Carmel were as plain to my eyes as they are now.' (p. 39)

Despite these familiar motifs of political and national comparison, Tobias does not draw parallels between the physical appearance of the countries. Indeed the observations by Isaac Tudor might indicate that comparisons are not necessarily the equations John Harvey suggests them to be in *Image of the Invisible.*

The tender attitude to Palestine and the respect for its biblical landscape expressed by this Welshman, Isaac Tudor, is in sharp contrast to that of an English Mandate official who intervenes in an Arab riot, a riot which provides the opening scene of the novel:

> 'Blasted women! Blasted niggers! Blasted sheenies!' He wiped his face . . . Bad enough to stew in this filthy hole when all was quiet, the natives behaving themselves, and only an impudent colonist poking his nose in occasionally. Nearly two years since he'd left Tilbury – it seemed like ten. A vision of London streets, Hyde Park, the river, Hampstead Garden Suburb . . . flashed against the reeking cobbles of this arid mountain-side, sucked eternally by the Eastern sun.[33]

The distinction that Tobias makes between Welsh and English attitudes to the physical place and peoples of Palestine appeals simultaneously to two kinds of Welsh support for Jewish aspirations in Palestine: on the one hand, it plays on the resonances of the Welsh-Israelite biblical tradition, and on the other, it serves to give moral primacy to Welsh nationalist attitudes over English colonialist attitudes. Such a comparison and moral reinforcement was made implicitly in *Y Ddraig Goch* some years later, in the accounts, discussed in the previous chapter, by a returning soldier who compared English attitudes to the Welsh, the Jews and Arabs. The claim that attitudes to Jews are the barometer of 'morally pure' Welsh nationalism, which is implicit in the case of the soldier in *Y Ddraig Goch*, and explicit in the case of D. Wynne Evans, is powerfully underlined here and elsewhere by Tobias.

It is curious, however, that she does not invoke older linguistic and ethnic comparisons. Indeed, rather than an awareness of 'traditional Welsh historiography', her material suggests the influence of millenarian discourse, with its strong conversionist subtext.[34] Nevertheless, despite the insistence on Jewish separateness by Leah in 'The Nationalists', Tobias's work does not betray any anxiety about conversionism. Nor, except in passing, does she make reference to the British-Israel theory, and even when it does make a small appearance, in *My Mother's House*, it is arguably neutral: Simon, unable to account in any other way for Edith's revelation that she is a Jew, asks, '"You were not bringing up the British Israel, Lost Ten Tribes business, were you?"'[35]

Millenarian belief is portrayed by Tobias as a positive, if occasionally puzzling, phenomenon. The most notable example occurs in the short story 'Glasshouses', which, like 'The Nationalists', was largely written before the First World War. Sheba, a Jewish girl working in a village glazier's shop, objects to the derisive laughter that a co-worker directs at the poor English of an immigrant Jew named Zacutta. As evidence that it is not only immigrant Jews who lack mastery over English, Sheba produces a barely literate order for glass written by a 'Christmas Jones', whose first language is Welsh.[36] Christmas Jones, it transpires, is uncle of Sheba's co-worker, and when Sheba meets him to propose that he employ Zacutta, the destitute Jew, he greets her with a quintessential End-of-Days exclamation:

> 'Merch annwyl [dear girl], and proud I am to meet you, for sure. Why, I do love the Jews, indeed I do. You are the people of the book and the lord will show His wonders through you yet. You have got a big job in front of you my gell . . . the return to Zion . . . Oh that I could live to see the day!'[37]

Christmas Jones responds with delight to the idea of employing Zacutta, the refugee: '"I would be telling him it is the Lord's will, and the sign that the prophecies are coming true. For, indeed, if the afflictions have come true, it is certain that the joy and happiness will come after,"' he says.[38]

This character reappears in *The Samaritan*, where he is once again glad to help a Jewish refugee. He is passionately interested in Jews, buying the glass for his market garden greenhouses from a Jewish shop solely because of its owners' Jewishness. His response to the idea of hiring a Jew is a slight elaboration of that in 'Glasshouses':

'Tell him it is the Lord's will that the People of the Book should suffer persecution – it is a sign that the prophecies are coming true. For sure it is, if the
afflictions are come to pass, that the joy and happiness will be coming after. . .'
And he quoted Isaiah, 'The ransomed of the Lord shall return – sorrow and
sighing shall flee away.'[39]

However, if Christmas Jones believed in 'the Return to Zion', and his
enthusiasms in *The Samaritan* are portrayed in sympathetic terms, this
does not extend to his daughter, Tegwen Jones, who is intent on visiting
Palestine as a missionary. She claims the Balfour Declaration is a fulfilment of her father's predictions, but tells Edith and Musa, who are visiting
the unemployed worker settlement where she is employed as an assistant:
'"Only God could make the Jews return to Zion. It's like the Day of
Judgement, only previous-like."'[40] With Tegwen, unusually, Tobias
touches on the disjuncture between the notional Jews of the Bible and the
reality of present-day living Jews: Tegwen is deeply discomfited by Musa,
the Samaritan, who talks casually about '"the Jew of Nazareth . . . who
walked much about my home"', and by her employer, Dick Partingdale,
who reiterates Musa's point that Jesus was a Jew:

> Tegwen found herself confused always by Dick Partingdale. The trouble
> seemed to be that she was a believer in the Bible, not a Socialist. She believed
> in people keeping in their place. Of course Jews were in their place in the Old
> Testament. But in the New – well, one didn't think quite in that way of Jews
> and Jesus.[41]

As with Christmas Jones in *The Samaritan* and in 'Glasshouses', Tobias
puts millenarian rhetoric and understanding to Zionist use in the person of
Meurig Lloyd in *My Mother's House*. Meurig Lloyd, also known as 'Lloyd
Patagonia' because he has returned from the Welsh colony in Argentina, is
reported to be 'cracked on the Jews', and, according to his daughter, he
believes that 'the Jews are the best people in the world'.[42] Like Christmas
Jones, who is portrayed as an outsider to the anglicised middle-class town
environment in which both 'Glasshouses' and parts of *My Mother's House*
and *The Samaritan* are set, Meurig Lloyd is portrayed as an outsider to
Blaemawe (a fictionalised Ystalyfera) – in his case, on account of his
distinct north Wales Welsh pronunciation, his Sabbatarianism, his nationalism, and his 'amorphous humanism'.[43] The attitudes that they express
therefore towards 'the People of the Book' are representative of
Welsh-speaking Wales, but, at the same time, representative of a minority
view in the south Wales context.

In *The Samaritan*, Tobias promotes the mutual sympathy between the
two cultures, which in turn legitimises Zionist claims: here the Welsh

situation is very much a secondary concern. This contrasts with several of her stories and with the novel *My Mother's House*, where the purpose of the comparison appears to be more one of mutual political legitimisation. Nevertheless, evident in all her work is a concern with the importance of maintaining cultural identity and traditions. Her fiction as a whole can be seen as a polemical effort against assimilation and deracination, and while her primary concern is with Jewish culture and identity and the need for Jewish national self-determination, she consistently situates that concern within a comparative Welsh cultural and political context.

Alfred Zimmern: nationalism and Celtic Orientalism

Tobias's formulation of nationality owes a great deal to Alfred Zimmern, one of the progenitors of International Relations as a field of study. Zimmern held the first Chair in International Relations at Aberystwyth from 1919 to 1921, before he was forced to resign over what was seen as his scandalous marriage to a divorcee. He was the first writer to frame the tripartite social and economic structure of Wales that was picked up by historian Dai Smith; it was subsequently adapted by Denis Balsom in 'The Three Wales Model'.[44] Indeed, though Zimmern is not often acknowledged, his 'Welsh' Wales and 'American' Wales became something of a historical trope.[45] It was Zimmern who observed in 1921:

> Firstly, the Wales of to-day is not a unity. There is not one Wales; there are three Wales. There is Welsh Wales; there is industrial, or, as I sometimes think of it, American Wales; and there is upper-class or English Wales.[46]

In 1985 Denis Balsom adapts this structure in his 'The Three Wales Model' to map political and language demographics, but in 2003 the challenge to this tripartite structure by Jane Aaron suggests that the neat division made by Zimmern in 1921 is no longer such a useful one.[47]

Zimmern lectured in Cardiff to the Jewish Student Union on the subject of Martin Buber in 1921, and the same year published the pamphlet *My Impressions of Wales*, but this was preceded by several articles on the subject of nationality and nationalism in *The Welsh Outlook*, in which he often criticises the Welsh for their lack of pride in their own culture.

In *My Impressions of Wales*, Zimmern develops the motif of an oriental origin for the Welsh, which had been proposed earlier by D. Wynne Evans (and centuries before that by Theophilus Evans, compiling from Charles Edwards and other sources). It is the same motif that was to be repeated just two years later, in 1923, by Caradoc Evans. The chronology suggests again that Evans's formulation was expressing something very much more complex than a stereotyped hostility to Jews. Zimmern's proposal of oriental origins, however, is conjoined with the immediately recognisable motif of Welsh familiarity with the geography of biblical Palestine:

> There is, indeed, something Eastern in the quality of the Welsh soul. It is not an accident which sets a Bethel and a Moriah, a Salem and a Shiloh, in Welsh countryside hamlets, or causes Welsh boys and girls to be almost more familiar with the geography of Palestine than of their own country.[48]

Zimmern goes further, however, for earlier, in 1917, he had depicted the Welsh as a colonised people with an eastern soul, thus situating the Welsh within the colonial and imperial Orientalist discourse explored by Edward Said in *Orientalism*.[49] In 'The Oldest British Colony', published in *The Welsh Outlook*, Zimmern describes England's first colony, Wales, as a pre-conquest untouched paradise, in which the Welsh disport themselves as a species of Celtic Noble Savage, as per the characterisation of the Welsh by Henry Rowlands in his 1723 publication, *Mona Antiqua Restaurata*.[50] Wales is, 'or was, before its colonisation, a beautiful land of rolling downs and pastures and running waters, framed by nature to be the home of a proud and independent race of dalesmen'.[51] However, the Celtic native differs from other colonial subjects: according to Zimmern, the natives in this 'oldest of the British possession . . . unlike the natives in many of our Colonies, are not heathens, but agelong and fervent adherents of the Christian faith'.[52]

Some years later he warns against the poisonous effects of a sense of inferiority among the Welsh, observing that 'there can be detected in the life of Wales today characteristics that are the mark, not of a great free people, but of a small and subject people'.[53] His imaging of the Welsh as simultaneously colonised subject and Celtic Noble Savage infused with a (Jewish) semitic soul and origin, constitutes a rather different kind of Orientalism than that explored by postcolonialist critics such as Edward Said.

Although from a fully assimilated family that was also Christian by faith, Zimmern explains that his outlook was informed by an awareness of his ineradicable Jewishness (though he carefully avoids identifying himself as such); like those hapless assimilated Jews in Lily Tobias's work who wanted to pass, but couldn't, his nationality (or ethnicity) means that he cannot be quite an Englishman. This, he explains, in an essay entitled 'True or False Nationalisms', is the source of his politicisation:

> I learnt to value Nationality, not from reading Mazzini's essays . . . nor from sympathising with European Nationalist movements . . . but from realising, as I grew to manhood, that I was not an Englishman, and from my sense of the

debt I owe to the heritage with which I am connected by blood and tradition.[54]

Although Zimmern only examines Welsh and Jewish national aspirations in the context of a wider survey of small nationalities, including Irish, Armenian and Polish examples, he does, like Lily Tobias, once again draw connections between Welsh and Jewish resistance to cultural assimilation.[55] In 'The International Settlement and Small Nationalities', published in *The Welsh Outlook* in 1919, he asks:

> just as in Park Lane and Maida Vale we can watch the unhappy transformation of the genuine Jew into what has been described as the amateur Gentile, is there not, I would ask in some of our Welsh institutions and social circles a similar tendency to turn the sons and daughters of the Principality, fresh from their native hills and tingling with the rude and perennial vigour of ancestral Wales, into amateur Englishmen and English-women, painfully adjusting their natural joyousness and Celtic *abandon* to the stiff collar, the starched shirt front and the impeccable self-control of the traditional type of English gentleman?[56]

This combination of 'wild Celt' and 'genuine Jew' is echoed in a reference to the Welsh-Israelite biblical tradition in the later *My Impressions of Wales*, where Zimmern observes that, unlike England, 'Wales has always set her gaze in a very different direction – towards the far hills of the Promised Land. When the young Welshman finds that his Pisgah-vision sets towards Downing Street and Whitehall . . . it is time that he reflected and sought to take his bearings once again.'[57]

In these publications, Zimmern, unlike Tobias, was not seeking to legitimise a Zionist ideology, or reinforce Jewish 'welcome' in Wales; instead, he was arguing in a Welsh context for the value of Welsh cultural particularity and Welsh political and national – if not necessarily nationalist – consciousness.

REFUGE AND RETREAT

Such subject matter almost entirely bypasses the next generation of Welsh Jewish writers, including Dannie Abse, Bernice Rubens, Maurice Edelman, Mervyn Levy and Sonia Birch-Jones. When, rarely, it does appear in the work of Bernice Rubens, for example, Welsh national identification and national aspirations are the target of satire or mockery. In her novels *Yesterday in the Back Lane* (1995), and *The Waiting Game* (1997), one-dimensional Welsh and Scottish characters who express nationalist sentiments are lampooned. In the latter novel, they provide the rather over-stated comic relief, in contrast to the more fully realised Jewish protagonist.[58] Reference by Rubens to a relationship between the two cultures is equally glancing. In her epic novel *Brothers*, a Welsh woman is untroubled by a new Jewish son-in-law because of that familiar eastern origin: 'The fact that he was a Jew did not disturb her. She regarded the Welsh as part of the lost tribes of Israel.'[59]

What several of these writers share instead, both with one another and with earlier writers such as Tobias, is an anxiety about 'dominant culture' hostility to Jews, and a related designation of Wales as a refuge from Jewish affliction. However, as I have argued elsewhere, such refuge is nevertheless usually qualified by an understanding of Jews as being perpetually vulnerable.[60] Although this is most explicit in the work of Tobias, who is the only overtly Zionist Welsh Jewish writer, such a qualification among other authors still effectively reinforces the legitimacy of the Zionist narrative: the possibility of only ever finding an uneasy haven from affliction often implicitly presents Jewish statehood as, ultimately, the sole viable refuge.

The designation of Wales as a refuge, or even in some cases as a shtetl, constitutes a perhaps not entirely coincidental variation on the image of Wales as a bulwark against the dangers of modernity, which appears in Saunders Lewis's *Buchedd Garmon*, Geraint Goodwin's Welsh border village anxieties, Harri Webb's 'green desert', or the repeating motif of 'y pentre gwyn', which Hywel Teifi Edwards explores so compellingly. Rather tellingly, in a discussion of Bernice Rubens's novel *Set on Edge*, Michael Woolf suggests that 'the location could be Rubens' native Wales or any other small town'.[61] Reconstituting Wales in its entirety as a small town reflects accurately – if in an accidental slippage – the underlying orientation of Rubens's own work, an orientation that may also be found in that of Dannie Abse.

The critical response to these best-known Welsh Jewish writers has helped to reinforce such a reduction of Welsh cultural complexity, but this perception is more explicit among the group of émigré Jewish writers and artists (and their critics) who took up residence or bought holiday homes in Wales between the 1940s and 1960s. Part of the so-called Bloomsbury of north Wales, these émigré Jews, clustered in and around the Croesor valley, discuss Wales not as a refuge from antisemitism so much as a retreat from metropolitan England. For many of them, including Eric Hobsbawm, Wales is imagined in reduced and simplistic terms, and the cultural and political reality around them registers almost exclusively as a hostile and unpalatable nationalism, to which they in turn respond with suspicion and denigration. But there are exceptions, too – most notably the case of two Jewish refugees from Nazi persecution: the painter Josef Herman and the writer and archaeologist Kate Bosse-Griffiths.

Josef Herman and Kate Bosse-Griffiths: from refuge to home
The artist Josef Herman made a home in Wales after he fled Poland in the 1930s. He had grown up in Warsaw, and his early work focused primarily on Jewish subject matter. Although his writing reveals a privileging of his Jewish identity, and although his well-known depiction of Welsh miners suggests something of the role of spectator, he is nevertheless sensitive in his work to the Welsh cultural environment. He allegedly found the subject matter and the 'idiom' for his life's work in Ystradgynlais and, according to his second wife, Nini Herman, he 'lost his heart to Wales – where his memory is enshrined as a legend, part of the folklore, a myth'.[62] Nevertheless, the manner in which he depicted the mining community was not universally embraced. Art critic John Berger claimed that in his paintings of miners Herman substituted endurance for hope. In an obituary of Herman, Ozi Rhys Osmond cites the imaging of endurance as a response to the 'group solidarity of communitarian culture which the mining tribe represented' to the artist, but Herman's writing itself goes some way to reinforcing the claim made by Berger.[63] In his diary, Herman notes 'the splendid symmetry of the tip so clear; within its triangular body the secret of long endurance', and of slate workers in north Wales he remarks: 'Quarrymen like miners, a million years of work.'[64]

Herman's writing also suggests how he saw those around him as monumental, universalised figures, for he renders them in simplified and representative terms, citing 'those splendid Welsh voices and their primitive veracity', or describing how 'it is this traditional passion, this monumental appearance, that broadens the local and incidental, and the once individual becomes typical and symbolic'.[65] Perhaps as suggestive of his attitude is his assertion that 'what makes the group so singular outside is but the strong similarity within the group'.[66] Herman's designation of the miner as a 'walking monument to labour'[67] certainly reduces individual and social complexity in problematic ways, but the objection by John Berger that Herman depicted the miners 'as if they were peasants, instead of one of the most lively and militant sections of the proletariat' highlights the de-politicisation that is also evident in Herman's work.[68] An objection similar to that made by Berger could be made against Herman's later imaging of and commentary on kibbutzniks, whose extreme left politicisation doubles the visual resonance between these images and those of the miners in Ystradgynlais. Interestingly, Herman's kibbutznik images differ as strongly from his Polish and Scottish-era imaging of the Jewish community as does the language he uses to describe them: the 'new Jew', he writes, has 'an entity and completeness all its own, typified in one particular representative . . . the kibbutznik . . . who transmits his example and purpose to his fellow countrymen. Earthy, in pale khaki, heavy-postured, he differs from peasants the world over by his wider consciousness . . . larger than life, proud of his humanity.'[69]

While this description clearly privileges his Jewish consciousness, nevertheless the visual idiom Herman developed in Wales entailed the loss of Jewish sensitivity and subject matter in his painting. His images of Jewish life in Poland – rendered as a memorialisation on his arrival as a refugee in Scotland – are intimate and personal, and, it might be said, more sensitive in cultural terms than his Welsh painting. However, this work of the early 1940s is largely forgotten and was certainly marginalised by him: it was while in a state of distress in Ystradgynlais in 1948, after hearing the detail of how his family had been killed by the Nazis, that he burnt material from this period, dismissing it as sentimental and derivative. 'I was not at all sorry to part with a lot of the works I did in Glasgow', he writes in his journal. 'I know exactly how I got on to this Chagallic trick but it has no longer any interest for me. Charm cannot be a substitute for good painting.'[70] It was only later that he found some surviving paintings, which led to his exhibition entitled 'Memory of Memories' in 1985. In the catalogue to that exhibition, he presents a more forgiving attitude to his work than the one revealed in his journal of 1948. 'At that time I painted and drew solely Jewish themes', he recalls. 'They may well belong to that Jewish tradition which culminated in the genius of Chagall, but I believe there is something in them which I can rightly call my own . . . deep down I know that they are part of me, a memory of memories. People, theatre, stories, life, they all evoked nostalgia; and this nostalgia is the background of these drawings.'[71]

Herman's nostalgia for the Yiddish-language environment in which he grew up is palpable in the account he gives of meeting a Welsh Jewish miner called Moishe. This account appears in a *Jewish Quarterly* article entitled 'Strange Son of the Valley'. Here his description of a Yiddish book, published by the Swansea Jewish Debating Society in 1904 and shown to him by Moishe, is wistful and yearning: 'The pages of cheap paper were yellowish and smelt like wet chalk, yet they breathed as if alive, sounded alive like an echo of times that never really disappear, for they are layers in the mountain of our history.'[72]

Not surprisingly, Herman's description of Moishe and his Yiddish book suggests a sensitivity to the complex world of Jewish linguistic and cultural history that is absent from his descriptions of the Welsh environment. It is ironic that, arguably, it was by abandoning this particularity in his work that he achieved popular success: by abandoning Jewish subject matter, and transforming particular Welsh experience into something universal, he became a successful Jewish artist. Consequently, although his so-called epiphany on the bridge in Ystradgynlais is read as a moment of inspiration, in the consideration of Herman as a *Jewish* artist, it may be read as a moment of loss.[73]

Herman was not included in the first survey of Welsh Jewish writing, which Mimi Josephson attempted in 1958 in the influential journal *Wales*. In that article, she laments that 'the ranks of Jewish-Welsh writers today are so thin' – but if she had included immigrants and Welsh-language writing in her survey, she would have had less cause for regret.[74] Aside from Josef Herman, one of the most important authors she overlooks on both counts is Kate Bosse-Griffiths, a writer who, like Herman, genuinely did find unqualified refuge in Wales.

Born into an upper-class German family with an assimilated mother, Kate Bosse-Griffiths worked as an Egyptologist until in 1936 she was dismissed from her post at the Berlin State Museums because she was Jewish. She left for the UK, where she met and married J. Gwyn Griffiths, and moved with him in 1939 to Pentre, in the Rhondda. There they hosted the Cylch Cadwgan literary group which drew together a number of left-wing, pacifist, nationalist writers who sought to bring a new international influence to bear on Welsh-language literature. Together with others, they also edited the monthly literary journal *Y Fflam*, and subsequent to their move to Swansea, Bosse-Griffiths became honorary curator of the Swansea Museum.

Bosse-Griffiths's mother died in Ravensbrück, but this family background and Jewish questions are largely absent from her published work. Nevertheless, it may be read as a subtext in her writing, and its influence is clearest in her poetry, most of which is written in German. Robat Gruffudd observes of his mother that 'her terrible experiences in the war, and her mother's death in Ravensbrück, formed her attitude to life. She took few things seriously and was totally anti-materialist . . . I believe her attitudes were very Jewish. Certainly she was the archetypal Jewish mother, simultaneously generous and demanding.'[75] Robat's brother Heini Gruffudd suggests that after fleeing Germany their mother closed the door on the difficult past, and embraced fully her new life in Wales.[76]

Nevertheless, Bosse-Griffiths writes movingly of suffering and loss, particularly as experienced by those in exile. In the short story 'Y Crwban' (The Tortoise), which was published in 1941, she portrays the liberal émigré and refugee circles with which she herself was associated on her arrival in Britain, and the alienation experienced by political exiles, both Jewish and non-Jewish. The year after 'Y Crwban' appeared, she won a short story prize at the National Eisteddfod, where the complimentary adjudication by the giant of Welsh-language literature, Kate Roberts, was perhaps more valuable than the prize money of £2. This short story and 'Y Crwban' were included in Bosse-Griffiths's first collection, *Fy Chwaer Efa a Storïau Eraill* (My Sister Eva and Other Stories), which appeared in 1944 and was republished, with several additional stories, as *Cariadau* (Loves), in 1995.[77]

The treatment of women in her fiction, and her portrayal of sexually frank and liberal attitudes, was seen as radical and fresh within Welsh-language literature, and her first novel, *Anesmwyth Hoen* (1941) was also a prize-winner. Her controversial second novel, *Mae'r Galon wrth y Llyw* (The Heart is at the Helm), published in 1957, depicts the stifling of individual aspirations and desires in a constraining nonconformist chapel culture, and along the way touches sensitively on the social tensions that Muslims face in the West.[78]

Despite its clear Welsh location and cultural context, she incorporates aspects of a personal family story whose protagonists perhaps encountered a similar Protestant constraint in the Germany of her youth. Here, as in the story 'Fy Chwaer Efa', Bosse-Griffiths criticises what she sees as the hollowness and hypocrisy of socially organised religion. However, according to her husband, what caused controversy with this novel was not the pejorative depiction of religious attitudes so much as the failure on the part of the author to condemn as immoral the adultery of the protagonists.[79]

Curiously, in the same novel, the discussion between the protagonists at an exhibition of paintings by Evan Walters reinforces, by its sensitivity to the local and particular in Walters's work, the problems that have been identified in Herman's depiction of depoliticised and de-localised miners. The protagonist, Arthur, musing on what he might paint were he an artist, imagines paintings that are attributable to Walters: "'Dyna un darlun a fyddai'n siwr o'm gwneud yn enwog – 'Mater Dolorosa a'r Cwm Glo'. Mam yn dal glowr marw yn ei breichiau'" ('There's one picture that would be sure to make me famous – 'Mater Dolorosa and the Mining Valley'. A mother holding a dead miner in her arms').[80] This is evidently the now well-known *pietà* painted by Walters.

In addition to her fiction and poetry, Bosse-Griffiths published many non-fiction works in Welsh, and wrote voluminously on archaeology and Egyptology in Welsh, English and German. Indeed, according to her sons, she was more interested in Egyptian religion than Judaism, but her Jewishness was something she nevertheless embraced. Given the general post-war silence about the Holocaust, it is no surprise that she should not address her identity as a Jew in her published work. Nevertheless, the delicate evasion achieved by Marion Löffler who describes her as 'the daughter of a Jewish woman', is perhaps a misunderstanding of such silence.[81]

It was in her treatment of German culture that Bosse-Griffiths engaged subtextually with her German-Jewish identity, writing, for example, about three fellow German-speaking Jews – Arnold Zweig, Stefan Zweig and Ernst Toller – who, like her, had been forced to flee. However, rather than dwelling on their identity as Jews, she discusses their international, socialist and anti-war commitments.[82]

The efforts by Bosse-Griffiths in Wales, and in Welsh, to challenge the demonisation of Germany during the war must have been a lonely endeavour. In her first story, 'Rhosynnau' (Roses), published in 1940, the pariah status of a girl who is criticised for laying flowers on the grave of a German pilot shot down over her village, suggests something of the isolation that Bosse-Griffiths herself may have felt. This internationalist and pacifist ethos was intertwined with Bosse-Griffiths's Plaid Cymru politics and Cymdeithas yr Iaith Gymraeg activism, and was also central to the discussions and publications of Cylch Cadwgan, the influential group of writers who met in her home in the Rhondda in the 1940s.

The Bloomsbury of north Wales
Such an engagement by Kate Bosse-Griffiths was in sharp contrast to the group of Jewish writers and artists who congregated between the 1940s and the 1960s in and around Portmeirion and the highbrow culture created there by Clough and Amabel Williams-Ellis. The group included German-Jewish writer and painter Fred Uhlman; Arthur Koestler, who lived for five years in a farmhouse in Ffestiniog, where he wrote *Thieves in the Night*; German-Jewish novelist Robert Neumann, who owned a house in Penrhyndeudraeth; and, for a period, the painter Martin Bloch. Although Josef Herman lived in Ystradgynlais from 1944 to 1955, he also worked in

the north Wales slate quarries at the same time as Bloch. The group of writers and artists nicknamed 'the Welsh Bloomsbury set' by Rupert Crawshay Williams, according to Eric Hobsbawm, was by no means exclusively Jewish – on the contrary, Bertrand Russell was perhaps the best-known intellectual present, and served as a magnet for others.

The Jewish artists and intellectuals who had left continental Europe in the mid-1930s had been thrown together in London as an émigré community.[83] This was a community with which Kate Bosse-Griffiths was also briefly associated: she too had been assisted by Amabel Williams-Ellis. After the outbreak of war many German-Jewish intellectuals were interned together as enemy nationals on the Isle of Man, among them Fred Uhlman and Robert Neumann. It is not clear whether it was in London, or the Isle of Man, or through the Williams-Ellises that personal connections between them were forged, but these were considerable. Josef Herman and Martin Bloch knew one another well and exhibited together, and with Fred Uhlman, in London. Uhlman and Herman were also close associates.[84] Koestler, in Ffestiniog between 1944 and 1949, also knew Uhlman: he later wrote the introduction to Uhlman's novel *Reunion*.[85] David Cesarani suggests that Koestler probably knew Uhlman from London, where he was also a close associate of Robert Neumann, while Anna Plodeck believes that Uhlman probably made a connection with Wales when he and his wife holidayed in Portmeirion in 1941.[86] It is likely that it was Amabel Williams-Ellis who provided the connection in London, where she had been a journalist espousing left-wing causes.[87] Uhlman bought his farmhouse from the Williams-Ellises, and published *An Artist in North Wales* in 1946 with Clough Williams-Ellis.[88]

There are several accounts of this so-called north Wales Bloomsbury set, both historical and fictional. In his biography of Bertrand Russell, who owned a house in Ffestiniog from 1946, Rupert Crawshay Williams gives credit to the eccentric creators of Portmeirion, observing that 'it must I think be something to do with the "ambience" of Clough and Amabel Williams-Ellis themselves, which attracts interesting people. Indeed, as somebody once complained, one finds an intellectual under every stone in the Croesor valley.'[89] Bertrand Russell is reputed to have said that 'all one had to do . . . was to sit in Portmeirion or the Croesor valley and eventually everybody would pass by'.[90] In the foreword to Jeremy Brooks's *Jampot Smith*, republished in 2008 in the Library of Wales series, Mervyn Jones recalls this very community, of which his father and Jeremy Brooks were a part, but overlooks the quite significant portion of it made up by Jewish artists and writers.[91]

These artists and writers did not choose the rural retreat of the pictur-esque, but opted instead for the harsh realities of mining communities – in the south and in the north – and all found retreat in Welsh-speaking communities. A partial answer to whether they sought *refuge*, as such, in Wales, and from what they were seeking such refuge, may be found in Richard Dove's work on German-Jewish émigré writers. He cites a letter from Stefan Zweig to Robert Neumann, in which the author states that he seeks to 'emigrate from the emigration'.[92] One may infer that, quite aside from the effect of the wartime bombing of London, the stultifying and apparently neurotic atmosphere in the émigré Jewish community also proved difficult to manage. Another possible explanation is more specula-tive: as continental Jews, and in particular as German-speaking Jews, it is entirely possible that it was in Welsh-speaking Wales that some of these refugees could find peace – not so much from antisemitism, as from English anti-Germanism. Fred Uhlman's son makes the suggestive obser-vation that his father 'didn't really integrate with the Welsh community, but he had a knack of getting on with local people, partly because he wasn't English and spoke with an amusing German accent'.[93]

Nevertheless, in his autobiography, it is apparent that Uhlman's percep-tion of himself was as a nascent Englishman. One might therefore equally speculate that perhaps in north Wales some of these German-Jewish émigrés might have been seen as outsiders not because of their German or Jewish identity, but because of their association with English incomers. Indeed, to English intellectuals who were also visiting that part of Wales, the émigrés may have felt more familiar and safer than the Welsh-speaking Welsh – that, at least, appears to have been the case for Eric Hobsbawm, discussed below.

Uhlman says nothing in his autobiography about the time that he spent in Wales. Both by this erasing of Wales, which was not only a crucial retreat for him but which also provided the subject matter for a great deal of his painting, and by the title of his autobiography, *The Making of an Englishman*, he suggests the perceptions of Wales perhaps shared by many of these émigrés. Indeed, in a prepublication letter quoted by Clough Williams-Ellis in Uhlman's *An Artist in North Wales*, Uhlman explains his attraction to Penrhyndeudraeth as being one of landscape:

> if someone should ask me what were the essential features I would reply: the loneliness and overwhelming grandeur of the country, the natural and almost primeval simplicity of the rock-like cottages, and the character of the inhabitants.[94]

Eric Hobsbawm on the Welsh

This suggestion of primitive native is explicit in the work of another Jewish visitor to north Wales, Eric Hobsbawm. Hobsbawm's autobiography, *Interesting Times: a Twentieth-Century Life*, reinforces the impression that many Jewish incomers formed little connection with, and were largely unaware of, the Welsh cultural life around them. Although it was in the early 1960s that he took up holiday residence in north Wales, many of the same people – including Uhlman, for example – lived or still retained holiday homes in and near the Croesor valley.

Like Leo Abse, Hobsbawm's Marxist-informed reaction to nationalism extends equally to Plaid Cymru as it does to Zionism. 'Britishness probably immunized me, fortunately, against the temptations of a Jewish nationalism', he observes; 'I have no emotional obligation to the practices of an ancestral religion and even less to the small, militarist, culturally disappointing and politically aggressive nation-state which asks for my solidarity on racial grounds'.[95] He values the state of diaspora and is caustically dismissive of the 'most fashionable posture of the turn of the new century, that of "the victim", the Jew who, on the strength of the Shoah . . . asserts unique claims on the world's conscience as a victim of persecution' (pp. 24–5).

These are familiar views from Leo Abse and, like Abse, Hobsbawm repeatedly resorts to the descriptors 'strident nationalism' and 'sullenly nationalist', which are so much a mark of the response on the left to the rise of Plaid Cymru, particularly during the 1979 Devolution debates. His image of a backward and primitive Welsh-language culture goes hand in hand with a designation of primitive nationalism:

> For most of the mountain people the Welsh language was chiefly a Noah's Ark in which they could survive the flood [of Anglophone modern civilization] . . . They turned inwards because they felt themselves to be in that most desperate of situations, that of a beleaguered, hopeless and permanent minority. But for some there was a solution: compulsory Cymricization, imposed by nationalist political rule. (p. 242)

Although Hobsbawm describes the breakdown in this society with some sympathy, he has little sympathy for political responses to that breakdown: in his view, the 'irresistible Anglophone flood of modern civilization' meant that this society, kept together in the past by isolation, 'poetry, puritanism and . . . general poverty', could not be shored up (pp. 242–3). Despite his nominal sympathy, it is clear that he places little value on the threatened culture that he observes. Indeed, his suggestion that 'R. S.

Thomas's great poems should not mislead us into thinking of most North Wales hill farmers as unintellectual hulks. A lot of Welsh reading and thinking went on under those low roofs' (p. 244), reinforces rather than challenges the stereotype of the primitive Welsh, while his observation about 'the inhabitants' indifference to visual aesthetics, so surprising in a people as receptive to music and words as the Welsh', suggests how strangely ill-informed he is about the culture he describes so breezily (p. 236). It is more remarkable, given his politics, that he should remain silent, in this context at least, about the extraordinary industrial labour history of the area where he lived, a history that fundamentally informs the attitudes of which he is, apparently, contemptuous.[96]

Perhaps more original and interesting than his comments about the Welsh are Hobsbawm's observations about the incomers, who, he suggests, came to Wales for 'the sheer physical discomfort' it offered: 'it made us feel closer to nature, or at least to the constant struggle against the forces of climate and geology which gives such satisfaction'.[97] He describes his fellow visitors as 'a curious population of permanent and semi-permanent settlers, or rather refugees, from outside . . . This community of incomers lived side by side with the indigenous Welsh, but divided from them, not only by language but, perhaps even more, by class, lifestyle and the growing separatism of the locals' (pp. 241–2).

Apparently with no consciousness of the impact of 'holiday homers' on a small community, nor the semantic weight of the word 'locals', Hobsbawm observes that in the valley there had been 'few close friendships across the "interracial divide"'(p. 242), and that the 'growth of nationalism soured relations with the Welsh' (p. 245). Uhlman could acknowledge that, 'in one way it's a tragedy. All the young people move away to find work. The old people prefer to go into council houses. So half of Hampstead has moved in.'[98] But Hobsbawm failed to engage with this social breakdown when he bemoaned the change in housing policy instituted by Clough Williams-Ellis's son. It was only in an English-speaking part of mid-Wales, where he and his family bought a new home, that he was able to find relief from what he calls the 'growing tensions of Croesor'.[99]

There is much research still to be done on the perceptions held by this émigré and refugee community, and its reception in north Wales. The evidence indicates that despite their use of Wales as a retreat and as subject matter, and despite prolonged contact with their 'host' community, many of these writers and artists did not engage with the life of the place in which they took refuge. Whether this is true, and if so, whether such non-engagement is due to the dominance of their Jewish concerns or to the assumption of common English attitudes, still remains to be explored.

Suggestive in this regard, however, is the Anglo-Jewish understanding of these relationships with Wales. A reviewer in *The Jewish Quarterly*, writing about Herman's 'Memory of Memories' exhibition, expresses puzzlement over the reasons for his move to a mining village in Wales after his involvement in the metropolitan art environment of Warsaw and Brussels.[100] With Fred Uhlman's death in 1985, the *Quarterly* mourned the fact that 'a whole generation of central European émigrés who came to this country in the 1930s and contributed so much to British culture, is gradually disappearing', but despite publishing a Welsh landscape alongside Uhlman's obituary, the journal fails to recognise the significance of Wales in his work, and focuses instead on his role in the cultural life of Hampstead in the 1930s. Tellingly, the article is entitled *From Émigré to Englishman*.[101]

JEWISH REINFORCEMENTS

How much does the evidence considered in this chapter suggest Jewish influence on the twentieth-century Welsh tradition of identification with Jews? Certainly there is nothing in the writing of the 'north Wales Bloomsbury set' to suggest any engagement with such a 'tradition'. There is little in Bernice Rubens, and although Dannie Abse invokes a cultural connection ('the relationship of David and Dafydd'), he describes it in purely literary, biblical terms, claiming that 'the older tradition permeates the younger'.[102] Similarly, neither Kate Bosse-Griffiths nor Josef Herman engage in published work with any such 'tradition', and it is entirely absent from the published fiction of the other prolific Welsh-Jewish writer of the twentieth century, Maurice Edelman. However, in an article in *The Jewish Chronicle* in 1963, Edelman does comment on the relationship, in a way that will be immediately familiar:

> Despite a very short period of tension in Tredegar before the First World War, the Jewish refugees were quickly absorbed into the warm community around them. Welsh non-conformists, with their deep respect for the Old Testament had a quick feeling for the Jewish minority.[103]

In a rather interesting development of cultural comparisons, Edelman concludes: 'If it is true that the air of Eretz Israel [the Land of Israel] makes men wise, it can also be said, I think, that the air of Wales makes men liberal.'

Edelman's article, 'To me it means home', appeared in a supplement in *The Jewish Chronicle* that featured several pieces on Wales. Another, by Lionel Simmonds, makes many of the comparisons originally catalogued in 1902 by D. Wynne Evans:

> To say that Welshmen and Jews have much in common is a gross understate-ment: culturally, spiritually and socially the similarity of the two peoples is remarkable. Even territorially the parallel is striking – the Principality of Wales and Monmouthshire comprises 8,006 square miles compared with Israel's 7,992 square miles.[104]

Simmonds goes on to describe Welsh and Jewish national character in ways that suggest very strongly a reading of Alfred Zimmern:

> Common nobility through common sufferance is matched by similarity of temperament. Welshmen and Jews lack the Anglo-Saxon sang-froid and inhibitedness. The livelier imaginative Celt is as noisy and boisterous as the Jew, who fits into the Welsh atmosphere with facility and less obtrusively than in England.[105]

The intended readership of these pieces is, presumably, primarily a Jewish one, and they appear before the rise in political temperature in the 1970s, when the association made by Leo Abse between nationalism and antisemitism effectively qualified that story of 'tolerance' and 'welcome' experienced by Jews. This association was also reinforced in the period in a series of articles by Geoffrey Alderman on the 1911 riot in Tredegar. The timing of these articles, which attribute widespread antisemitism to Wales in the Edwardian period, cannot be entirely coincidental or politically neutral. In the debate in the 1970s, Judith Maro's participation can be seen as a very clear Jewish reassertion of the tropes of close cultural association – as, indeed, can Leo Abse's, on the other side of the political divide. But between the 1930s and the 1970s, among the better-known Jewish writers who emerged in Wales, or who were associated in some way with Wales, there appears little engagement with any such 'tradition of identification'.

The earlier evidence – in the *South Wales Jewish Review*, in Lily Tobias's fiction, and in Alfred Zimmern's influential writings – suggests that if such a 'tradition of identification' was not an act of Jewish inven-tion, it was certainly promoted by Jews; indeed, it was promoted in overt political ways by Lily Tobias.

Curiously, and rather suggestively, a *Western Mail* review of Tobias's second novel, *My Mother's House*, contextualises the book in just this way, indicating how such a reinforcement occurs in a kind of iterative dialogue: 'Those who insist on the affinity of the Welsh and Jewish peoples would do well to read and ponder this extraordinarily powerful study of a young Jew, bred and born in Wales', the reviewer concludes.[106] That the reviewer identifies some as 'insisting' on this affinity suggests that such claims were, at the very least, contested. A review in *The Welsh Outlook* a year later makes a more practical comparison, echoing Zimmern: 'The subject of "My Mother's House" – the conflicting loyalties of a young Jew – will be new to most readers of the Welsh Outlook', the reviewer begins. 'Miss Tobias's work appeals to readers of Jewish blood . . . [y]et the problems confronting Simon Black are not really different from those confronting any young Welshman of distinction, tempted by "glittering prizes" to renounce his birthright.'[107]

It is evidently the case that 'semitic discourse' in its widest sense does occur in a dialogue with its subject. Nowhere is this more obvious than in the case of Judith Maro quoting Harri Webb, or Lily Tobias creating Welsh-speaking characters who serve as mouthpieces for Zionist aspirations. However, the celebration of the purported welcome that Judith Maro received also suggests a purposeful exchange in the promulgation of Wales as peculiarly tolerant. It is a conflation, perhaps, of 'tolerance' and 'identification' that has led to the rather grander claims that were made about Welsh philosemitism in the later twentieth century. Nevertheless, as some of the work considered here shows, even if Jewish writers have not necessarily originated such ideas, they have been as actively engaged in constructing and promoting notions of tolerance and 'affinity' for equally clear, though different, political purposes.

Conclusion

When, in 1979, Gwyn A. Williams asked his now-famous BBC Radio question, 'When was Wales?', he answered himself using a telling conjoined metaphor to describe the emergence of the Welsh:

> The relatively rapid rise of a powerful England turned the Welsh, almost from birth, penned as they were in a harshly poor upland economy staked to a bony mountain spine, into a marginal people. Talented but marginal, the talent probably a function of marginality, light of foot, light of spirit, light of plough, they lived by their wits, the Jews of the British Isles.[1]

This depiction by Williams of an emergent Wales in which the Welsh are characterised as Jews should not come as a surprise. Nor should it come as a surprise that Williams effectively erases the living Jews of Britain in the twelfth- to thirteenth-century period that he describes, and replaces them with the Welsh – and this at precisely the time when Jews were suffering oppression and would soon be exiled. This is a particularly complex illustration of how central Jews have been in the Welsh imagination – it is particularly complex in this case, given that in that defining period described by Williams, Llywelyn ap Gruffudd, the last Welsh prince, compared English oppression of the Welsh with English oppression of the Jews.[2]

How might one characterise this example by Williams of a now-familiar association? It is not positive; it is not negative; it invokes the biblical Jews and the experience of historical Jews, and at the same time erases them. The comparison here – the equation and erasure – are written into one of the most important and influential Welsh historical texts of the twentieth century. A slightly different but related comparison – and a different implicit erasure – was made in another famous and influential BBC Radio lecture, one that changed the course of the Welsh language: Saunders Lewis's 1962 'Tynged yr Iaith' (The Fate of the Language). In that lecture, Lewis compares the situation of Welsh as a national language with that of Hebrew in Israel – but, in doing so, he neglects entirely the costs that came with the 'success' of Hebrew, not least the impact of the domination of the Hebrew language on minority cultures and languages in Israel.

This survey has only touched the surface of such cultural comparisons, and new evidence keeps turning up. Scholars and friends, associates and strangers draw my attention to example after example – in a novel, a play, a poem, an article; slightly different, in curious juxtaposition, suggesting new possibilities, reinforcing old familiar associations.[3]

'The Jews' in some way, notional and historical, are embedded in Welsh consciousness in the nineteenth and twentieth centuries, and in less historical and more notional ways for a great deal longer than that. The tradition of Welsh identification with Jews may be an invention of the twentieth century, but Welsh interest in Jews – or some version of them – does indeed have roots in the deep past.

Of course it is possible to make a very different map of this terrain: one could trace other paths, and draw different conclusions. There is, for example, a bias in this study towards writing by men, which in part reflects an imbalance in the literature. Writing by men is better known in general, and therefore likely to be republished and commented upon, and hence imaging of Jews is likely to be closer to the surface, whereas, despite great efforts by scholars, writing by women still remains a somewhat specialist field. This is evident, for example, in the gender imbalance in the titles republished so far in the Library of Wales series.

In her survey of women's writing in Wales in the twentieth century, Katie Gramich identifies in Dilys Cadwaladr's 'Yr Hen Oruchwyliaeth' in *Storïau*, published in 1936, the 'disquieting caricature of a "greasy", exploitative Jew, echoing some of the pervasive antisemitism of the period'.[4] Nevertheless, it appears to be the case that where women writers use Jewish imaging it is usually unremarkable, which is to say that it is incidental rather than significant that a character is Jewish. Some of Dorothy Edwards's stories, for example, include characters who might be read as Jewish, but their Jewishness is marginal to the story and the constrained, claustrophobic atmosphere she creates.[5] Her writing is so compressed and understated in style that although it might perhaps be possible to read particular forms of class and Bloomsbury alienation into some of this imaging, this operates in a wholly different register to the kind of unmistakeable (if flexible) identities in Geraint Goodwin or Caradoc Evans. Nevertheless, a consideration of that neutral and more realist imaging of Jews would help to contextualise the stereotyped depictions in a different way.

One might view conversionism in new ways, too. Shortly after I had completed the writing of this account, the Welsh-language publisher Y Lolfa brought out a new edition of the letters of Margaret Jones, which promised the possibility of new perspectives on missionary activity. The volume, *Y Gymraes o Ganaan: Anturiaethau Margaret Jones ar Bum Cyfandir*, combines the two books by Margaret Jones and some further material from her later years in Australia. It also includes a long and detailed introduction and contextualising chapters by the editor and compiler, Eirian Jones, and a preface by religious history scholar, E. Wyn James. Quite rightly, Eirian Jones makes a case for the author's literary style and the importance of women travellers' accounts. Sadly, and predict-ably, the tricky questions that conversionism brings up are elided, and for reasons that become clear: in the introductory notes, Yiddish is described as a 'jargon' – a truly bizarre and dated description of a minority language for a Welsh-language publication – and the source for this and for most of the information she provides about the Jewish context is given as *Jewish Intelligence*, the nineteenth-century missionary publication of the London Society for Promoting Christianity among the Jews.[6] In a similar fashion, when E. Wyn James suggests in the preface that the missionary movement should be reassessed, it appears that he means reassessed in terms of its value – that is, it should be rehabilitated:

> Fe aeth y mudiad cenhadol dan gwmwl yng Nghymru yn ystod yr ugeinfed ganrif, oherwydd twf rhyddfrydiaeth a seciwlariaeth a gwrth-imperialaeth. Ond, yn fy marn i, y mae'n hwyr bryd bellach inni fynd ati i ailarchwilio ac ailasesu'r mudiad hwnnw.[7]

> (The missionary movement came under a cloud in Wales during the twentieth century, because of the growth of liberalism and secularism and anti-imperialism. But, in my opinion, it is high time we re-examine and reas-sess this movement.)

Margaret Jones's evident respect for the subjects of her conversionist desires, and John Mills's proto-ethnography are positive attributes, but they do not lessen the assault on Jewish identity that is inflicted by a missionary's attempt to remove the Jewishness of Jews. To seek to qualify such an assault with arguments about sympathy or kindliness is indefen-sible in the present, and the failure to acknowledge and analyse this as a problem will continue to undermine claims of Welsh tolerance and liberalism. This difficulty is largely occluded by the antisemitic/ philosemitic blinkers that have restricted the view of imaging of Jews in Wales. Nevertheless, the alternative – to look at work in terms of how it operates as part of a wider semitic discourse – is also constraining. I have inevitably focused on what are primarily negative stereotypes, since these offer rich pickings (as Frank McCourt observes so elegantly of dwelling on his miserable childhood in his memoir, *Angela's Ashes*, 'the happy childhood is hardly worth your while').[8] But while it is certainly true that the exaggerated stereotypes in Caradoc Evans, for example, are fascinatingly grotesque, positive stereotypes are also suspect: they are still essentialised, and they reveal the shadow of their negative counterpart. They are therefore also part of a prescriptive discourse that determines what is acceptable behaviour for Jews, and at the same time indicates the trap of hostile stereotype that is awaiting anyone who deviates from that acceptable behaviour.

The notion of 'tolerance' in this context itself deserves further consideration: tolerance, after all, denotes a conditional acceptance – a distinction familiar in considerations of multiculturalism and cultural relativism. One of the limitations of liberal multicultural democracy is demarcated precisely by this contingent acceptance of difference. *Behave like good immigrants*, the dominant cultural discourse and political and legal structures demand; people from minority backgrounds are expected to keep cultural difference in the private sphere, and immigrants are expected to acclimatise and assimilate themselves to the dominant culture norms. Welsh speakers fail to keep their difference private in a British or a Welsh context and that failure provoked a great deal of anxiety both within Wales and in Britain generally in the 1960s and 1970s (and it still does). The failure of Jews in the late nineteenth and early twentieth century to keep their difference private was at least in part what provoked the kinds of debates around the immigration acts (debates that are repeated in similar form in the early twenty-first century about Muslims). Fundamental concerns in these debates are not new: the dominant majority fears culture change and those fears clearly identify the limitations of 'tolerance', and the boundaries between acceptable and unacceptable difference.

While tolerance is an acceptance contingent on good behaviour, the immigrant can't do too *well*, either, without the limitations of that toleration being once again exposed. The culturally or ethnically different 'other' may be viewed with suspicion if he or she achieves success, or wields perceived power within the framework of the dominant culture, as was the case, for example, with Alfred Mond (and hence in part the recurrent fears of a Jewish control of the media). An awareness all the time of the conditional nature of one's acceptance renders the ethnic minority or immigrant group always vulnerable and potentially anxious, so that there are inevitably sensitivities to hostile depictions that might seem at times like overreactions.

Semitic discourse in Wales does indeed indicate some of the admittedly shifting boundaries of the culture's tolerance of difference, using familiar motifs that help remind Jews of their place, and of the conditional nature of their acceptability, and at the same time reminds others of that contingent position enjoyed by Jews. Such discourse in Britain in the present can contribute to individually identifiable Jews being the target of violent attack as has been the case for Orthodox Jews in English cities, but it can also stimulate an anxiety that is never entirely quiet, even if the individual is, arguably, safe – hence, perhaps, the perpetual insecurity expressed by a writer like Dannie Abse, who, despite not having experienced antisemitism in his upbringing in Wales, nevertheless defines his Jewish identity in terms of antisemitism.[9]

This very insecurity is, it might be argued, the Zionist movement's strength, both in the past and in the present. Harri Webb's poem 'Israel' presents the Jew as being always vulnerable in the absence of a muscular ideology of militarised Zionism, and the assertion of perpetual Jewish vulnerability has constituted and continues to constitute the key argument in support of Jewish statehood.[10] This is something that Jewish writers help to perpetuate – Lily Tobias's depiction of the Jew as always vulnerable, for example, is very clearly deployed in an argument to reinforce Zionism as an ideology, and Jewish self-determination as a moral and practical necessity.

Consequently, my assertion that semitic discourse occurs in dialogue with its subject goes further than I suggested in the last chapter. The dialogue between Judith Maro and Harri Webb, or indeed between Judith Maro and Gwynfor Evans, is premised on the same articulation of vulnerability and the moral case for Jewish statehood. But here the omissions and elisions are rather serious ones. The long relationship between a Jewish fantasy about Palestine and a Welsh fantasy about Wales has until very recently emptied Palestine of much of its existing population. If the chapel deacons and preachers of the religious nonconformist movement in the nineteenth century dreamed into being a Wales-as-Israel depopulated of Jews, the preachers and deacons of the political awakening in the twentieth century dreamed into being an Israel-as-Wales depopulated of Arabs. The fantasy about what the Hebrew-language revival offered as a model (a

fantasy which, perhaps more than any other aspect of these cultural inter-
changes, had a measurable, practical impact on Wales), occurred in an
imaginary space in which it was separated from the conditions that enabled
it to occur: the *organised* Hebrew revival, and its success, took place after
the establishment of the Israeli state. No matter that the new state was offi-
cially bilingual, the *ulpan* system arose out of the political need to unify
the new state, its existing population and its immigrants, through one
language. Its success was built upon the Nakba, the Palestinian Catastrophe,
and upon the marginalisation of what became, in the new state, minority
languages – Arabic (for Arabs and Jews), Yiddish and Ladino, among
others – and minority ethnic groups, including Arabs, Druze and
Samaritans. The dominance of Hebrew also marginalised some Jewish
groups within the Jewish 'majority', such as Jews from Arab countries
and, subsequently, Jews from Ethiopia.

The example that Israel and the revival of Hebrew offered to Wales was
based on a fantasy rooted deep in the Welsh imagination – it was rooted in
the Welsh-Israelite biblical tradition, and its precursor in traditional Welsh
historiography, and was given sustenance also by what had been a strong
Welsh conversionist desire. But the Israel that existed in the hopes of
Zionists, and in the imaginative comparisons of the Welsh, ceased to be
one of the 'small' nations whose success is yet to come, and became one of
the 'successful' nations, according to Derec Llwyd Morgan's taxonomy;
and not just 'successful', and believing its own success to be signal of
divine favour, but expansionist, militant and colonising. How might that
be reconciled in the Welsh imagination with Israel as a Wales in the east, or
with Wales as an iteration of the Holy Land? The Welsh discourse on Israel
and on Hebrew was powerful and deeply influential. It may now be uncomfortable for many in Wales who view Israel and its actions (and inactions)
with a great deal of criticism, but it cannot easily be dropped from the
cultural record, and nor is the evidence or influence erased by beginning to
remove the word *wlpan* from Welsh course descriptions.

How is it possible to fold such cultural complexity and specificity into a
monolithic 'England', whether or not the term 'Britain' is used, as has so
often occurred in Jewish studies? The editor of the *South Wales Jewish
Review* remarked in 1904 on the *Jewish Chronicle* practice of placing in
the short 'provincial' announcements the news of the several Jewish
communities in Wales. 'In retaliation for the scant attention given to South
Wales news in our contemporaries,' he wrote, 'the staff have been thinking
of placing London jottings in the "Provincial" news'.[11] Six months later,

commenting on the new *Jewish Year Book*, he observes that many towns in Wales are included for the first time, but then he exclaims:

> Oh! if the Editor of the *Year Book* had only read his *Review*. And yet he must have done, for is not its appearance duly chronicled on page 422 amongst 'Magazines and Reviews published in *England*'? Evidently 'the Celtic fringe' has been destroyed so that the printer might be saved the trouble of setting up in type 'published in Wales'.[12]

That too is a long tradition: more than a hundred years of the British Jewish establishment – and its scholars – overlooking the rich cultural particularity of Wales, and overlooking also its particular language and religious history, its national self-image, and its unique, imaginative and complex interest in Jews, however they might be constituted.

Notes

Notes to Introduction

1. Prys Morgan, 'From a death to a view: the hunt for the Welsh past in the Romantic period', in Eric Hobsbawm and Terence Ranger (eds), *The Invention of Tradition* (Cambridge: Cambridge University Press, 1984), pp. 43–100.
2. Gwyn A. Williams, *The Welsh in their History* (London: Croom Helm, 1982), p. 200.
3. Shlomo Sand, *The Invention of the Jewish People*, trans. Yael Lotan (London: Verso, 2010), p. x.
4. Sand, *The Invention of the Jewish People*, p. 15.
5. It's also possible that this Star of David is nothing of the sort, that it was merely a decorative motif when it was affixed in 1858, without the cultural meanings that we might retroactively impose on it. Nevertheless, because of those present-day meanings of the six-pointed star, local oral tradition identifies the building as a former synagogue, and people in the valley report that Orthodox Jews make pilgrimages to see it every summer. In fact, members of the three communities of Orthodox Jews who spend two weeks each year in Aberystwyth are merely having a holiday, which, for many, includes day-trips to nearby sites, including the scenic Rheidol valley.
6. David Cesarani, 'Reporting Antisemitism: The *Jewish Chronicle* 1879–1979', in Siân James, Tony Kushner and Sarah Pierce (eds), *Cultures of Ambivalence. Studies in Jewish – Non-Jewish Relations* (London: Vallentine and Mitchell, 1998), p. 255.
7. I have made this argument previously in '"By whom shall she arise? For she is small": the Wales-Israel tradition in the Edwardian period', in Nadia Valman and Eitan Bar-Yosef (eds), *The Jew in Late-Victorian and Edwardian Culture: Between the East End and East Africa* (London: Palgrave, 2009), pp. 161–82.
8. Michael Woolf, 'Negotiating the Self: Jewish Fiction in Britain Since 1945', in A. Robert Lee (ed.), *Other Britain, Other British: Contemporary Multicultural Fiction* (London: Pluto Press, 1996), p. 136.

9 Others have been challenging that notion for some time. See for example Neil Evans, Paul O'Leary and Charlotte Williams (eds), *A Tolerant Nation?: Exploring Ethnic Diversity in Wales* (Cardiff: University of Wales Press, 2003) and Charlotte Williams, *Sugar and Slate* (Aberystwyth: Planet, 2002).

10 W. D. Rubinstein, 'The anti-Jewish riots of 1911 in south Wales: a re-examination', *Welsh History Review* 18/4 (1997), 670.

11 Eitan Bar-Yosef, *The Holy Land in English Culture 1799–1917* (Oxford: Oxford University Press, 2005), p. 4.

12 Ibid., p. 4, note 8.

13 Dorian Llywelyn, *Sacred Place, Chosen People: Land and National Identity in Welsh Spirituality* (Cardiff: University of Wales Press, 1999); John Harvey, *Image of the Invisible: the Visualization of Religion in Welsh Nonconformist Tradition* (Cardiff: University of Wales Press, 1999).

14 Kirsti Bohata, *Postcolonialism Revisited* (Cardiff: University of Wales Press, 2004); Stephen Knight, *A Hundred Years of Fiction* (Cardiff: University of Wales Press, 2004); Bryan Cheyette, *Constructions of 'the Jew' in English Literature and Society: Racial Representations 1875–1945* (Cambridge: Cambridge University Press, 1993), and Bryan Cheyette, 'Neither black nor white: the figure of "the Jew" in Imperial British literature', in Linda Nochlin and Tamar Garb (eds), *The Jew in the Text: Modernity and the Construction of Identity* (London: Thames and Hudson, 1995), pp. 31–41.

15 Benedict Anderson, *Imagined Communities: Reflections on the Origin and Spread of Nationalism* (1983; London: Verso, 1991).

16 See for example Nadia Valman, *The Jewess in Nineteenth-Century British Literary Culture* (Cambridge: Cambridge University Press, 2007).

17 Bryan Cheyette (ed.), *Between 'Race' and Culture: Representations of 'the Jew' in English and American Literature* (Stanford: Stanford University Press, 1996), p. 14.

18 M. Wynn Thomas, for example, explores such Discourse – the dominant 'discourse' of nonconformity in nineteenth-century Wales – and the challenge to it by the emerging Welsh writing in English of the twentieth century in *In the Shadow of the Pulpit: Literature and Nonconformist Wales* (Cardiff: University of Wales Press, 2010), pp. 124–5.

19 See for example Chris Williams and Jane Aaron (eds), *Postcolonial Wales* (Cardiff: University of Wales Press, 2005).

Notes to Chapter 1

1 Meic Stephens (ed.), *The New Companion to the Literature of Wales* (Cardiff: University of Wales Press, 1998); Peter Lord, *The Visual Culture of Wales: Industrial Society* (Cardiff: University of Wales Press, 1998); *The Visual Culture of Wales: Imaging the Nation* (Cardiff: University of Wales Press, 2000); *The Visual Culture of Wales: Medieval Vision* (Cardiff: University of Wales Press, 2003).

2 Ralph Fevre and Andrew Thompson (eds), *Nation, Identity and Social Theory: Perspectives from Wales* (Cardiff: University of Wales Press, 1999), and Neil Evans, Paul O'Leary and Charlotte Williams (eds), *A Tolerant Nation?: Exploring Ethnic Diversity in Wales* (Cardiff: University of Wales Press, 2003).

3 Charlotte Williams, *Sugar and Slate* (Aberystwyth: Planet, 2002); Grahame Davies (ed.), *Chosen People: Wales and the Jews* (Bridgend: Seren, 2002).

4 W. D. Rubinstein, 'The anti-Jewish riots of 1911 in south Wales: a re-examination', *Welsh History Review*, 18/4 (1997), 667–99.

5 I include in the early twentieth-century date range the years in which the *South Wales Jewish Review* appeared, as it too published material dealing with these questions, as discussed in chapter 5.

6 See Jasmine Donahaye, 'Jewish writing in Wales' (unpublished Ph.D. thesis, Swansea University, 2004), chs 1–3.

7 *The South Wales Jewish Review*, for example, appeared for only two or three years. For a discussion of Welsh-language cultural magazines in the period, see Hazel Davies, 'The early travel books and periodicals of O. M. Edwards', in Hywel Teifi Edwards (ed.), *A Guide to Welsh Literature c.1800–1900* (Cardiff: University of Wales Press, 2000), pp. 186–209. See also *Young Wales, The Welsh Outlook, Wales* and others, and the discussion by Malcolm Ballin, 'Welsh periodicals in English 1880–1965: literary form and cultural substance', *Yearbook of Welsh Writing in English*, 9 (Cardiff: New Welsh Review, 2004), pp. 1–32.

8 Benedict Anderson, *Imagined Communities: Reflections on the Origin and Spread of Nationalism* (1983; London: Verso, 1991).

9 Bryan Cheyette, *Constructions of 'the Jew' in English Literature and Society: Racial Representations 1875–1945* (Cambridge: Cambridge University Press, 1993), p. 8, footnote.

10 Dorian Llywelyn, *Sacred Place, Chosen People: Land and National Identity in Welsh Spirituality* (Cardiff: University of Wales Press, 1999).

11 I use the term 'abject' in a non-theoretical way here to describe what evangelical Christians saw as Jewish wretchedness, both material and spiritual (a consequence of their rejecting Jesus as Messiah). Nevertheless, examining Welsh conversionist commentary on Jewish abjection according to Julia Kristeva's meaning of the term would no doubt be a very fruitful enquiry. See Julia Kristeva, *Powers of Horror: An Essay on Abjection*, trans. Leon S. Roudiez (New York: Columbia University Press, 1982).

12 Eitan Bar-Yosef, *The Holy Land in English Culture 1799–1917* (Oxford: Oxford University Press, 2005).

13 See, for example, W. D. Rubinstein, *Philosemitism – Admiration and Support in the English-speaking World for Jews 1840–1939* (London: MacMillan Press, 1999), and W. D. and Hilary L. Rubinstein, 'Philosemitism in Britain and in the English-speaking world, 1840–1939: Patterns and Typology', *Jewish Journal of Sociology* 40/1–2 (1998), 5–47.

14 W. D. Rubinstein, 'The anti-Jewish riots', 670. For a discussion of how these events have been interpreted, and the use to which they have been put, see J. Donahaye, 'Jewish Writing in Wales', ch. 1. See also *www.bbc.co.uk/news/uk-wales-14582378*.

[15] W. D. Rubinstein, 'The anti-Jewish riots', 669.

[16] Ibid., 671–2.

[17] Ibid., 676–7.

[18] W. D. Rubinstein, 'The Chosen People: Wales and the Jews', *New Welsh Review*, 57 (2002), 110.

[19] G. Davies, *The Chosen People*, p. 11.

[20] Such equivocation might also be seen in the 1942 poem 'Yr Iddewon' (The Jews) and *Plasau'r Brenin* (Mansions of the King) (Aberystwyth: Gwasg Gomer, 1934), Gwenallt's fictionalised account of his prison experiences as a conscientious objector. Davies argues that both of these indicate Gwenallt's attempt to expose antisemitic attitudes rather than giving an indication of his own antisemitism.

[21] Daniel Evans, *Golwg ar gyflwr yr Iuddewon* (Aberystwyth, 1826), pp. 15 and 19.

[22] Reproduced in translation by G. Davies, *Chosen People*, p. 66 from *Y Geninen*, 36 (1 January 1918). No page numbers given.

[23] H. Davies, 'The Early Travel Books and Periodicals of O. M. Edwards', p. 192.

[24] Neil Evans, 'Immigrants and minorities in Wales, 1840–1990: a comparative perspective', *Llafur*, 5/4 (1991), 5.

[25] In her earlier volume on O. M. Edwards in the Writers of Wales series, Hazel Walford Davies was perhaps working from this later version, for she does not comment on the passage. See Hazel Davies, *O. M. Edwards* (Cardiff: University of Wales Press, 1988).

[26] G. Davies, *Chosen People*, p. 168.

[27] Ibid., p. 157.

[28] See for example Neil Evans, Paul O'Leary and Charlotte Williams, *A Tolerant Nation?*, and Glenn Jordan, '"We never really noticed you were coloured": post-colonialist reflections on immigrants and minorities in Wales', in Jane Aaron and Chris Williams (eds), *Postcolonial Wales* (Cardiff: University of Wales Press, 2005).

[29] John Harvey, *Image of the Invisible: the Visualization of Religion in Welsh Nonconformist Tradition* (Cardiff: University of Wales Press, 1999), p. 95.

[30] See frontispiece, p. ii.

[31] Harvey, *Image of the Invisible*, p. 98. Although Harvey gives a *c.*1901 date and no artist, the map is dated 1900 and signed with the name Ap Dewi (a generic name for a Welshman). In his chapter in a survey of biblical art in Wales, Harvey describes the means of this transmission: 'In the nineteenth century, images of the biblical land and stories entered the chapel culture and the imagination of Nonconformists in the form of steel-plate engravings in pulpit and family Bibles, Bible dictionaries, commentaries, devotional books, coloured lithographs, and Sunday-school banners.' See Harvey, 'The Bible and Art in Wales: A Nonconformist Perspective', in Martin O'Kane and John Morgan-Guy (eds), *Biblical Art from Wales* (Sheffield: Sheffield Phoenix Press, 2010), p. 77.

[32] A survey of biblical imaging in Welsh visual culture also shows little evidence of such a widespread tradition – see Martin O'Kane and John Morgan-Guy (eds), *Biblical Art from Wales*. While there is a lack of compelling imagery to support Harvey's claim, biblical imagery does appear in the work of some of the industrial painters of south Wales. According to Peter Lord this work reflects the same

tensions between biblical and Marxist ideologies that are manifested in the work of Gwenallt, but constitute clearly Christian biblical references. See Peter Lord, *The Visual Culture of Wales: Industrial Society*. However the artisan work that is produced via the patronage of those who might articulate such a tradition is almost exclusively portraiture, while Hugh Hughes and William Roos, the foremost nonconformist painters of the nineteenth century (the former married to the grand-daughter of a converted Jew), produce no such work. See Peter Lord, *Hugh Hughes: Arlunydd Gwlad* (Llandysul: Gomer, 1995) and *The Visual Culture of Wales: Imaging the Nation*.

[33]   Indeed it might well have been Evans who alerted him to the image of Moses in O. M. Edwards's *Hanes Cymru*, because this is discussed by Evans in his essay 'Studies in Britannic-Hebraic Eschatology V', *Young Wales*, 8/90 (June 1902), 121–7.

[34]   Derec Llwyd Morgan, *'Canys Bechan Yw': y Genedl Etholedig yn Ein Llenyddiaeth* ('For she is small': the chosen people in our literature) (Aberystwyth: University of Wales, 1994) and Glanmor Williams, *Religion, Language and Nationality in Wales: Historical Essays* (Cardiff: University of Wales Press, 1979). The work of both is discussed below.

[35]   Llywelyn relies on Michael Winterbottom (ed. and trans.), *Gildas' 'The Ruin of Britain' and other works* (London: Phillimore and Co., 1978).

[36]   Llywelyn, *Sacred Place, Chosen People*, p. 80.

[37]   Ibid.

[38]   Ibid., p. 89.

[39]   Stephens (ed.), *The New Companion to the Literature of Wales*, p. 201.

[40]   Llywelyn, *Sacred Place, Chosen People*, p. 95.

[41]   Ibid., p. 101.

[42]   Theophilus Evans, *Drych Y Prif Oesoedd* (Shrewsbury, 1716), and Henry Rowlands, *Mona Antiqua Restaurata – an Archaeological Discourse on the Antiquities, Natural and Historical, of the Isle of Anglesey, the Antient Seat of the British Druids in Two ESSAYS* (1723; Macclesfield: Redesmere Press Ltd, 1993).

[43]   Llywelyn, *Sacred Place, Chosen People*, p. 102.

[44]   See for example Orin Gensler, 'A Typological Evaluation of the Celtic/Hamo-Semitic Syntactic Parallels' (unpublished Ph.D. thesis, University of California, Berkeley, 1993).

[45]   Llywelyn, *Sacred Place, Chosen People*, p. 102.

[46]   Ibid., quoted in translation from Charles Edwards, *Y Ffydd Ddi-ffuant*, p. 150.

[47]   Llywelyn, *Sacred Place, Chosen People*, p. 102. Quoted in translation from *Y Ffydd Ddi-ffuant*, p. 214. This matter is of particular interest in the context of distinctions made in the Anglo-Israel or British-Israel theory, which is discussed in chapter 2.

[48]   It should be noted that while Jews might object to the Christian belief, expressed in I Peter 2:9, that Christians as a whole have inherited the mantle of being God's 'chosen people', this chosen state is often seen by Jews in terms of affliction. Nowhere is this more succinctly expressed than by the mother of Welsh-Jewish poet Dannie Abse: '"Chosen . . . chosen to be persecuted"' she complains. Dannie Abse, *Goodbye Twentieth Century: An Autobiography* (London: Pimlico, 2001), p. 17.

[49]   This occurs in parallel but different form in the English imagination – Eitan
       Bar-Yosef concludes that 'it was quite possible, then, for Englishmen to think of
       themselves as a – or even *the* – chosen people, the true Israel, and yet to manifest
       an interest in the Jews as the descendents of the ancient Israelites; to imagine the
       Kingdom of God in England and yet ponder the role designated to Jerusalem in
       the East'. Bar-Yosef, *The Holy Land in English Culture*, p. 35.
[50]   See the re-examination of Methodism by E. Wyn James, '"The New Birth of a
       People": Welsh Language and Identity and the Welsh Methodists *c*.1740–1820',
       in Robert Pope (ed.), *Religion and National Identity: Wales and Scotland c. 1700–
       2000* (Cardiff: University of Wales Press, 2001), pp. 14–42. Methodism in Wales
       is predominantly Calvinistic Methodism, as opposed to the Wesleyan Methodism
       prevalent in England. Some authors refer to Welsh Methodism interchangeably as
       Methodism, Calvinistic Methodism or (Welsh) Presbyterianism. The Calvinist
       Methodists as a denominational body date to 1811, when they separated from the
       Church of England.
[51]   Prys Morgan, 'The clouds of witnesses: the Welsh historical tradition' in R.
       Brinley Jones (ed.), *Anatomy of Wales* (Peterson-super-Ely: Gwerin Publications,
       1972), quoted by James in 'The New Birth of a People', p. 23; Glanmor Williams,
       Religion, Language and Nationality in Wales, p. 23.
[52]   Williams, *Religion, Language and Nationality in Wales*, p. 23.
[53]   Ibid., p. 24.
[54]   James, 'The New Birth of a People', p. 23.
[55]   Williams, *Religion, Language and Nationality in Wales*, p. 24–5.
[56]   James, 'The New Birth of a People', pp. 18 and 21.
[57]   Ibid., p. 35.
[58]   Eryn White, 'The Established Church, Dissent and the Welsh Language', in
       Geraint H. Jenkins (ed.), *The Welsh Language Before the Industrial Revolution*
       (Cardiff: University of Wales Press, 1997), p. 265.
[59]   Llywelyn, *Sacred Place, Chosen People*, p. 106.
[60]   Ibid.
[61]   Presenting any kind of general Welsh nonconformist attitude with deep roots is
       more problematic when the denominational allegiances of 'traditional historiog-
       raphers' are taken into account: David Charles was a Dissenter, for example, but
       Theophilus Evans was an Anglican clergyman. As discussed below, the Calvinistic
       Methodists remained within the Anglican Church until 1811, unlike Dissenting
       groups such as the Independents, and continued to be wary of other noncon-
       formist groups even after the shared response to the attack on Welsh morals in the
       1847 Blue Books. For a broader history of Christian belief in Wales, see various
       works by R. Tudur Jones, including (on the Independents) *Hanes Annibynwyr
       Cymru* (Abertawe: Undeb yr Annibynwyr Cymraeg, 1966), and *Grym y Gair a
       Fflam y Ffydd: Ysgrifau ar Hanes Crefydd yng Nghymru*, gol. D. Densil Morgan
       (Bangor: Canolfan Uwch-Efrydiau Crefydd yng Nghymru, 1998). See also
       M. Wynn Thomas's study *In the Shadow of the Pulpit: Literature and
       Nonconformist Wales* (Cardiff: University of Wales Press, 2010).
[62]   E. T. Davies, *Religion and Society in the Nineteenth Century* (Christopher Davies:
       Llandybïe, 1981), p. 20.

[63] Ibid., p. 18.

[64] See Eitan Bar-Yosef for an account of the dissemination in England of imagery of Ottoman Palestine up to 1917, particularly chapter 3, 'Popular Palestine: the Holy Land as Printed Image, Spectacle and Commodity'. A survey of Welsh visual imaging of Palestine during the same period would no doubt yield answers to this speculation on my part. As discussed in the next chapter, John Mills provided detailed accounts of Palestine from the 1850s, but through a decidedly Calvinistic Methodist filter.

[65] In a textual equivalent to this map, E. T. Davies reports that a Welsh writer at the end of the nineteenth century described Wales as 'the Palestine of Christendom'. E. T. Davies, *Religion and Society in the Nineteenth Century*, p. 37.

[66] E. T. Davies, *Religion and Society*, p. 37. This statement also appears in the novel *The Samaritan* by Lily Tobias, which is discussed in chapter 5.

[67] See e.g., work by Lily Tobias, discussed in chapter 5.

[68] Eitan Bar-Yosef, *The Holy Land in English Culture*, pp. 182 and 245–6. W. D. Rubinstein also cites Thomas Ellis. Rubinstein, 'The anti-Jewish riots', 670.

[69] Llywelyn, *Sacred Place, Chosen People*, p. 77.

[70] Derec Llwyd Morgan's use of this biblical reference is mirrored by Ahad Ha'am, who observes: 'Destroy a land, and a living people shall rebuild it. But destroy a people, and who will arise, and from whence comes its strength?' Quoted in Bernard Avishai, *The Tragedy of Zionism: Revolution and Democracy in the Land of Israel* (New York: Farrar, Strauss Giroux 1985), p. 58.

[71] Llwyd Morgan, *'Canys Bechan Yw'*, p. 6.

[72] Ibid., p. 8.

[73] Ibid., p. 10. This reference to the Welsh as 'the last remnant' also appears in R. S. Thomas's lecture on mythical 'Abercuawg'. R. S. Thomas, *Abercuawg* (Aberteifi: Eisteddfod Genedlaethol Cymru Aberteifi a'r Cylch, 1976), p. 18.

[74] 'Rhaid derbyn, mewn ffydd, y bydd yr Arglwydd Dduw yn tosturio wrth Walia Wen yn union fel y tosturiodd dro ar ôl tro wrth Israel'. Llwyd Morgan, *'Canys Bechan Yw'*, p. 11.

[75] 'myth ein Israeliaeth', ibid., p. 12.

[76] Ibid., p. 12.

[77] Gwenallt (D. Gwenallt Jones), *Gwreiddiau* (Aberystwyth: Gwasg Aberystwyth, 1959), p. 39.

[78] Gwenallt, *Gwreiddiau*, p. 46 and *Eples* (Llandysul: Gwasg Gomer, 1951), p. 24.

[79] Benedict Anderson, *Imagined Communities*, p. 6. In this context, a consideration of *blason populaire*, that body of folklore concerned with determining who is within and who is outside the folkgroup, might lend itself usefully to the discussion – see, for example, Elliott Oring, 'Ethnic Groups and Ethnic Folklore', in Elliott Oring (ed.), *Folk Groups and Folklore Genres: an Introduction* (Logan, Utah: Utah State University Press, 1986), pp. 23–44.

[80] Anderson, *Imagined Communities*, p. 6.

[81] Anderson, *Imagined Communities*, p. 5.

[82] Anderson, *Imagined Communities*, 'Cultural Roots', pp. 9–36.

[83] These are considered in detail in chapter 3.

[84] Eric Hobsbawm, 'Introduction: Inventing Traditions', in Eric Hobsbawm and Terence Ranger (eds), *The Invention of Tradition* (Cambridge: Cambridge University Press, 1984), p. 1.

[85] Ibid., p. 1.

[86] One may see in Dorian Llywelyn's work, published in 1999, a warning not dissimilar to that made by some of the authors whom he discusses. He is concerned with political morality, or perhaps even purity, in the context of devolution, and calls for a vigilance against a kind of nationalist idolatry.

[87] 'Ac y mae'r Israel fodern yn enghraifft odidocach fyth'. J. R. Jones, *Gwaedd yng Nghymru* (Liverpool and Pontypridd: Cyhoeddiadau Modern Cymreig Cyf., 1970), p. 67.

[88] Ibid., p. 68.

[89] Rubinstein, 'The anti-Jewish riots', 669.

[90] Rubinstein, 'The Chosen People: Wales and the Jews', 110.

Notes to Chapter 2

[1] Michael Ragussis *Figures of Conversion: 'The Jewish Question' and English National Identity* (Durham: Duke University Press, 1995), pp. 17–18. Eitan Bar-Yosef, *The Holy Land in English Culture 1799–1917* (Oxford: Oxford University Press, 2005), p. 189.

[2] This association between the conversion of the Jews (and Muslims) and the End of Days derives from an interpretation of the prophecies in the book of Isaiah. It found strong expression in the Puritan period and can be seen, for example, in the work of Welsh Puritan mystic Morgan Llwyd, who is discussed below.

[3] See Ursula Henriques (ed.), *The Jews of South Wales: Historical Studies* (Cardiff: University of Wales Press, 1993). Leo Abse, recalling his grandfather's attitudes, has speculated that established Anglo-Jewish communities helped the new arrivals to move on to Wales, as they felt this foreign, impoverished, religiously observant mass reflected poorly on them. 'The bulk of the Jews . . . in Cardiff weren't very nice. Bernice Rubens has written some books cruelly about the Jews in Cardiff. But justifiably . . . What she was depicting wasn't very nice because they weren't very nice . . . They were ghetto Jews who had come over – and I strongly suspect, but I can't prove it – but some of the Jews that came to south Wales were the ones which the establishment Jews in London didn't want to keep in their lives. Because there was a move that's historically recorded that they helped the Jews and I don't know if they would have chosen the ones they wanted to get rid of to get them out of London because they . . . reflected badly. And I think Wales had more than its quota of some of the refuse from the ghettos. They weren't criminals, but they were anti-social and they only lived – that group – they only lived within themselves to such an extent because, of course, they prayed morning, noon and night, and played cards almost morning noon and night.' Interview with the author, 2002. Lily Tobias's stories and first novel indicate how 'established' Jews in the south Wales cities also distanced themselves from the recent immigrants and encouraged their relocation outside urban centres: see *The*

Nationalists and Other Goluth Studies and *My Mother's House*, both discussed in chapter 5.

4   See e.g. Ursula Henriques, 'Lyons versus Thomas: The Jewess Abduction Case, 1867–8', in Henriques, *The Jews of South Wales*, 131–49.

5   Geoffrey Alderman, 'The Jew as scapegoat? The settlement and reception of Jews in south Wales before 1914', *Jewish Historical Society of England, Transactions*, 26 (1974–8), 67; W. D. Rubinstein, 'The anti-Jewish riots of 1911 in south Wales: a re-examination', *Welsh History Review*, 18/4 (1997), 681–2.

6   Such a lacuna is evident in W. D. Rubinstein's apologia for John Mills in 'The anti-Jewish riots', 676, note 34; W. D. Rubinstein, *Philosemitism – Admiration and Support in the English-speaking World for Jews 1840–1939* (London: Macmillan Press, 1999); W. D. and Hilary L. Rubinstein, 'Philosemitism in Britain and in the English Speaking World, 1840–1939: Patterns and Typology', *Jewish Journal of Sociology*, 40/1–2 (1998), 5–47; and David Morris, 'The Formation and Decline of Jewish Communities in Wales' (unpublished Ph.D. thesis, University of Wales, Aberystwyth, 1999).

7   For studies of Morgan Llwyd's writings, see M. Wynn Thomas, *Morgan Llwyd: ei Gyfeillion a'i Gyfnod* (Cardiff: University of Wales Press, 1991), and M. Wynn Thomas, 'Seventeenth-century Puritan writers: Morgan Llwyd and Charles Edwards', in R. Geraint Gruffydd (ed.), *A Guide to Welsh Literature, c.1530–1700* (Cardiff: University of Wales Press, 1997), pp. 190–209.

8   Matthew Biberman, *Masculinity, Anti-Semitism and Early Modern English Literature: from the Satanic to the Effeminate Jew* (Aldershot: Ashgate, 2004), p. 121. Biberman proposes the following model for his survey: 'it is clear that the logic of the survey methodology is to assess antisemitism in a way that can organize the phenomenon along a continuum where the measured quality is "virulence." At one end you have a banal antisemitism that is almost without virulence, and at the other you have virulent Nazism.'

9   D. Wynne Evans, 'Studies in Welsh Chiliastic History I', *Young Wales*, 7/75 (March 1901), 55–7; 'Studies in Iberic=Hebraic Eschatology II', *Young Wales*, 7/78 (June 1901), 121–5; 'Studies in Iberic=Hebraic Eschatology III', *Young Wales*, 7/80 (August 1901), 172–7; 'Studies in Britannic-Hebraic Eschatology IV', *Young Wales*, 8/88 (April 1902), 87–91, and 'Studies in Britannic-Hebraic Eschatology V', *Young Wales*, 8/90 (June 1902), 121–7.

10 Theophilus Evans, *Drych Y Prif Oesoedd* (Shrewsbury, 1716); Charles Edwards, *Y Ffydd Ddi-ffuant* (1667; Oxford, 1677).

11 Mary Garrard gives the following account in her biography of Jessie Penn Lewis: 'At Keswick that year were two Welsh Ministers (the Revs. J. Rhys Davies and D. Wynne Evans) who told how thirteen Welsh people had met one day at the 1896 Convention, to pray that God would give Wales a Convention for the deepening of spiritual life; and from that time on, they had been holding this petition before the Lord. Now the "fullness of time" seemed to have come. "Let us go and see Mrs. Penn-Lewis and confer with her," Mr. Rhys Davies said to his friend; and every succeeding step evidenced that the Lord was going before, to bring into being the Convention which afterwards became one of the channels for the "rivers" of life to Wales – an important factor in the outbreak of Revival in the Principality in

'1904–5.' Mary N. Garrard, *Mrs Penn Lewis: A Memoir* (London: The Overcomer Book Room, 1931), p. 221. Also available online under the heading 'Mrs Penn Lewis and the Welsh Revival', *www.revival-library.org/catalogues/1904ff/garrard.html*.

12   Evans, 'Studies in Welsh Chiliastic History I', 57.

13   Morgan Llwyd (1648). Evans, 'Studies in Iberic=Hebraic Eschatology II', 121.

14   Evans, 'Studies in Iberic=Hebraic Eschatology II', 122. This 'Prof. Lloyd' may well be the historian J. E. Lloyd, who was associated with the Cymru Fydd movement, and who would later publish the influential *A History of Wales* in 1911. In 1893 he was bemoaning the kind of 'entertaining and ancient traditions' to which Evans was still making reference: 'The true history of Wales has lain for so long under a heap of legends that some Welshmen may, perhaps, barely recognize their country in the pages that follow.' J. E. Lloyd, *Llyfr Cyntaf Hanes* (Caernarfon 1893), quoted in translation in Huw Pryce's definitive biography, *J. E. Lloyd and the Creation of Welsh History: Renewing a Nation's Past* (Cardiff: University of Wales Press, 2011), pp. 101–2.

15   For a somewhat different view, see David Katz, *Philo-Semitism and the Readmission of the Jews to England 1603–1655* (Oxford: Oxford University Press, 1982), and David Katz, *The Jews in the History of England 1485–1850* (Oxford: Oxford University Press, 1994).

16   Evans, 'Studies in Iberic=Hebraic Eschatology II', 122.

17   Evans, 'Studies in Iberic=Hebraic Eschatology II', 123. Quoted from Rhys, 'Welsh Literary Notes', *Manchester Guardian* (April 13, 1901), 9.

18   Evans, 'Studies in Iberic=Hebraic Eschatology II', 123.

19   Ibid. Evans adds in a footnote that this had also occurred to Dean Arthur Penrhyn Stanley in Stanley's *Bible in the Holy Land*. Evans lists other comparisons made by David Howell, including parallels between hymnology and the book of psalms, and between Welsh music and Jewish synagogue music.

20   Originally published in Transactions of the Liverpool Welsh National Society. It is perhaps considered such a representative specimen of the writing and attitudes of the time that it has been digitised and included in the online 'Gathering the Jewels' project at *www.gtj.org.uk/en/small/item/GTJ76989*.

21   Evans, 'Studies in Iberic=Hebraic Eschatology II', 123.

22   Evans, 'Studies in Iberic=Hebraic Eschatology III', 173.

23   Evans, 'Studies in Britannic-Hebraic Eschatology IV', 87.

24   Rubinstein, 'The anti-Jewish riots', 671.

25   The latter-day racist aspect of the British-Israel theory is detailed in David S. Katz and Richard H. Popkin, *Messianic Revolution: Radical Religious Politics to the End of the Second Millennium* (London: Allen Lane/Penguin Press, 1999). In his chapter 'Eccentric Zion', Eitan Bar-Yosef usefully considers the movement or theory in the context of the wider (marginal) 'restoration' movement. See *The Holy Land in English Culture*, pp. 182–246.

26   Derec Llwyd Morgan, *'Canys Bechan Yw': y Genedl Etholedig yn Ein Llenyddiaeth* (Aberystwyth: University of Wales, 1994).

27   Dorian Llywelyn, *Sacred Place, Chosen People: Land and National Identity in Welsh Spirituality* (Cardiff: University of Wales Press, 1999), p. 102, quoted from Edwards, *Y Ffydd Ddi-ffuant*, p. 214.

[28]   Evans, 'Studies in Britannic-Hebraic Eschatology V', 124.

[29]   Henry Rowlands, *Mona Antiqua Restaurata – an Archaeological Discourse on the Antiquities, Natural and Historical, of the Isle of Anglesey, the Antient Seat of the British Druids in Two ESSAYS* (1723; Macclesfield: Redesmere Press Ltd, 1993).

[30]   F. W. Phillips, *The historical, ethnic and philological arguments in proof of British Identity with the lost Ten Tribes of Israel. . .* (London, 1879); F. W. Phillips, *Proofs for the Welsh that the British are the lost tribes of Israel. The Abrahamic Covenant* (Bangor: 'The North Wales Chronicle', 1880), and *Y Genedl Gymreig yn deillio oddiwrth ddeg llwyth colledig Tŷ Israel: sef, epistol at y Cymry* (Bangor: 'The North Wales Chronicle', 1880). F. W. Phillips wrote under the pen name 'Philo-Israel', whom Katz and Popkin identify as Edward Wheler Bird, the founder of the Anglo-Israel Association. Nevertheless, the publications by Philo-Israel identify him as F. W. Phillips. Katz and Popkin identify two strands in the Anglo-Israel movement – the Teutonists, who saw the Anglo-Saxons, and sometimes the Scandinavians, as part of the elect, and the British-Israelites, who restricted membership to the English or British. Katz and Popkin do not appear to distinguish between 'England' and 'Britain', and hence the significance of the inclusion of the Celts by Philo-Israel is overlooked.

[31]   I have lost count of how many times an individual, learning something about the subject of this research, reports to me that a parent, or a grandparent, or 'the Welsh' more widely believed themselves to be descended from the lost ten tribes. One of the more curious published examples appears in a novel by Thomas Pynchon: 'How they *persist*. The poor, the black. And the Jews! The Welsh, the Welsh once upon a time were Jew*ish* too? one of the Lost Tribes of Israel.' Thomas Pynchon, *Gravity's Rainbow* (1973; London: Penguin, 1995), p. 170. I am grateful to Amy Feinstein for this reference.

[32]   Llywelyn, *Sacred Place, Chosen People*, p. 102.

[33]   Eric Michael Reisenauer, 'Anti-Jewish philosemitism: Hebrew and British affinity and nineteenth-century British antisemitism', *British Scholar*, 1/1 (September 2008), 79–104.

[34]   Evans, 'Studies in Britannic-Hebraic Eschatology IV', 90.

[35]   Ibid.

[36]   Ibid., 89.

[37]   Ibid., 89–90. Evans also comments on the legend among mid-nineteenth century Palestinian Jews, which was reported by John Mills, concerning restitution by the British, and on the connection between the Patagonian Welsh settlement and Colonel Goldsmid's Cardiff, Zionist and Patagonian interests (Goldsmid was responsible for the Welsh regiment in Cardiff, and was a prominent Zionist in the 1890s who met Theodor Herzl). Evans traces this tradition back to the British or Brythonic pre-Saxon foot soldiers in Roman legions posted from Wales to Judea, and comments on the parallels between the two peoples then both 'under the heel' of Rome.

[38]   Perhaps an explanation may lie in his concluding exclamation: 'God Save the King'. Edward VII was about to be crowned.

39 J. E. Lloyd, *A History of Wales: from the Earliest Times to the Edwardian Conquest* (London: Longmans, Green and Co., 1911).

40 Evans, 'Studies in Britannic-Hebraic Eschatology V', 126.

41 Reisenauer, 'Anti-Jewish philosemitism', 81.

42 Daniel Evans, *Golwg ar gyflwr yr Iuddewon* (Aberystwyth, 1826).

43 Evans, *Golwg ar gyflwr yr Iuddewon*, pp. 15 and 19.

44 See entry in Meic Stephens (ed.), *The New Companion to the Literature of Wales* (Cardiff: University of Wales Press, 1998), p. 431.

45 H. Elvet Lewis, *Israel and Other Poems* (London: Foyles, 1930), p. 11.

46 Ibid., pp. 12 and 15.

47 Ibid., p. 16.

48 Derec Llwyd Morgan, 'Morgan Llwyd a'r Iddewon', *Ysgrifau Beirniadol*, 21 (1996), pp. 81–96.

49 As explained in the previous chapter, I use the term 'abject' and 'abjection' to describe what evangelical Christians saw as the material and spiritual wretchedness of Jews arising from their refusal to recognise Jesus as Messiah, but again, exploring such Jewish abjection here in more theoretical terms along the lines of Julia Kristeva's *Powers of Horror: An Essay on Abjection* (New York: Columbia University Press, 1982) would no doubt yield fascinating insights.

50 Evans, 'Studies in Iberic=Hebraic Eschatology II', 124.

51 Back cover text to John Mills, *Palestina: sef Hanes Taith Ymweld ag Iuddewon Gwlad Canaan* (1858).

52 See the entry on Mills in *Y Bywgraffiadur Cymreig* (London: Cymdeithas y Cymmrodorion, 1953), p. 597.

53 Nigel Jenkins, *Gwalia in Khasia* (Llandysul: Gomer, 1995), p. 28.

54 John Mills, 'Y Genadaeth Iuddewig', *Y Drysorfa* (Chwefror 1847), 60.

55 'Y maent mor ddyeithr i'r Hen Destament ag yw y Pabyddion i'r Testament Newydd . . . Y mae enwau Esaiah, Jeremiah, Daniel &c. mor ddyeithr i'r rhan luosocaf o Iuddewon y lle hwn, ac ydyw enwau Taliesin, Tydain, neu Dafydd ab [*sic*] Gwilym'. *Y Drysorfa* (Chwefror 1847), 61.

56 '. . . yr ysbryd masnachol sydd yn llenwi y genedl', *Y Drysorfa* (Chwefror 1847), 61.

57 See for example Bryan Cheyette, *Constructions of 'the Jew' in English Literature and Society: Racial Representations 1875–1945* (Cambridge: Cambridge University Press, 1993).

58 'Y mae sefyllfa y meddwl Iuddewig yn bresennol yn debyg iawn i'r hyn yw meddwl bachgen o dua phymtheg oed nes y bo tua phump ar hugain'. *Y Drysorfa* (Chwefror 1847), 90. 'Y mae yn dechreu teimlo nad yw gair Rabbi ond gair dyn ffaeledig . . . Mae ysbryd y genedl fel pe b'ai yn deffroi o hir gwsg. Y mae y llanc wedi ymryddâu o dan ddeddf ei dad, ac yn dechreu cerdded yn ei nerth ei hun'. *Y Drysorfa* (Chwefror 1847), 91.

59 Robert Knox, *The Races of Men* (London, 1850), p. 206.

60 John Hughes Morris, *The History of the Welsh Calvinistic Methodists' Foreign Mission to the end of the year 1904* (Caernarfon: CM Book Room, 1910).

61 Peter Lord, *Words with Pictures: Images of Wales and Welsh Images in the Popular Press, 1640–1860* (Aberystwyth: Planet, 1995), pp. 153–4.

[62] Lord, *Words with Pictures*, p. 154.

[63] John Mills, *The British Jews* (London, 1853), n. p.

[64] '. . . amcan penaf yr ysgrifenydd yn ei baratoi oedd ennill teimladau cristionogol ei gydwladwyr i weddio dros y genedl Iuddewig, ac i ymdrechu i'w hennill i'r gwirionedd fel y mae yn yr Iesu.' Mills, *Iuddewon Prydain* (London, 1852), n. p.

[65] Mills, *The British Jews*, p. 347.

[66] There is still a community in Khasia in India, for example, that shows the legacy of the Welsh mission there in the form of singing Welsh hymns and a version of the Welsh national anthem. Some members of the community retain links with Wales. For a discussion of anglicisation in a Welsh context, see my chapter, '"By Whom Shall She Arise? For She Is Small"', in Eitan Bar-Yosef and Nadia Valman (eds), *The Jew in Late-Victorian and Edwardian Culture* (London: Palgrave, 2009), pp. 161–82.

[67] The book appeared first in monthly serial form.

[68] '. . . y man goraf [*sic*] yn y byd'. Mills, *Palestina*, p. 500.

[69] '. . . dylem grybwyll, y byddai gwrthwynebiad anorfod i wneyd Palestina ei hun yn wladychfa yn meddwl pawb sydd yn credu mai Israel a'i pia, ac mai hwynt a'i meddianna eto'. Mills, *Palestina*, p. 500.

[70] '. . . byddai Gwladychfa Gymreig yn Palestina dan lygaid parhaus y gwahanol alluoedd Ewropeaidd, a byddai hyn yn sicrwydd na chae neb ymyryd â'i hannibyniaeth'. Mills, *Palestina*, p. 505.

[71] 'Ond am Palestina y mae natur yn gwneyd mwy na hanner y gwaith yno.' Mills, *Palestina*, p. 501.

[72] '. . . yn ngwasanaeth rhinwedd a chrefydd'. Mills, *Palestina*, p. 501.

[73] '. . . lle y gallent fyw fel cymundeb o Gymry – byw are eu tir eu hunain, ennill eu bara eu hunain, siarad eu iaith eu hunain, ffurfio eu deddfau eu hunain, mewn gair cario yn mlaen eu holl achosion fel cymundeb annibynol ar bob llywodraeth arall'. Mills, *Palestina*, p. 504.

[74] '. . . y mae y lle mor anhysbell [*sic*], ac allan o olwg y byd gwareiddedig, fel nad oes gobaith y deuai byth y sylw. Ond am Palestina, y mae pob cenedl yn teimlo cymaint o ddawr ynddi, fel y byddai y cymundeb lleiaf yno o gymaint pwys ag i gael lle yn y fan yn naearyddiaeth ac ar *fap* y byd'. Mills, *Palestina*, p. 505.

[75] 'Yr ydym yn teimlo yn sicr y byddai Mahommetaniaid, yn gystal a Christionogion brodorol, ac yn neillduol yr Iuddewon, yn bur fuan, yn llawn o deimladau caredig at y wladychfa, ac yn awyddus i'w gwasanaethu'. Mills, *Palestina*, p. 506.

[76] See Eitan Bar-Yosef, *The Holy Land in English Culture*, pp. 182–225.

[77] A report on such a lecture appears in *Y Drysorfa*. D. Evans, *Y Drysorfa* (Hydref, 1860), 353–4.

[78] Evans, 'Studies in Iberic=Hebraic Eschatology II', 124.

[79] '. . . arwyddion fod Rhagluniaeth Ddwyfol yn agor y ffordd i wneyd daioni iddynt'. John Mills, *Y Drysorfa* (Mehefin, 1859), 251.

[80] John Mills, *Three Months' Residence at Nablus and an Account of the Modern Samaritans* (1864), pp. vii–viii.

[81] Besharan Doumani, *Rediscovering Palestine: Merchants and Peasants in Jabal Nablus, 1700–1900* (Berkeley: University of California Press, 1995).

82   Lily Tobias, *The Samaritan. An Anglo-Palestinian Novel* (London: Robert Hale, 1939). The Samaritans now only number some 350 individuals, with half the community living in the West Bank near Mount Gerizim, which has an Israeli military installation at its summit. The other half of the community lives in Cholon, within Israel. Cut off from each other by the 1948 war, the communities were reconnected after the 1967 war, but are now once again separated. Men in the community have recently been marrying out, bringing in Russian and Ukrainian nominal converts as brides in order to safeguard the culture against extinction. Not a large community in Mills's time either, they were as subject then as they are now to the whims of successive administrations, and maintain a neutral position when it comes to political and ethnic conflicts. Photographer Ahikam Seri has documented Samaritan traditions near Nablus in recent years – see *www. ahikamseri.com*.

83   Mills, *Three Months' Residence at Nablus*, p. viii.

84   H. B. Tristram, *The Land of Israel* (1865), pp. 140–1.

85   None of this conveys how entertaining and sharp Mills can be as a writer – particularly on questions of personal hygiene. Staying in Nablus, with a family of Christian Arabs, he found the son, Silman, 'filthily dirty to the last degree . . . I always felt a solicitude lest he should come too near me. He had a thriving colony upon his person, and his continual motions showed that they roved over all the territory; but his head was the capital' (p. 124). Silman's father was 'anxious lest [Silman] should have a wife before he learnt to read; and I felt anxious lest he should have one before he had learnt to comb his head' (p. 124). Mills was equally worried about food hygiene. 'Sometimes it became very intolerable,' he remarks, 'when the idea would suggest itself that perhaps Silman . . . had been rummaging after his live stock during the cooking process' (p. 130).

86   Mills, 'Y Genadaeth Iuddewig', *Y Drysorfa* (Ionawr 1847), 61.

87   See the entries on Margaret Jones in Stephens (ed.), *The New Companion to the Literature of Wales*, p. 393, and in *Y Bywgraffiadur Cymreig*, p. 464.

88   Margaret Jones, *Llythyrau Cymraes o Wlad Canaan* (1869), p. 4.

89   '. . . daethant tuag atom, gan afael â'u bysedd yn eu dannedd blaen, fel pe buasent am eu tynnu allan o'u safnau, yr hyn sydd gan yr Arabiaid yn nod o amddifadrwydd'. Jones, *Llythyrau Cymraes o Wlad Canaan*, p. 15.

90   'Y mae y rhan fwyaf o'r Iuddewon yn dlodion a thruenus'. Jones, *Llythyrau Cymraes o Wlad Canaan*, pp. 41–2.

91   'Eu prif bechod, sef gwrthod a chroeshoelio Arglwydd y Bywyd . . . y rhai oedd yn yr amser gynt yn arglwyddi y tir wedi eu gostwng trwy bechod i raddau mor isel'. Jones, *Llythyrau Cymraes o Wlad Canaan*, p. 42. Similar sentiments appear in her account of Jews in Morocco.

92   Since this chapter was completed, a new expanded edition of Margaret Jones's letters has been published and this is discussed briefly in the conclusion.

Notes to Chapter 3

[1]   Bryan Cheyette (ed.), *Between Race and Culture: Representations of 'the Jew' in English and American Literature* (Stanford: Stanford University Press, 1996), p. 14.
[2]   Matthew Biberman, *Masculinity, Anti-Semitism and Early Modern English Literature: from the Satanic to the Effeminate Jew* (Aldershot: Ashgate, 2004), p. 121.
[3]   See, for example, David G. Goodman and Masanori Miyasawa, *Jews in the Japanese Mind: the History and Uses of a Cultural Stereotype* (1995; Lanham, MA: Lexington Books, 2000). The authors claim in the preface to the expanded later edition that the Japanese example 'confirms that antisemitism has nothing to do with Jews and everything to do with antisemites' (p. xvi), and while this is perhaps extreme, the study nevertheless shows the strength of semitic discourse largely divorced from living Jews.
[4]   Gwyn A. Williams, *When Was Wales? A History of the Welsh* (London: Black Raven, 1985), p. 5.
[5]   W. D. and Hilary L. Rubinstein, 'Philosemitism in Britain and in the English Speaking World, 1840–1939: Patterns and Typology', *Jewish Journal of Sociology*, 40/1–2 (1998), 5.
[6]   W. D. Rubinstein, 'The anti-Jewish riots of 1911 in south Wales: a re-examination', *Welsh History Review*, 18/4 (1997), 669.
[7]   David Cesarani, 'Reporting Antisemitism: The *Jewish Chronicle* 1879–1979', in Siân James, Tony Kushner and Sarah Pierce (eds), *Cultures of Ambivalence. Studies in Jewish – Non-Jewish Relations* (London: Vallentine and Mitchell, 1998), p. 255.
[8]   See in particular Bryan Cheyette, *Constructions of 'the Jew' in English Literature and Society: Racial Representations 1875–1945* (Cambridge: Cambridge University Press, 1993), and 'Neither black nor white: the figure of "the Jew" in Imperial British literature', in Linda Nochlin and Tamar Garb (eds), *The Jew in the Text: Modernity and the Construction of Identity* (London: Thames and Hudson, 1995), pp. 31–41.
[9]   See, for example, Bernard Gowers's review of Anthony Julius's *Trials of the Diaspora: A History of Anti-Semitism in England*, in *Jewish Quarterly*, 215 (2010), 80–1.
[10] Cheyette, *Constructions of the Jew*, 3.
[11] See for example both Hywel Teifi Edwards's and Grahame Davies's treatment of Caradoc Evans, discussed below.
[12] I am referring here to the register in which antisemitism is discussed, rather than to a psychological analysis of it. In the Welsh context there has not been, as far as I am aware, a psychoanalytic approach to imaging of Jews, such as Sander Gilman's *Jewish Self-Hatred: Anti-Semitism and the Hidden Language of the Jews* (Baltimore: John Hopkins University Press, 1988), or Matthew Biberman's *Masculinity, Anti-Semitism and Early Modern English Literature*.
[13] Cesarani, 'Reporting Antisemitism', p. 225.
[14] Cheyette, *Constructions of the Jew*, p. 5.

[15] A comparison of Arnold's formulations of Celtic literature and character and his formulation of Hebraism would no doubt reveal some suggestive resonances.

[16] David Lloyd George, *Is It Peace?* (London: Hodder and Stoughton, 1923), pp. 246–7.

[17] Ivor Wynne Jones, *Lloyd George's New Jerusalem* (Llandudno: Ivor Wynne Jones, *c.*1999), p. 13; Geoffrey Alderman, 'The anti-Jewish riots of August 1911 in South Wales: a response', *Welsh History Review*, 20/3 (2001), 566.

[18] John Grigg, *The Young Lloyd George* (Berkeley: University of California Press, 1973), p. 260.

[19] Grigg, *The Young Lloyd George*, p. 260.

[20] David Lloyd George, *Is it Peace?*, p. 247.

[21] Grigg, *The Young Lloyd George*, p. 260.

[22] David Berry, 'Introduction', in David Berry and Simon Horrocks (eds), *David Lloyd George: The Movie Mystery* (Cardiff: University of Wales Press, 1998), p. 19.

[23] Ron Berry, *So Long, Hector Bebb* (London: Macmillan, 1970). The novel was republished by Parthian in 2006 under the Library of Wales imprint, but the references that follow are to the original 1970 edition.

[24] Berry, *So Long, Hector Bebb*, p. 15.

[25] Ibid., p. 18.

[26] Geraint Goodwin, *The White Farm and Other Stories* (London: Jonathan Cape, 1937), p. 223.

[27] Ibid., p. 225.

[28] Geraint Goodwin, *The Heyday in the Blood* (1936; Cardigan: Library of Wales, 2008).

[29] Goodwin, *The White Farm*, p. 87.

[30] Ibid., pp. 88–9.

[31] Goodwin, *The Heyday in the Blood*, p. 23. All references are to the 2008 Library of Wales edition.

[32] Sam Adams, *Geraint Goodwin* (Cardiff: University of Wales Press, 1975), p. 46–7.

[33] Stephen Knight, *A Hundred Years of Fiction* (Cardiff: University of Wales Press, 2004), p. 45.

[34] Bryan Cheyette, 'White Skin, Black Masks: Jews and Jewishness in the Writings of George Eliot and Frantz Fanon', in Keith Ansell-Pearson, Benita Parry and Judith Squires (eds), *Cultural Readings of Imperialism: Edward Said and the Gravity of History* (London: Lawrence & Wishart, 1997), p. 107.

[35] Katie Gramich, Foreword to Geraint Goodwin, *The Heyday in the Blood*, p. xii.

[36] Ibid., p. xii.

[37] Letter to the author, 2000.

[38] In a letter to novelist Kate Roberts, Saunders Lewis observes of F. R. Leavis: 'Dylwn ddweud wrthych nad Cristion mo Leavis, Iddew ac agnostig, yn ôl a ddeallaf, yw ef, – ond Iddew amlwg iawn, Iddew Iddewig' (I should tell you that Leavis isn't a Christian but, as far as I understand, a Jew and an agnostic – but a very prominent Jew, a Jewish Jew'). Dafydd Ifans (gol.), *Annwyl Kate, Annwyl Saunders: Gohebiaeth, 1923–83* (Aberystwyth: Llyfrgell Genedlaethol Cymru, 1992), p. 153.

[39] The play was published in a two-play volume under the title *Esther* a *Serch Yw'r Doctor* (1960; Abertawe: Christopher Davies, 1977).

[40] The continued deployment of Lewis against Plaid Cymru may be seen, for example, in a 2001 debate on the Government of Wales Act 1998, in which Llew Smith, Labour MP for Blaenau Gwent, remarked: 'It is important that we understand the reasons for the demands of the nationalists and why they are pushing for independence. Anti-English prejudices have run throughout their party since its birth. Saunders Lewis, a founding member and former leader, saw the Jews and the English as enemies, while admiring Hitler and Mussolini. [Interruption.] Of course, the nationalists do not want to hear this. Of Hitler, Saunders Lewis declared: "At once he fulfilled his promise – a promise which was greatly mocked by the London papers months before that – to completely abolish the financial strength of the Jews in the economic life of Germany."' *www.publications.parliament.uk/pa/cm200102/cmhansrd/vo011205/halltext/11205h02.htm*. But see also Geoffrey Alderman's review of Anthony Julius's *Trials of the Diaspora: A History of Anti-Semitism in England* in the *Times Education Supplement* of 29 April 2010 for an outburst against both Saunders Lewis and Gwynfor Evans: *www.timeshighereducation.co.uk/story.asp?storyCode=411427&sectioncode=26*.

[41] In the fifth century, Bishop Germanus sought to slow the deterioration of British Christianity in its post-Roman crisis; Lewis's play was written in 1937 after his arrest for the symbolic arson at Penyberth, when he and two others protested against the building of a bombing school that would destroy a site that was of historical importance to Wales, and at the heart of a Welsh-language community. Passages from Lewis's play subsequently took on great significance in the nationalist movement.

[42] Ned Thomas, *The Welsh Extremist* (1970; Talybont: Y Lolfa, 1973), p. 64.

[43] Dorian Llywelyn, *Sacred Place, Chosen People: Land and National Identity in Welsh Spirituality* (Cardiff: University of Wales Press, 1999), p. 109.

[44] Llywelyn, *Sacred Place, Chosen People*, p. 110.

[45] By contrast, Alun Lewis's story, 'The Wanderers', published in the journal *Welsh Review* in 1939, shares features with Geraint Goodwin's short-story Jewish stereotypes, but does not share the extra rhetorical load that can be seen in Goodwin's work and in the writing of Saunders Lewis. Perhaps what is more uncomfortable to a reader in the twenty-first century is the designation of his character as 'the Jew': 'The Jew bent over [the earrings], fondling them with his skinny fingers'. Lewis's unnamed 'Jew' then rushes out to shovel up a pile of horse droppings newly deposited in the street (suggesting, perhaps, a desire to profit even in manure), and he rubs his hands in another representative Jewish gesture. But this does not carry the extra powerful international associations of the capitalist or cosmopolitan Jew. Alun Lewis, 'The Wanderers', *Welsh Review* (October 1939), 130.

[46] Saunders Lewis, 'The Deluge 1939', in Alun R. Jones and Gwyn Thomas (eds), *Presenting Saunders Lewis* (Cardiff: University of Wales Press, 1983), p. 178. The translation is by Gwyn Thomas.

[47] Caradoc Evans, *My People* (1915; Bridgend: Seren, 1987) and *Capel Sion* (1916; Bridgend: Seren, 2002).

[48] For critical work that bridges the divide see M. Wynn Thomas, *Corresponding Cultures: the Two Literatures of Wales* (Cardiff: University of Wales Press, 1999).

[49] Eryn White, 'The Established Church, Dissent and the Welsh Language', in Geraint H. Jenkins (ed.), *The Welsh Language Before the Industrial Revolution* (Cardiff: University of Wales Press, 1997), p. 268.

[50] Quoted in translation in Llywelyn, *Sacred Place: Chosen People*, p. 112, from Derec Llwyd Morgan, 'Y Beibl a Llenyddiaeth Gymraeg', in R. Geraint Gruffydd (gol.), *Y Gair ar Waith: Ysgrifau ar yr Etifeddiaeth Feiblaidd yng Nghymru* (Cardiff: University of Wales Press, 1988), p. 84.

[51] Aneirin Talfan Davies, 'A Question of Language', *The Welsh Anvil*, 5 (1953), 28.

[52] Aneirin Talfan Davies, 'A Question of Language', 27–8. Welsh writing in English, whose beginnings have in the past been located in the publication of *My People*, has been definitively pushed back well into the nineteenth century by feminist scholar Jane Aaron and others through their consideration of Welsh women's writing. For another intervention in the making of the Welsh writing in English canon, see Jane Aaron, 'Gendering the Canon', *Planet*, 201 (January 2011), 4–15.

[53] Ivor John, 'My People!', *The Welsh Outlook* (March 1916), 83.

[54] Hywel Teifi Edwards 'O'r Pentre Gwyn i Llaregyb', in M. Wynn Thomas (gol.), *DiFfinio Dwy Lenyddiaeth Cymru* (Cardiff, University of Wales Press, 1995), pp. 7–41.

[55] Edwards, 'O'r Pentre Gwyn i Llaregyb', pp. 25–6.

[56] Edwards writes: 'A chan dapio pwll o grawn o'i fewn, chwaraeodd ran yr hilgi er difyrrwch i ddarllenwyr y *Sunday Express*' (and in vomiting up a pool of pus from inside, he played the part of a racist for the delectation of *Sunday Express* readers). 'O'r Pentre Gwyn i Llaregyb', p. 26.

[57] Quoted from Edwards, 'O'r Pentre Gwyn i Llaregyb', p. 26.

[58] Derec Llwyd Morgan, 'Y Beibl a Llenyddiaeth Gymraeg', p. 84. To travel through Wales is to travel through biblical Israel or Palestine: you might see signs for or find yourself in Nebo, Bethlehem, Hebron, Caersalem (Jerusalem), Bethania, Moriah and many other biblical places.

[59] Ursula Henriques, *The Jews of South Wales: Historical Studies* (Cardiff: University of Wales Press, 1993), p. 13.

[60] Caradoc Evans, *Capel Sion*, p. 64.

[61] Oliver Sandys, *Caradoc Evans* (London: Hurst & Blackett, 1946), p. 73. The journal extracts are published in the biography, and are also reproduced as a companion piece in the republished novella *Morgan Bible* (1943; Aberystwyth: Planet, 2006).

[62] Lara Trubowitz, 'Acting like an Alien: "Civil" Antisemitism, the Rhetoricized Jew and Early Twentieth-Century British Immigration Law', in Eitan Bar-Yosef and Nadia Valman (eds), *'The Jew' in Late-Victorian and Edwardian Culture* (London: Palgrave, 2009), pp. 65–79.

[63] See, for example, John Harris's introduction to Caradoc Evans, *My People*, and T. L. Williams, *Caradoc Evans* (Cardiff: University of Wales Press, 1970).

[64] Draig Glas (Arthur Tyssilio Johnson), *The Perfidious Welshman* (London: S. Paul, 1910).

[65] The two authors moved in some of the same circles – for example they both knew Thomas Burke, author of *Limehouse Nights*.

[66] See, for example, Meri-Jane Rochelson (ed.), *Children of the Ghetto* (Detroit: Wayne State University Press, 1998), and the biography by Joseph H. Udelson, *Dreamer of the Ghetto: the Life and Works of Israel Zangwill* (Tuscaloosa: University of Alabama Press, 1990).

[67] My thanks to Alyce von Rothkirch for bringing these to my attention.

[68] T. L. Williams, *Caradoc Evans*, p. 94.

[69] Caradoc Evans, *This Way to Heaven* (London: Rich & Cowan, 1934), p. 15.

[70] Meic Stephens (ed.), *The New Companion to the Literature of Wales* (Cardiff: University of Wales Press, 1998), p. 228. Caradoc Evans, *Mother's Marvel* (London: Andrew Dakers, 1949).

[71] Indeed in the interwar period, Jews were heavily involved in the early film world, and the account may well portray particular historical individuals. However, John Harris suggests that the model for Tony, the 'mummy's boy', is clearly the son of Evans's wife (interview with John Harris, September 2010). The frantic rate of poor, quick film production locates the novel in the period of post-1927 legislation that introduced British film quotas, which led to a proliferation of cheap, popular film, much of which is now lost. Suggestively, the 'Ideal Pawnshops Company' mentioned in *This Way to Heaven* (p. 133) is no doubt a play on the Ideal Film Company, the Jewish company that in 1918 had made *The Life Story of David Lloyd George*, which was later suppressed. For discussion of the Ideal Film Company, see Berry and Horrocks (eds), *David Lloyd George: the Movie Mystery*. For Jews in early British film, see Nathan Abrams, 'Hidden: Jewish Film in the United Kingdom, past and present', *Journal of European Popular Culture*, 1/1 (2010), 53–68, and Edward Marshall, '"The dark, alien executive": Jewish producers, émigrés and the British film industry in the 1930s', in Geoffrey Alderman (ed.), *New Directions in Anglo-Jewish History* (Brighton, MA: Academic Studies Press, 2010), pp. 163–87.

[72] Harri Garrod Roberts has produced a fascinating study of 'abjection' in the work of Welsh writers including Caradoc Evans, which might be extended very usefully to this forgotten novel. Undoubtedly Julia Kristeva's theoretical meanings of 'abjection' has interesting applications to understanding Welsh imaging of self and Jew. See Harri Garrod Roberts, *Embodying Identity: Representations of the Body in Welsh Literature* (Cardiff: University of Wales Press, 2009).

[73] John Harris, *Fury Never Leaves Us: A Miscellany of Caradoc Evans* (Bridgend, Poetry Wales Press, 1985), p. 41.

[74] Evans, *Mother's Marvel*, p. 166.

[75] Evans, *This Way to Heaven*, pp. 262–3.

[76] Evans, *The Earth Gives All and Takes All* (London: Andrew Dakers, 1946), pp. 39–49. In the diary excerpts in the biography by Evans's wife, a brief entry suggests a delightfully humorous possible source for this oddity: 'The servant here, a German Jewess refugee, went for a walk yesterday and she met a man. The man said to her: "I have five cows, seven pigs, and so on. Will you marry me? Let me know next Sunday. You will know me by my dog."' Sandys, *Caradoc Evans*, p. 130.

[77] Evans, *This Way to Heaven*, p. 310.

Notes to Chapter 4

1   Harri Webb, 'Manuscript found in a bottle', *Collected Poems* (Llandysul: Gwasg Gomer, 1995), p. 95.
2   Plaid Cymru was founded in 1925 as Plaid Genedlaethol Cymru, the Welsh Nationalist Party. From 1945 onwards it was known as Plaid Cymru, the Party of Wales. To avoid confusion, the shorter name 'Plaid Cymru' is used here.
3   The journal published articles about Judaism and its latter-day developments; about Jewish belief, and about the influence of Jewish theology on Christianity – all through a Christian lens.
4   John Jones, 'Seioniaeth (Zionism)', *Y Traethodydd*, 58.251 (1903), 181.
5   Thomas J. Jones, 'Yr Iddewon a'r Rhyfel', *Y Traethodydd*, 73/327 (1918), 150.
6   Ibid.
7   Interview with Lyn Ebenezer, Pontrhydfendigaid, 2005.
8   Interview with Leo Abse, London, 2002.
9   D. Hywel Davies, *The Welsh Nationalist Party 1925–1945: A Call to Nationhood* (Cardiff: University of Wales Press, 1983), p. 166.
10 Quoted in Simon Griver, 'Learning from Hebrew', Israel Ministry of Foreign Affairs (originally Israel Government Press Office), *www.mfa.gov.il/MFA/go.asp?MFAH0kx50* (1 October 2001). Schapiro, a researcher at the Academy of the Hebrew Language, continues: '"In the 1960s, a national network of Welsh language classes was set up based on the Hebrew model . . . Of course the Welsh are confronted by a different problem . . . There the number of native Welsh speakers was eroded by the influence of English. With the help of the ulpanim, the trend has been reversed."'
11 See the discussion of Leo Abse, below. See also W. D. Rubinstein, 'The anti-Jewish riots of 1911 in south Wales: a re-examination', *Welsh History Review*, 18/4 (1997), 667–99.
12 'Un o'r aelodau Cymreig yn senedd Loegr yw'r Cymro bondigrybwyll hwnnw, y Syr Alfred Mond. Byddai Mond yn gyff gwawd a chwerthin digymar fel aelod Cymreig onibai ei fod yn un o'r cymeriadau mwyaf sinister a pheryglus yng ngwleidyddiaeth ein hoes ni.' J. Arthur Price, *Y Ddraig Goch*, 1/7 (Rhagfyr 1926), 1.
13 The 'Cook' referred to here is A. J. Cook, General Secretary of the Miners' Federation of Great Britain during the time of the general strike of 1926, who had Communist leanings and was also a target of criticism in this article. Alfred Mond was sensitive to his outsider status: in an article entitled 'Should Wales want Home Rule?' which had appeared in *Wales* in 1912, he suggests: 'Perhaps one who stands, in a certain sense, outside old controversies, and who has not been engaged in the efforts made in the past to deal with these difficulties, may be in a better position to form an unbiassed [*sic*] judgement, or may be more sanguine that the difficulties can be overcome than those whose greater knowledge and experience of the past tends to a certain feeling of discouragement.' *Wales*, 2/8 (August 1912), 420.
14 *The Protocols of the Elders of Zion*, a Russian publication alleging an international Jewish conspiracy, had been translated and published in England in 1920,

and had been prominently debunked in *The Times* the following year. Notoriously, Henry Ford had published *The Protocols* in America; just as notoriously, elements continued in circulation among Arab leaders, and form part of Hamas's now discarded Charter.

[15]   Mallt Williams, 'The Welsh Nation', *The Welsh Nationalist* (March 1934), 4.

[16]   J. E. Daniel, 'Eire a Phalesteina – Cymhariaeth' (Ireland and Palestine – A Comparison), *Y Ddraig Goch* (Chwefror 1938), 7.

[17]   Ibid.

[18]   Ibid. 'Tra y myn yr Iddewon lynu wrth wlad fel Loegr nad oes ganddi rithyn o ddiddordeb ond yn ei buddiannau ymerodrol ym Mhalesteina, ni welir yno heddwch'.

[19]   Lewis Valentine, 'Beddau'r Byw', *Y Ddraig Goch* (Gorfennaf 1938), 9.

[20]   'Ni allai taeogrwydd fynd ymhellach nag argraffu ar furiau'r Synagog weddi arbennig dros y brenin' (Servility could go no further than print on the walls of the Synagogue a special prayer for the king). Ibid., 12.

[21]   'triniaeth y Sais o'r brodor – y "bloody wops" fel y gelwid pob math o Arab o Gasablanca i Deheran, a'r "bloody Yids"'.

[22]   Anon., 'Profiad Milwr', *Y Ddraig Goch* (Ionawr 1945), 2.

[23]   Ibid., 2–3.

[24]   Anon., 'Oliver Brown o'r Alban yn dweud "Ni ellir dibynu ar Gymru"', *Y Ddraig Goch* (Ebrill 1945), 5.

[25]   Ibid. 'Y mae goreuon yr Iddewon ymhell y tu hwnt i'r Scotiaid a'r Cymry, a'r gwaethaf ohonynt i'r un graddau'n is na'r Scotiaid a'r Cymry am eu bod wedi dioddef yn drymach ac yn hwy . . . Cyfodwn ein Caersalem yn ein gwlad ein hun, pa le bynnag y bo; canys honno yw ein Tir Santaidd ni.'

[26]   Gwynfor Evans, 'Neges Palesteina i Gymru: Camp Iddewon Heddiw', *Y Ddraig Goch* (Hydref 1946), 3.

[27]   Ibid.

[28]   Anon. (assistant editor), 'Hebrew re-birth after 1500 years', *Welsh Nation* (February 1969), 3. The heading, in Hebrew (with one letter printed upside down), is translated as 'The spirit of the nation revives the most ancient living language in the world'.

[29]   'A ellid gweithio'r cynllun yma yng Nghymru ynglŷn â gwerthu tir i Saeson?' Letters page, *Y Ddraig Goch* (October 1947), 2.

[30]   Wyn Jones, 'Pentrefi Cydweithredol Palestina', *Y Ddraig Goch* (Tachwedd 1947), 6.

[31]   Davies, *The Welsh Nationalist Party*, p. 112.

[32]   Gwynfor Evans, 'Eu Hiaith a Gadwant?', *Y Ddraig Goch* (Gorffennaf 1937), 8.

[33]   If such a parallel was no doubt informed by the Welsh-Israelite biblical tradition of his chapel background, it is interesting to note that this was the Independent, not Calvinistic denomination – the Independents having supported the lifting of Jewish and Catholic disabilities considerably earlier than the Calvinistic Methodists. Such denominational difference in attitudes to Jews deserves closer study.

[34]   Rhys Evans, *Gwynfor Evans: Portrait of a Patriot* (Talybont: Y Lolfa, 2008), p. 110.

35 Ibid., p. 119.
36 Saunders Lewis, 'The Fate of the Language', trans. Elizabeth Edwards, *Planet*, 203 (2011), 20. Originally published in *Planet*, 4 (1971), 13–27.
37 Lewis, 'The Fate of the Language' (2011), 10–11.
38 R. Evans, *Gwynfor Evans*, p. 218.
39 Ibid., p. 217.
40 See John Humphries, *Freedom Fighters: Wales's Forgotten 'War', 1963–1993* (Cardiff: University of Wales Press, 2008).
41 Humphries, *Freedom Fighters*, p. 97.
42 R. Evans, *Gwynfor Evans*, pp. 143–4.
43 Conversation with Cynog Dafis, Aberystwyth, 2005.
44 The date of Judith Maro's arrival in Wales is given inconsistently: the *New Companion to the Literature of Wales* states that she has lived in Wales since 1949; in correspondence she gave the date of her arrival as the early 1950s. Letter to the author, 5 March 2004.
45 Y Lolfa was founded by Robat Gruffudd, the son of German-Jewish refugee writer Kate Bosse-Griffiths.
46 *Welsh Nation* replaced *The Welsh Nationalist*, which was published from 1932 to 1949.
47 Judith Maro, *Hen Wlad Newydd* (Talybont: Y Lolfa, 1974), p. 16–17: '. . . teimlais ar unwaith rywfaint o berthynas rhwng Cymru ac Israel . . . a dyma beth y byddwn yn dod i sylwi arno dro ar ôl tro, atsain rhwng fy ngwlad fy hun a'r wlad roeddwn yn mynd i fyw ynddi . . . Roeddwn i gartref – bron.'
48 Judith Maro, 'Adfer yr Hebraeg', *Taliesin* (Rhagfyr 1971), 52–73; 'The Hebrew revival – a lesson for Wales', *Welsh Nation* (1 June 1973), 4, and 'Welsh "Ulpans": the way for a major linguistic breakthrough?', *Welsh Nation* (8 June 1973), 5.
49 Gwynfor Evans, 'Cyflwyniad', in Maro, *Hen Wlad Newydd*, p. 4.
50 Gwynfor Evans, 'Digwyddodd yn Israel', *Barn* (April 1969), 152–3.
51 Ned Thomas, *The Welsh Extremist* (1971; Talybont: Y Lolfa, 1991).
52 Thomas, *The Welsh Extremist*, p. 17.
53 Ned Thomas, 'Israel/Wales: An Interview with Judith Maro', *Planet*, 31 (1976), 16.
54 Ibid.
55 Ibid., 19.
56 Raymond Garlick, 'Roll Call', *Planet*, 31 (1976), 20.
57 S. Ariel, 'This is not a Fairytale', *Planet*, 4 (1971), 39.
58 Thomas, *The Welsh Extremist*, p. 122.
59 Ibid., pp. 127–8.
60 The longevity and ubiquity of this notion of Jewish influence on or control of media and capital can make the most apparently benign observation suspect to those for whom its motifs are familiar, but outside Jewish scholarly circles knowledge of such conspiracy theories is limited. Hence even though Thomas is in all likelihood making a quite neutral comparison between relative Welsh and Jewish influence, the resonance cannot be ignored. The website *www.jewwatch.com* stands as exemplar of the conspiracy theory in its modern form.
61 Thomas, *The Welsh Extremist*, p. 123.

[62] Ibid. Judith Maro herself claims, in correspondence, that she discussed with the BBC and Saunders Lewis her possible translation of *Esther* into Hebrew for the Hebrew hour on the World Service. She admired and liked him immensely, and revealed that she only learned later about his attitudes to Jews, of which he repented. Undated letter, 2000.

[63] Bernard Susser, 'The Ideology of Affliction: Reconsidering the Adversity Thesis', in Howard Wettstein (ed.), *Diasporas and Exiles: Varieties of Jewish Identity* (Berkeley: University of California Press, 2002), pp. 221–33. Bernard Gowers, reviewing Anthony Julius's 2009 *Trials of the Diaspora: a History of Anti-Semitism in England*, suggests both the continuing strength of that tradition and its limitations – see Bernard Gowers, *Jewish Quarterly*, 215 (Summer 2010), 80–1.

[64] For a discussion of this phenomenon more widely in Welsh poetry in English, see J. Donahaye, 'Identification, Rejection and Cultural Co-option in Welsh Poetry in English', in Daniel Williams (ed.), *Slanderous Tongues: Essays on Welsh Poetry in English, 1970–2005* (Bridgend: Seren, 2010), pp. 226–46.

[65] Judith Maro, undated letter to the author, 2000.

[66] Maro, 'Wisdom be thy chief thought', *The Anglo-Welsh Review*, 10/26 (1960), 54. This was republished under the title 'Addysg' (Education) in *Hen Wlad Newydd*.

[67] Interview with Leo Abse, London, 2002. See J. Donahaye, 'Cultivating irreverence', *Planet*, 160 (August/September 2003), 7–17.

[68] Gwynfor Evans, *For the Sake of Wales* (1996; Caernarfon: Welsh Academic Press, 2001), pp. 182–3. Originally published as *Bywyd Cymro* (Caernarfon: Gwasg Gwynedd, 1982).

[69] National Library of Wales Leo Abse archive d/f/7 and 1–14. All letters quoted are from the same source.

[70] Ibid. This reads, 'capitulate to the mean concept of a nation state' in *Wotan My Enemy: Can Britain Live with the Germans in the European Union?* (London: Robson Books, 1994), p. 24.

[71] NLW Leo Abse archive d/f/7 and 1–14.

[72] See J. Donahaye, '"A dislocation called a blessing": three Welsh-Jewish perspectives', in *Welsh Writing in English: A Yearbook of Critical Essays*, 7 (2001–2), pp. 154–73.

[73] Leo Abse, 'A tale of collaboration not conflict with the "people of the book"', *New Welsh Review*, 6/2 (1993), 20.

[74] Dannie Abse, *Goodbye Twentieth Century: An Autobiography* (London: Pimlico, 2001), p. 16. In 'The anti-Jewish riots', Rubinstein describes Thomas as a 'notable recent Welsh sympathizer with Jewish causes' (677, footnote 36).

[75] Interview with Leo Abse, London, 2002.

[76] Ibid.

[77] Perhaps as telling is his remark about another motivation behind his often vituperative anti-nationalism: 'in my mind all the time, was the consequences of extreme nationalism to wherever Jews were. The nationalism that grew up in Wales was exactly the same sort of nationalism that Theodor Herzl had reacted to and adopted. Theodor Herzl for whom I've no time, right?' Herzl was a founding figure in the political Zionist movement.

78   Gwynfor Evans, *For the Sake of Wales*, p. 163.
79   Ali Yassine, 2009, during the recording, with the author, of 'Y Ferch a'i Chrefydd' for Radio Cymru.
80   The poem was first published in *Welsh Nation* in 1969, when Harri Webb was editor. Meic Stephens, editor of *Harri Webb: Collected Poems*, gives 1966 with a question mark as the year of composition.
81   Harri Webb, *The Green Desert: Collected Poems 1950–1969* (Llandysul: Gomer, 1969), p. 59. Reproduced by kind permission of Meic Stephens.
82   At the time Harri Webb was associated with the underground direct action groups that found inspiration in the Haganah and the Irgun, among others. A Republican, he left Plaid Cymru for a period, but his actual involvement wasn't widely known until after his death. See John Humphries, *Freedom Fighters*, pp. 6 and 68.
83   In *The Informed Heart* (1960; London: Penguin, 1986), Bruno Bettelheim details the psychological means by which a profound passivity was created among Jews in Europe. His attribution to Jews in the extermination camps of a kind of death wish (as explanation of why relatively few rebelled) has caused angry controversy ever since. Webb's depiction, again, might usefully be examined, like conversionist depictions, in terms of Julia Kristeva's understandings of 'the abject'.
84   For a discussion of Harri Webb's Republicanism and his political models, see Nicholas Jones, '"Marching Backwards": Nationalism, Tradition and Ambivalence in the Poetry of Harri Webb', in Williams (ed.), *Slanderous Tongues*, pp. 60–86.
85   Ephraim Nimni (ed.), *The Challenge of Post-Zionism: Alternatives to Israeli Fundamentalist Politics* (London: Zed Books, 2003), pp. 1–2.
86   Nimni, *The Challenge of Post-Zionism*, p. 3, discussing Chaim Waxman, 'Critical sociology and the end of ideology in Israel', *Israel Studies*, 2/1 (1997), 194–210. As Nimni claims, post-Zionism is a term of hope as well as one of abuse. 'The debate about the importance or triviality of post-Zionism is iconoclastic, comprehensive, bitter, subversive of cherished beliefs, collective memories and emotions, and not lacking in vilification and *ad hominem* attacks.'
87   In *The Holocaust Industry*, for all its sometimes overstated and inflammatory rhetoric, Norman Finkelstein disturbingly analyses the way in which the image of the vulnerable diaspora Jew has continued to be utilised by Israel (and by fundraising groups). Norman Finkelstein, *The Holocaust Industry* (London: Verso 2000).
88   Ilan Pappe, *The Ethnic Cleansing of Palestine* (Oxford: Oneworld Publications, 2006).
89   See Eitan Bronstein and others, *www.zochrot.org.il*, and J. Donahaye, 'The Pain of Remembering', *Planet*, 196 (Winter 2010), 65–76.
90   *The Green Desert* is the name of the collection in which this poem first appears. See Brian Morris's monograph on Harri Webb in the Writers of Wales series (Cardiff: University of Wales Press, 1993). 'Eretz Israel' – the Land of Israel – differs significantly in register from 'Medinat Israel', the State of Israel, and in this distinction lies the concern at the heart of post-Zionism: Israel as a Jewish state and/or Israel as a multicultural liberal democracy.

[91] Maro, *Hen Wlad Newydd*, pp. 72–3.
[92] Letter to the author, 21 December 2000.

Notes to Chapter 5

[1] See Michael Ragussis, *Figures of Conversion: 'The Jewish Question' and English National Identity* (Durham: Duke University Press, 1995), and Nadia Valman, *The Jewess in Nineteenth-Century British Literary Culture* (Cambridge: Cambridge University Press, 2007).

[2] Isaiah Berlin, *The Crooked Timber of Humanity: Chapters in the History of Human Ideas* (London: Fontana, 1991), p. 245.

[3] Lara Trubowitz, 'Acting like an Alien: "Civil" Antisemitism, the Rhetoricized Jew and Early Twentieth-Century British Immigration Law', in Eitan Bar-Yosef and Nadia Valman (eds), *'The Jew' in Late-Victorian and Edwardian Culture* (London: Palgrave, 2009), p. 70.

[4] Israel Zangwill, *Children of the Ghetto: a Study of a Peculiar People* (1892); Grace Aguilar, *The Vale of Cedars* (1850).

[5] The only copies I have been able to find are those published in these two years that are held by Cardiff Public Library.

[6] Anthony Glaser and Ursula Henriques, 'The Valleys communities', in Ursula Henriques (ed.), *The Jews of South Wales: Historical Studies* (Cardiff: University of Wales Press, 1993), pp. 45–67. Glaser and Henriques observe that, in the valleys, the Jewish literary societies often became amalgamated with Zionist societies and they were therefore both cultural and political in outlook and purpose. The societies were also given considerable support by the London Union of Jewish Literary Societies and it was reputedly at a conference of this union that the writer Lily Tobias met her future husband Phillip Tobias.

[7] See for example Robert Pope, *Building Jerusalem: Nonconformity, Labour and the Social Question in Wales, 1906–1939* (Cardiff: University of Wales Press, 1998), and Robert Smith, *'In the direct and homely speech of the workers': Llais Llafur 1898–1915* (Aberystwyth: University of Wales Centre for Advanced Welsh and Celtic Studies, 2000).

[8] *The South Wales Jewish Review* (hereafter *SWJR*) (September 1904), 132. This could, of course, be read as a potential cause of resentment by non-Jewish workers.

[9] *SWJR* (November 1904), 169. This suggests the presence of recent immigrants. The strained relationship between established and immigrant Jews is examined by Leonard Mars in 'Immigration and anglicisation: religious education as an issue in the Swansea Hebrew Congregation, 1894–1910', *Jewish Journal of Sociology*, 39/1–2 (1997), 76–86, and 'The Ministry of the Reverend Simon Fyne in Swansea, 1899–1906', in Henriques (ed.), *The Jews of South Wales*, pp. 111–30. See also Jasmine Donahaye, '"By Whom Shall She Arise? For She Is Small": the Wales-Israel Tradition in the Edwardian Period', in Eitan Bar-Yosef and Nadia Valman (eds), *'The Jew' in Late-Victorian and Edwardian Culture*, pp. 161–82.

[10] For an assessment of analysis of the Tredegar riots, see Jasmine Donahaye, 'Jewish writing in Wales' (unpublished Ph.D. thesis, Swansea University, 2004), chapter 1.

[11] *SWJR* (April 1904), 49. In 1895, Goldsmid had met in Cardiff with Theodor Herzl, introduced by Israel Zangwill in an important precursor to the first Zionist Congress. See Raphael Patai (ed.), *The Complete Diaries of Theodor Herzl*, trans. Harry Zohn, vol. 1 (New York: Herzl Press and Thomas Yoseloff Press, 1960).

[12] *SWJR* (January 1904), 16; (February 1904), 30.

[13] *SWJR* (February 1904), 30 and 32.

[14] *SWJR* (September 1904), 130. The score of 'The Captivity' by D. Emlyn Evans was published in Aberystwyth by D. Jenkins in 1903. The Welsh translation of Oliver Goldsmith was by none other than H. Elvet Lewis – Elfed – whose conversionist sentiments in the collection *Israel and Other Poems* are discussed in chapter 2.

[15] *SWJR* (September 1904), 130.

[16] *SWJR* (September 1904), 6–7. Contrary to this claim, it should be observed that Yiddish-speaking maids working for the nouveau-riche Jewish families in the 1920s and 1930s appear in *A First Class Funeral* by Sonia Birch-Jones (Lantzville, British Columbia: Oolichan Books, 1983). See also Simon Joseph, *My Formative Years: a Jewish Boy's Childhood in South Wales in the Early 1900s* (London: Multifarious Publications, 1993), p. 29.

[17] '. . . a'u cywaid cyfalafwyr Iuddewig' and 'hanes dinystrio rhyddid ac anibyniaeth mân genhedloedd', from *Llais Llafur* (9 December 1905), quoted in Robert Smith, *'In the direct and homely speech of the workers'*, p. 8. Leo Abse claimed that Tobias had written for the 'famed socialist *Red Dragon* published in Ystalyfera', but *Llais Llafur* was the well-known socialist paper published in the town. In a portrait of Tobias in the *Western Mail* on 22 January 1927, she mentions 'a local paper' whose staff she joined (p. 7). A review of her novel *Eunice Fleet* in the *Western Mail* on 4 May 1933 identifies her as having once been on the staff of the *Western Mail* (p. 13).

[18] Leo Abse, 'A tale of collaboration not conflict with the "people of the book"', *New Welsh Review*, 6/2 (1993), 20.

[19] Tobias, *The Nationalists and Other Goluth Studies* (London: C. W. Daniel, 1921), p. 16.

[20] *Western Mail* (22 January 1927), 7. I am grateful to Alyce von Rothkirch for this and previous *Western Mail* references.

[21] Harri Webb, *The Green Desert: Collected Poems 1950–1969* (Llandysul: Gomer, 1969), p. 59.

[22] Tobias, *The Nationalists*, p. 17.

[23] Ibid., p. 80.

[24] *The Nationalists*, pp. 81–3.

[25] Lily Tobias, *My Mother's House* (London: George Allen & Unwin, 1931), p. 175.

[26] For a stimulating deployment of queer terminology in an exploration of Jewish assimilation, see Jon Stratton, *Coming Out Jewish: Constructing Ambivalent Identities* (London: Routledge, 2000).

[27] Tobias, *My Mother's House*, pp. 164–5.

[28] Lily Tobias, *The Samaritan. An Anglo-Palestinian Novel* (London: Robert Hale, 1939). As indicated in the author note, the novel was largely finished in 1938, but

Tobias's husband was killed in a riot in Haifa that summer, and she was unable to rework it substantially afterwards. It was published in 1939.

29 Tobias, *The Samaritan*, p. 178.

30 Ibid., pp. 178–9.

31 Ibid., p. 178. Perhaps this 'famous parallel' refers to Arthur Balfour's maiden speech delivered on 21 June 1922, in which he observed: 'Here you have a small race, originally inhabiting a small country, I think about the size of Wales or Belgium'. Quoted in Christopher Sykes, *Cross Roads to Israel* (London: Collins, 1965), p. 18. See also Alfred Zimmern's comparison in *Nationality and Government and Other Wartime Essays* (London: Chatto & Windus, 1919), in which he asks: 'Why [does] Palestine, which is the size of Wales . . . mean more to mankind than the whole of the New World?' (pp. 99–100). The comparison, in terms of size, of Israel with Wales is very widespread. For a variant, see Betty Miller, *Farewell Leicester Square* (1941; London: Persephone, 2000): 'there's only an area about a quarter the size of Wales for sixteen million Jews to redeem themselves on' (p. 182).

32 Tobias, *The Samaritan*, 178.

33 Tobias, *The Samaritan*, p. 14. The reference to a colonist here is not to the colonial administration under the British Mandate, but to a 'Jewish colonist', when the term was free, at least in Zionist circles, of its now largely pejorative associations.

34 This may well be a consequence of exposure to such attitudes that were widespread in the 1904–5 religious revival in Wales.

35 Tobias, *My Mother's House*, p. 188.

36 It is unclear whether Tobias is referring to the famous Welsh preacher Christmas Evans in the naming of this character.

37 Tobias, *The Nationalists*, p. 46.

38 Ibid., p. 47.

39 Tobias, *The Samaritan*, p. 181.

40 Ibid., p. 182.

41 Ibid., p. 183.

42 Tobias, *My Mother's House*, pp. 30 and 35.

43 Ibid., p. 45.

44 Dai Smith, Preface, *Aneurin Bevan and the World of South Wales* (Cardiff: University of Wales Press, 1993); Denis Balsom, 'The Three Wales Model', in John Osmond (ed.), *The National Question Again: Welsh Political Identity in the 1980s* (Llandysul: Gomer, 1985), pp. 1–17.

45 Gwyn A. Williams's 'American' Wales in *The Welsh in Their History* differs somewhat, perhaps – but the nickname 'American' Wales that he and others refer to often points back to Zimmern's *My Impressions of Wales* (London: Mills and Boon, 1921).

46 Zimmern, *My Impressions of Wales*, p. 29.

47 Jane Aaron, *The Welsh Survival Gene: The 'Despite Culture' in the Two Language Communities of Wales* (Cardiff: Institute of Welsh Affairs, 2003), p. 2.

48 Zimmern, *My Impressions of Wales*, p. 19.

49 Edward Said, *Orientalism* (1978; Harmondsworth; Penguin, 1985).

50 Alfred Zimmern, 'The Oldest British Colony', *The Welsh Outlook* (April 1917), 124. Henry Rowlands, *Mona Antiqua Restaurata – an Archaeological Discourse on the Antiquities, Natural and Historical, of the Isle of Anglesey, the Antient Seat of the British Druids in Two ESSAYS* (1723; Macclesfield: Redesmere Press Ltd, 1993).

51 Zimmern, 'The Oldest British Colony', 124.

52 Ibid.

53 Alfred Zimmern, 'Wales and the World', *The Welsh Outlook* (September 1920), 213.

54 Alfred Zimmern, 'True or False Nationalisms', *The Welsh Outlook* (March 1916), 80.

55 Zimmern identifies Jewish and Armenian national consciousness as the oldest (presumably the oldest in Europe). Curiously, Shmuel Niger includes a chapter on the Welsh and Armenian languages and traditions of bilingualism in his survey of Jewish literature, *Bilingualism in the History of Jewish Literature*, trans. Joshua A. Fogel (Lanham: University Press of America, 1990).

56 Alfred Zimmern, 'The International Settlement and Small Nationalities', *The Welsh Outlook* (July 1919), 175.

57 Zimmern, *My Impressions of Wales*, pp. 40–1.

58 Bernice Rubens, *Yesterday in the Back Lane* (London: Little, Brown and Co., 1995), and *The Waiting Game* (London: Little, Brown & Co., 1997).

59 Bernice Rubens, *Brothers* (1983; London: Abacus, 1984), p. 204.

60 Jasmine Donahaye, '"Gartref – bron": adversity and refuge in the Jewish literature of Wales', in Daniel Williams and Alyce von Rothkirch (eds), *Beyond the Difference: Welsh Literature in Comparative Contexts* (Cardiff: University of Wales Press, 2004), pp. 38–53.

61 Michael Woolf, 'Negotiating the Self: Jewish Fiction in Britain Since 1945', in Robert A. Lee (ed.), *Other Britain, Other British* (London: Pluto Press, 1995), p. 136.

62 Nini Herman, Foreword in Josef Herman, *Related Twilights: Notes from an Artist's Diary* (1975; Bridgend: Seren, 2002), p. 10.

63 Ozi Rhys Osmond, 'Epiphany in Ystradgynlais', *New Welsh Review*, 48 (2000), 9.

64 Josef Herman, *Notes from a Welsh Diary 1944–1955* (London: Free Association Books, 1988), pp. vii–ix.

65 Josef Herman, *The Early Years in Scotland and Wales* (Llandybïe: Christopher Davies, 1984), p. 89.

66 Ibid., pp. 85–6.

67 Ibid., p. 85.

68 Ibid, p. 85. John Berger, *Permanent Red: Essays in Seeing* (London: Methuen & Co. Ltd, 1960), p. 92.

69 Herman, *Related Twilights*, p. 110.

70 Herman, *The Journals* (London: Peter Halban, 2003), p. 17.

71 Josef Herman, *'Memory of Memories': The Glasgow Drawings 1940–43* (Glasgow: Third Eye Centre, 1985), p. 7.

[72] Josef Herman, 'A Strange Son of the Valley', *The Jewish Quarterly*, 21/1–2 (1973), 133. Moishe was not the only Jewish miner – see also Morris Silverglit from Aberfan. Recorded by David Jacobs, 1978, Oral History Archive, Museum of Welsh Life, tape 6017.

[73] For an excellent discussion of the problematic notion of Jewish art and Jewish artists see Margaret Olin, *The Nation without Art: Examining Modern Discourses in Jewish Art* (Lincoln: University of Nebraska Press, 2001).

[74] Mimi Josephson, 'Dual Loyalties', *Wales*, 4 (December 1958), 17.

[75] Robat Gruffudd, letter to the author, 25 February 2001.

[76] Interview with Heini Gruffudd, 5 June 2003. For an account of her life, upon which this discussion draws, see Heini Gruffudd, 'Cofio Kate Bosse-Griffiths', *Taliesin*, 102 (1998), 100–9, in which he observes: '[D]ihangodd [hi] yn fwyaf dianaf [o'i theulu], er na all neb fesur anaf i enaid. O hynny ymlaen mesurai anawsterau bywyd yn ôl graddfa Ravensbrück, a bach iawn oedd ei phwys ar foethau materol' (105) (She escaped the least harmed [of her family], although the injury to her soul cannot be measured. From then on she would measure life's difficulties according to the scale of Ravensbrück, and she had little concern with material luxuries).

[77] This was published by Y Lolfa in 1995.

[78] Kate Bosse-Griffiths, *Mae'r Galon wrth y Llyw* (Aberystwyth: Gwasg Aberystwyth, 1957).

[79] Interview with J. Gwyn Griffiths, Swansea, 2003.

[80] Bosse-Griffiths, *Mae'r Galon wrth y Llyw*, p. 77.

[81] Marion Löffler, 'A Tribute to Dr Kate', *Minerva: Transactions of the Royal Institution of South Wales*, 7 (1999), 6.

[82] The choice to use Jews to present German-language culture perhaps met a double need: on the one hand, she was reclaiming liberal German-language culture from the prevailing Nazi ethos and image; on the other she was reclaiming her right to be identified with that culture, reaffirming as she did the humanism and internationalism of Germany, and reaffirming the Germanness (and hence also the internationalism) of German Jews. She was certainly not alone in the effort: in England the formation of the Free German League of Culture by émigrés Fred Uhlman and Oskar Kokoschka had a similar purpose. This project soon disintegrated, according to Uhlman's hotly anti-Communist rhetoric in *The Making of an Englishman* (London: Gollancz, 1960), because of infiltration by German Communists.

[83] This community is described in Fred Uhlman, *The Making of an Englishman*, and in Josef Herman's *Journals*.

[84] Anna Plodeck, letter to the author, November 2003; Anna Plodeck, 'Fred Uhlman in Exile: Painter, Writer, Collector' (unpublished Ph.D. thesis, Courtauld Institute, 2004).

[85] Fred Uhlman, *Reunion* (1971; 1985; London: Harvill, 1997). The edition with Koestler's introduction was published by Fontana in 1978.

[86] David Cesarani, *Arthur Koestler: The Homeless Mind* (London: Vintage, 1999); Anna Plodeck, letter to the author, November 2003.

[87] See Mervyn Jones, Foreword to Jeremy Brooks, *Jampot Smith* (Cardigan: Library of Wales, 2008), p. xiii.

88   Clough Williams-Ellis, *An Artist in North Wales: Pictures by Fred Uhlman* (London: P. Eleck, 1946).
89   Rupert Crawshay-Williams, *Russell Remembered* (London: Oxford University Press, 1970), p. 120. Also quoted by Clough Williams-Ellis in his memoir *Architect Errant* (London: Constable, 1971), pp. 212–13.
90   Crawshay-Williams, *Russell Remembered*, p. 120.
91   Jones, *Jampot Smith*, pp. viii–xv.
92   Richard Dove, *Journey of No Return: Five German-speaking Literary Exiles in Britain 1933–45* (London: Libris, 2000), p. 163. Stefan Zweig was closely associated, along with Uhlman and Kokoschka, with the Free German League of Culture, which was founded in Uhlman's house in 1938. According to an anonymous obituary, Uhlman's home provided 'a welcome haven for large numbers of émigré artists and intellectuals'. See 'From émigré to Englishman', *The Jewish Quarterly*, 32/3 (1985), 5.
93   Letter from Francis Uhlman to the author, 29 November 2003.
94   Williams-Ellis, *An Artist in North Wales*, p. 40.
95   Eric Hobsbawm, *Interesting Times: a Twentieth-Century Life* (London: Abacus, 2002), pp. 23–4.
96   This is not to suggest that Hobsbawm was unaware of this history. On the contrary, he commented extensively on Welsh labour history. Hence his silence in this context is peculiar. See Dai Smith's account in 'Left Historic', *New Welsh Review*, 59 (Spring 2003), 11–19.
97   Hobsbawm, *Interesting Times*, pp. 240–1.
98   Graham Samuel, 'Artist Who Fled', *Western Mail* (11 March 1968), 6.
99   Hobsbawm, *Interesting Times*, p. 242.
100 Agi Katz, 'Josef Herman's "Memory of Memories"', *The Jewish Quarterly*, 32/1 (1985), 15–16.
101 Anon., 'From émigré to Englishman', *The Jewish Quarterly*, 32/3 (1985), 119.
102 Donahaye, '"Gartref – bron"', p. 167.
103 Maurice Edelman, 'To me it means home', *Jewish Chronicle* (20 September 1963), vii.
104 Lionel Simmonds, 'The Welsh and Ourselves', *Jewish Chronicle* (20 September 1963), v.
105 Ibid.
106 W. H. J., 'A Jew of Wales', *Western Mail* (21 March 1931), 13. I am grateful to Alyce von Rothkirch for this reference.
107 GWR, 'My Mother's House', *The Welsh Outlook* (April 1932), 12.

Notes to Conclusion

1   Gwyn A. Williams, *The Welsh in Their History* (London: Croom Helm, 1982), p. 191. The radio broadcast was published by the BBC as a pamphlet, before being included in this collection of essays.
2   *Western Mail* (22 January 1927), 7. I am grateful to Alyce von Rothkirch for this reference.

3   For example, towards the end of Emyr Humphreys's novel *Jones*, a character observes: "'My mother was Jewish and I feel myself getting more Jewish year by year. And that's what the Welsh nonconformists are, or were, I suppose. Pale imitation Jews. Natural born ghetto-dwellers.'" Emyr Humphreys, *Jones* (London: J. M. Dent & Sons, 1984), p. 118. My thanks to M. Wynn Thomas for this reference.

4   Katie Gramich, *Twentieth-Century Women's Writing in Wales: Law, Gender, Belonging* (Cardiff: University of Wales Press, 2007), p. 101. The Jew in question, although undoubtedly representing the stereotype of the Jewish capitalist, is himself depicted more in threatening than obsequious or 'greasy' terms. As with Geraint Goodwin's stories and novel, he is also more troublingly worldly and *English* than Jewish for the monolingual Welsh-speaking couple that he targets.

5   See Dorothy Edwards, *Rhapsody* (1927; Cardigan: Library of Wales, 2007).

6   Eirian Jones, *Y Gymraes o Ganaan: Anturiaethau Margaret Jones ar Bum Cyfandir* (Talybont: Y Lolfa, 2011), p. 41.

7   E. Wyn James, 'Rhagair', *Y Gymraes o Ganaan*, p. 12.

8   Frank McCourt, *Angela's Ashes* (New York: Touchstone, 1999), p. 9.

9   See, for example, Dannie Abse, *Goodbye Twentieth Century* (London: Pimlico, 2001), p. 15 and p. 195, where he describes an upbringing without encountering antisemitism, and pp. 67–9 for his discussion of an antisemitism-determined Jewishness, albeit one rooted in knowledge of the Holocaust.

10 That formula of Jewish vulnerability being redeemed by Jewish statehood is discredited by many post-Zionists, who assert that statehood and what it has entailed has rendered Jews more rather than less vulnerable in the world. Others assert that Jewish vulnerability in the world has lessened in proportion to the development of liberal democracies.

11 *SWJR* (February 1904), 25.

12 *SWJR* (September 1904), 131.

Index